Creating Reports & Charts For Alpha Five Desktop Applications Made Easy

By Dr. Indera E. Murphy

Tolana Publishing
Teaneck, New Jersey

Published By:
Tolana Publishing
PO Box 719
Teaneck, NJ 07666 USA

Find us online at www.tolanapublishing.com
Inquiries may be sent to the publisher: tolanapub@yahoo.com

Our books are available online at www.barnesandnoble.com. They can also be ordered from Ingram.

Quantity discounts are available for corporations, non-profit organizations and educational institutions for educational purposes, fundraising or resale. www.tolana.com/wholesale.html

ISBN-13: 978-1-935208-26-6
ISBN-10: 1-935208-26-8

Library of Congress Control Number: 2013940470

Printed and bound in the United States Of America

Cover by Mary Kramer, owner of Milkweed Graphics, www.milkweedgraphics.com

v1.0

About The No Stress Tech Guide Series

Creating Reports & Charts For Alpha Five Desktop Applications Made Easy is part of a series of computer software books that are designed to be used as a self-paced learning tool. Our books can also be used in a classroom setting or in an online class. The books in this series contain an abundance of step-by-step instructions and screen shots to help reduce the "stress" often associated with learning new software. This book is geared towards the intermediate user. The other audience for this book is people that have already created basic desktop applications in Alpha Five and now want to take their report writing skills to the next level.

Titles In The Series

	ISBN
ACT! 2007	978-0-9773912-5-7
ACT! 2009	978-1-935208-07-5
ACT! 2010	978-1-935208-09-9
ACT! Pro 2011	978-1-935208-13-6
ACT! Pro 2012	978-1-935208-17-4
Sage ACT! Pro 2013	978-1-935208-22-8
Using Crystal Reports 2008 With ACT! 2010 Databases	978-1-935208-10-5
Getting Started With Alpha Five Desktop Applications	978-1-935208-23-5
Alpha Five Desktop Applications Beyond The Basics	978-1-935208-24-2
Creating Reports & Charts For Alpha Five Desktop Applications Made Easy	978-1-935208-26-6
Using SAP Crystal Reports With Alpha Five Databases Made Easy	978-1-935208-25-9
Crystal Reports XI For Beginners (2nd Edition)	978-1-935208-00-6
What's New In Crystal Reports 2008	978-1-935208-01-3
Crystal Reports 2008 For Beginners	978-0-9773912-9-5
Crystal Reports 2011 For Beginners (2nd Edition)	978-1-935208-15-0
Crystal Reports Beyond The Basics	978-1-935208-18-1
Crystal Reports For Visual Studio 2005	978-0-9773912-6-4
Crystal Reports Basic For Visual Studio 2008	978-0-9773912-8-8
Crystal Reports For Visual Studio 2010	978-1-935208-12-9
Crystal Xcelsius 4.5	978-1-935208-02-0
Xcelsius 2008	978-1-935208-05-1
SAP Crystal Dashboard Design 2011 For Beginners	978-1-935208-11-2
OpenOffice.org 2 Writer	978-0-9773912-4-0
OpenOffice.org 3 Writer	978-1-935208-08-2
Microsoft Office Starter 2010 (Word & Excel)	978-1-935208-14-3
Microsoft PowerPivot For Excel 2010	978-1-935208-16-7
Microsoft Works 7	978-0-9773912-2-6
Microsoft Works 8 & 8.5	978-0-9773912-1-9
Microsoft Works 9	978-0-9773912-7-1
Windows XP	978-0-9773912-0-2

Why A Book On Creating Reports and Charts For Alpha Five?

Reports and charts are used to view data in a variety of ways. They are often used in the decision making process. There are a lot of options for creating reports and charts in Alpha Five and I felt that these topics deserved a book of their own.

The goal of this book is to provide coverage of report and chart topics that can help make the project that you are working on look as professional as possible. Many of the topics covered are often ones that have made me ask "How did they do that?"

About The Author

Dr. Indera Murphy is an author, educator and IT professional that has over 20 years of experience in the Information Technology field. She has held a variety of positions including technical writer, programmer, online adjunct professor, consultant, web designer, course developer and project leader. Indera has designed and developed software applications and websites, as well as, manage technology driven projects in several industries. In addition to being an Executive Director, she has taught courses in a variety of areas including project management, technical writing, Crystal Reports, information processing, Access, HTML, Windows, Excel, Dreamweaver and critical thinking.

Thank you for purchasing this book!

CONTENTS

GETTING STARTED WITH REPORTS & CHARTS IN ALPHA FIVE

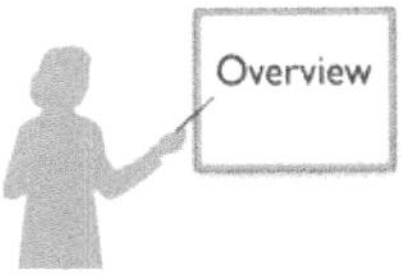

This chapter provides a brief overview of what this book covers and shows you how to download the practice files for this book.

CHAPTER 1

Welcome To Creating Reports & Charts In Alpha Five Desktop Applications!

The topics covered in this book will show you how to create a variety of reports and charts. While this book provides a lot of detailed information and steps, it cuts to the chase. That is possible because this book is geared towards people that have already used the Desktop Edition of Alpha Five, version 11 or higher.

It is my sincere hope that whatever your current skill level is with Alpha Five, that you will learn more about the report and chart features that you are already familiar with as you go through this book and that you learn about report or chart features that you did not know existed. Learning new tips and shortcuts will let you work faster and smarter. The more that you know about creating reports and charts in Alpha Five, the easier your report writing experiences will be.

So sit back, relax and lets get started!

How This Book Is Organized

Each chapter covers specific topics. This book is designed to be read from cover to cover. I do not advise skipping around in the book because some of the files needed in later chapters are created in earlier chapters. Below is an overview of what is covered in each chapter.

Chapter 1, Getting Started With Alpha Five covers background information, conventions that I use in this book and downloading the practice files.

Chapter 2, Report Basics covers report control options and the Quick Report Genie.

Chapter 3, Report Editor Basics covers using the Report Editor, creating free-form reports and learning about report properties.

Chapter 4, Enhancing Reports Part 1 covers creating reports from scratch, Free-Form reports and enhancing reports with groups, totals and calculated fields.

Chapter 5, Introduction To Layout Table Reports covers using the Report Genie to create a Layout Table report and features specific to Layout Table reports.

Chapter 6, Creating Letters, Labels And Envelopes covers creating form letters, different types of labels and envelopes.

Chapter 7, Enhancing Reports Part 2 covers creating hyperlinks, customized headers and footers, expressions and suppression techniques to make reports look more professional.

Chapter 8, Adding Bookmarks, An Index And Table Of Contents To A Report covers adding these features to a report.

Chapter 9, Enhancing Reports With Arguments covers adding functionality to reports that allows users to select filter criteria for the report at run-time.

Chapter 10, Creating Charts covers creating a variety of chart types.

Objectives Of This Book

The primary objective of this book is to introduce a variety of report and chart features in Alpha Five that can take the applications that you create to the next level. Because this is not a beginners book, you should know how to do the following in Alpha Five.

- ☑ Create forms from scratch
- ☑ Create basic expressions
- ☑ Use functions
- ☑ Create basic reports

Many of the options used to create and format reports are the same as the ones for creating forms. The options specifically for reports or mostly used for reports are explained in this book.

This book is a visual guide that shows you how to use a large number of the report and chart features in Alpha Five. There are over 350 illustrations that practically eliminate the guess work and let you know that you are doing the steps correctly.

Step-by-step instructions are included throughout this book. This book takes a hands-on approach to teaching you how to use report and chart features in Alpha Five to provide the skills required to enhance desktop applications. After completing the exercises in this book, you will be able to create the following types of reports and charts and more:

- ☑ Reports with continuation footers
- ☑ Subreports
- ☑ Reports with arguments
- ☑ Top N reports and charts
- ☑ Display data conditionally
- ☑ Reports with bookmarks and an index
- ☑ Linked reports
- ☑ Bar, Pie, Spline Area and Line charts

> **What I Know For Sure . . .**
> Having designed more applications and reports than I can count and being called upon to review and fix reports created by other people, it is clear that a lot of people either do not test the reports that they create or do not know how to test reports, especially reports that have formulas. I can tell you that from appearances, formulas may look like they are working because a system error was not generated and the report produces output. If the only thing that you take away from this book is to thoroughly test your formulas before putting reports into production, then my mission will be accomplished.

Conventions Used In This Book

I designed the following conventions to make it easier for you to follow the instructions in this book.

- ☑ The `Courier` font is used to indicate what you should type.
- ☑ **Drag** means to press and hold down the left mouse button while moving the mouse.
- ☑ **Right-click** means to press the right mouse button once, which will open a shortcut menu.
- ☑ **Click OK** means to click the OK button on the dialog box.

☑ **Press Enter** means to press the Enter key on your keyboard.

☑ **Press Next** means to click the Next button on the dialog box.

☑ **Click Finish** means to click the Finish button on the dialog box.

☑ **SMALL CAPS** are used to indicate an option to click on or to bring something to your attention.

☑  This icon indicates a shortcut or another way to complete the task that is being discussed. It can also indicate a tip or additional information about the topic that is being discussed. Some of this information comes from my experience in the IT field.

☑  This icon indicates a warning, like a feature that has been removed or information that you need to be aware of. This icon can also represent what I call a quirk, meaning a feature that did not work as I expected it to.

☑  This icon represents what I call an "Alpha Five-Ism". This means that the term or concept being presented is called something different in Alpha Five then it is commonly known as or called in many other software packages. Hopefully, this will help in the transition, if you have used other database or report design software.

☑ All of the reports that you create and save will start with the letter "a". This will put them at the top of the list of file names on the Alpha Five Control Panel. This will make is easy to tell which files you create versus the practice files.

☑ [See Chapter 3, Database Concepts] refers to a section in a different chapter then the one you are currently viewing that you can use as a reference for the topic that is being discussed.

☑ [See Chapter 2, Figure 2-8] refers to an illustration (screen shot) in a different chapter then the one you are currently viewing that you can use as a reference for the topic that is being discussed.

☑ [See Show Break] or [See Figure 6-7] refers to a section or figure in the chapter that you are currently in.

☑ When you see the instruction "Click the (field or option name) button", it means to click the button at the end of the field or option.

☑ Many of the dialog boxes in Alpha Five have OK, Cancel and Help buttons on the right side or bottom. Viewing these buttons on all of the screen shots adds no value, so they are not shown in the figures.

☑ When you see "**YOU SHOULD HAVE THE OPTIONS SHOWN IN FIGURE X-X**", or something similar in the exercises, check to make sure that your screen does look like the figure. If it does, continue with the next set of instructions. If your screen does not look like the figure, redo the steps that you just completed so that your screen does match the figure. Not doing so may cause you problems when trying to complete exercises later in the book.

☑ The section heading **EXERCISE X.Y:** (where X equals the chapter number and Y equals the exercise number) represents exercises that have step-by-step instructions that you should complete. You will also see sections that have step-by-step instructions that are not an exercise. Completing them as you go through the book is optional, but recommended.

☑ **TOOLS ⇒ FEATURE PACKS ⇒ INSTALL OPTIONAL FEATURE PACKS** means to open the **TOOLS** menu, select the option **FEATURE PACKS**, then select the **INSTALL OPTIONAL FEATURE PACKS** option, as shown in Figure 1-1.

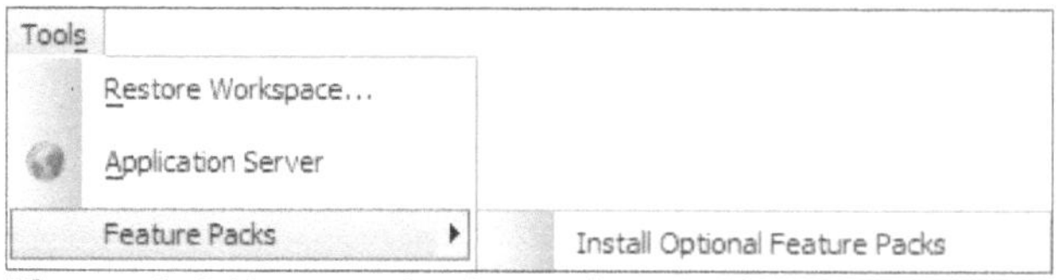

Figure 1-1 Menu navigation technique shown

Assumptions

Yes, I know one should never assume anything, but the following assumptions have been made. It is assumed that you . . . .

☑ Have Alpha Five version 11 or higher installed on your computer. If you are not sure what version you have installed, open Alpha Five, then select Help ⇒ About Alpha Five. You will see the version that is installed, at the bottom of the dialog box.

☑ Know that the version of Alpha Five used to write this book is Alpha Five, version 11.

☑ Know that you can select whether the term "Workspace" or "Database" is displayed in the software. For example, if Workspace is selected as the default option, when the Recent button on the Control Panel is clicked, the dialog box that opens will display "Select Workspace", as shown in the upper left corner of Figure 1-2, instead of "Select Databases". If you have Database selected as the default, keep this in mind when going through the book because your software will not look like some of the screen shots.

☑ Know that the operating system used to write this book is Windows 7. If you are using a different version of Windows, any or all of the following can apply:

① Some of the screen shots may have a slightly different look.

② Some of the instructions for Windows tasks may be different.

③ The path to folders and files on your computer may be different then the paths listed in this book.

☑ Understand that from time to time, I will point out functionality that may not work as expected. When I do this, I am not complaining, merely pointing out things that you should be aware of.

☑ Know that I am not perfect and sadly, you may find minor mistakes in this book. It is not intentional and I apologize for any inconvenience.

☑ Know that when you see <smile> in this book, it signifies my attempt of adding humor to the learning process.

☑ Understand that most objects are saved as one word (for example, CustomerList) and are displayed that way on the Control Panel. In the instructions in this book, the object names are displayed with spaces between the words (for example Customer List) to make them easier to read.

☑ Have access to the Internet to download the practice files needed to complete the exercises in this book.

☑ Understand that there will be options on dialog boxes that will not be referenced in the step-by-step instructions. When that is the case, accept the default value.

☑ That you know to click OK or the appropriate button to close a dialog box and know to save the changes.

☑ Optional: That you have access to a printer, if you want to print any of the reports that you create while using this book.

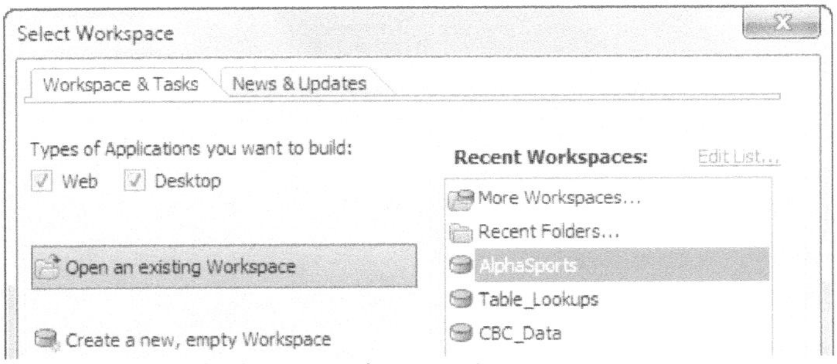

Figure 1-2 Default terminology setting

Exercise 1.1: Create A Folder For This Book And Download The Practice Files

In this book, you will learn how to create reports and charts that would be used in a database application. It is a good idea to store all of the files in the same folder on your computers hard drive so that you can find them easily. I will refer to this folder as "your folder" throughout the book. The instructions below show you how to create the folder at the root of the C drive. If you want to create the folder in another location or under an existing folder, navigate to that location prior to starting step 2.

1. Open Windows Explorer, then click on the C drive.
2. File ⇒ New ⇒ Folder.
3. Type `A5 Reports Book` as the folder name, then press Enter.
4. The practice files for this book are in a zip file named a5reports.zip. To have the link for the zip file sent to you, send an email to a5reports@tolanapublishing.com. If you do not receive an email in a few minutes with the subject line Alpha 5 Reports & Charts Files, check the spam folder in your email software.
5. When you have the zip file, extract the files to your folder.
6. Open Alpha Five. On the Select Workspace dialog box shown above in Figure 1-2, click on the **MORE WORKSPACES** folder, then click OK. Navigate to your folder, then double-click on the a5reports.dbf file.

REPORT BASICS

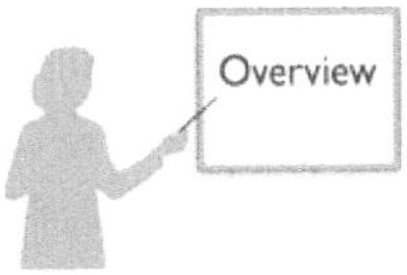

In addition to learning how to create basic reports in this chapter, you will learn about the following report features.

- ☑ Control Panel options for reports
- ☑ Quick Report Genie

CHAPTER 2

Overview

For many readers, this is the book that you have been waiting for because your application to-do list has at least 20 reports. Creating reports is similar to creating a form in that you can select where the fields and other objects are placed on the layout. Creating reports has more steps then creating forms.

This chapter covers the basic options used to create a report. The goal of this chapter is to introduce you to the two key tools used to create reports: The Quick Report Genie and the Report Editor.

Reports Tab Control Panel Options

The Preview button on the Control Panel displays the options shown in Figure 2-1.

The **PREVIEW** option displays the report in preview mode.

The **PRINT GENIE** option opens the Print Genie with the Preview option selected.

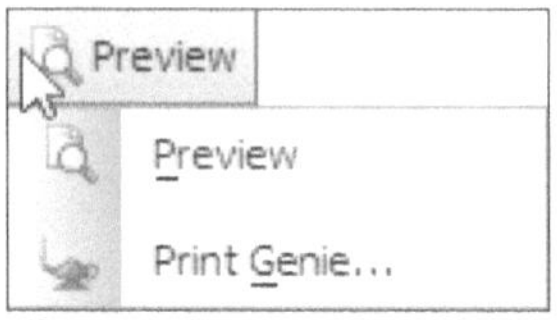

Figure 2-1 Preview button options

Report Types

There are two types of reports that you can create, as explained below.

① **FREE FORM REPORT** This report type is the most flexible and is best suited for printed reports and reports that need to be saved in PDF format.
② **LAYOUT TABLE** This report type is best suited for exporting the data in a report to Excel and for creating linked reports. Layout Table reports can also be used as stand alone reports like free form reports.

Subreports

Subreports are a very powerful and flexible tool. A subreport is a report within a report. They are created the same way any other report is created - either from scratch or by using the Report Genie. There are two types of subreports, as explained below.

① **SUBREPORTS** This is the standard subreport type that you may already be familiar with. It can only be added to a Free Form report.
② **LINKED REPORTS** Can be added to Free Form and Layout Table reports, which is why they are considered a subreport. They have more functionality then standard subreports because calculated fields from this report type can be added to the main report.

Quick Report Genie

This tool is very helpful in creating both Free Form and Layout Table reports. Actually, this genie has to be used to create a Layout Table report. The Quick Report Genie shown later in Figure 2-9, has the following tabs: Columns, Groups, Report Settings, Filter/Order, Calculated Fields, Style and Preview.

Are you sitting down? If you have not been a fan of the genies up to now, the Report Genie may change your mind because unlike the other genies that have been covered in this book, you can preview the report before closing the genie. Wait! It gets better. You can save your report genie selections and reopen the genie and change them to either update the existing report or to create a new report! Yes, Really!

Instead of explaining the options on each tab on the genie now, lets create a basic report and I will explain as we go.

> Unless stated otherwise, you should have the Reports tab on the Control Panel displayed before starting an exercise in this chapter.

Exercise 2.1: Create A Basic Report

In this exercise you will learn how to create a basic list report. In the next exercise you will learn how to use options on the Quick Report Genies Groups, Filter/Order and Style tabs.

New Report Dialog Box

This dialog box is used to select the table or set that the report will be based on.

1. On the Reports tab, click the New button, then select the Contacts data source.

2. Select the Use Quick Report option.

   You should have the options shown in Figure 2-2.

   Click OK.

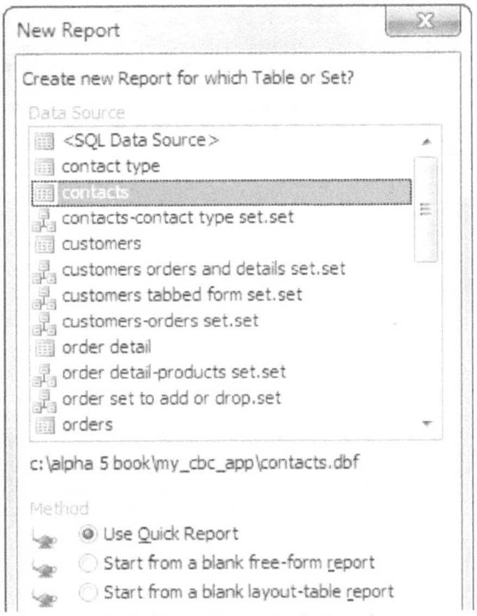

Figure 2-2 New Report dialog box

Report Methods

As shown above in Figure 2-2, there are three ways that you can create a report. The options are explained below.

① **USE QUICK REPORT** Will use the Quick Report Genie.

② **START FROM A BLANK FREE-FORM REPORT** Opens the Report Editor and displays a blank Free Form report.

③ **START FROM A BLANK LAYOUT-TABLE REPORT** Opens the Report Editor and displays a blank Layout Table report.

Report Genie Menu

The Report Genie menu is shown in Figure 2-3. The menus with options specifically for reports are explained in Tables 2-1 and 2-2.

Figure 2-3 Report Genie menu

File Menu

The options shown in Figure 2-4 are explained in Table 2-1.

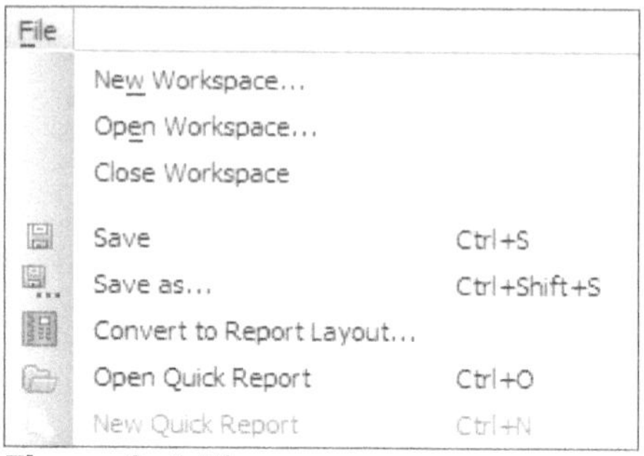

Figure 2-4 File menu

Option	Description
Convert to Report Layout	Is used to select the report type (Layout Table or Free Form) that you want to convert the report (that was created with the Genie) to.
Open Quick Report	Opens the dialog box shown in Figure 2-5, which is used to select a different report to open.
New Quick Report	Opens the dialog box shown in Figure 2-5. It is used to select an existing report to use as the starting point for another report. After I updated the software, this option was no longer enabled.

Table 2-1 File menu options explained

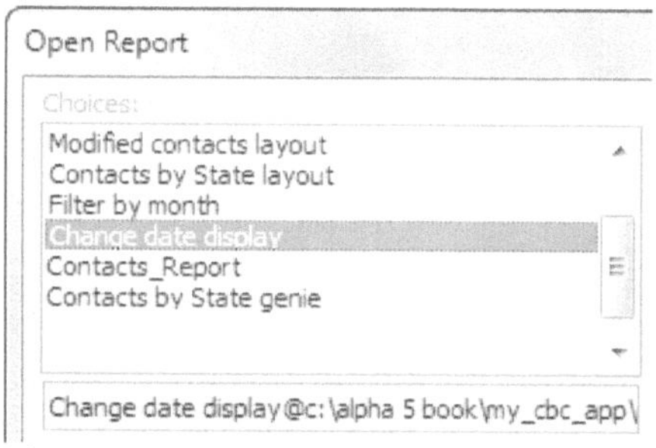

Figure 2-5 Open Report dialog box

Report Menu

The options shown in Figure 2-6 are explained in Table 2-2.

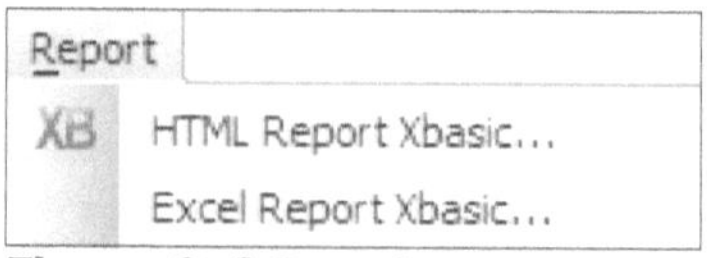

Figure 2-6 Report menu

Option	Displays The Code That Is Used To Create The Report In . . .
HTML Report Xbasic	HTML format.
Excel Report Xbasic	Excel format, as shown in Figure 2-7.

Table 2-2 Report menu options explained

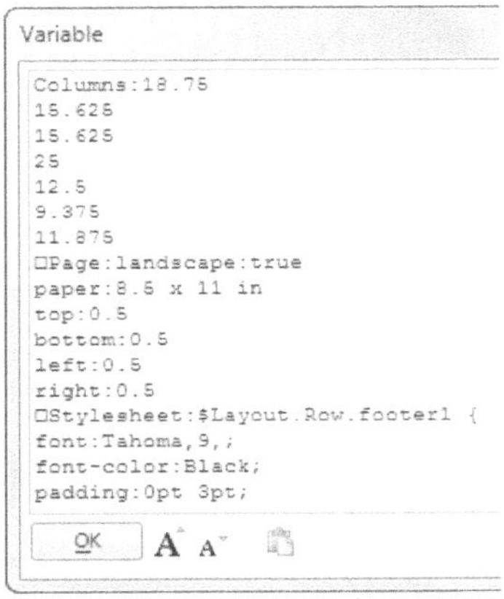

Figure 2-7 Xbasic code to create the report in Excel

Report Genie Toolbar

The options shown in Figure 2-8 are explained in Table 2-3.

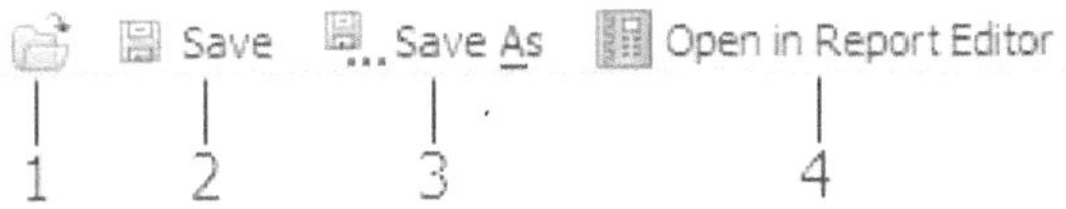

Figure 2-8 Report Genie toolbar

Button	Description
1	[See Table 2-1, New Quick Report] The difference between this option and the one on the File menu is that this option is always available, unlike the one on the File menu.
2	Save the Report Genie options.
3	Save the Report Genie options with a new file name.
4	Opens the **REPORT DEFINITION** (aka Report Genie options) in the Report Editor.

Table 2-3 Report Genie toolbar buttons explained

Using The Quick Report Genie

As you see in Figure 2-9, this genie has a lot of options for you to create a report.

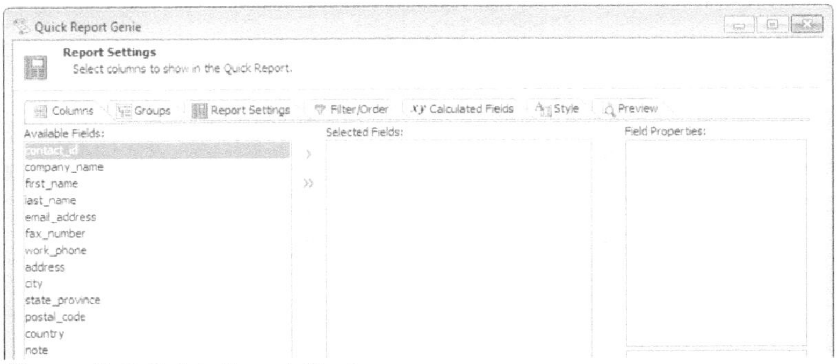

Figure 2-9 Quick Report Genie

Columns Tab

The options on this tab, shown above in Figure 2-9, are used to select the fields that will be displayed in the Detail section of the report.

1. Select the following fields in the Available Fields list and add them to the Selected Fields list: Company Name, First Name, Last Name, Address, City, State Province and Postal Code.

   Notice that once you add a field to the Selected Fields list, the field is bold in the Available Fields list. That is done to indicate that the field has already been added to the report.

Field Properties

The options shown in Figure 2-10 (on the Columns tab) are used to customize the fields that will be displayed on the report.

The options in the **COLUMN SECTION** are used to customize how the field is displayed on the report. The options are explained below.

The **LABEL** option displays the heading for the field.

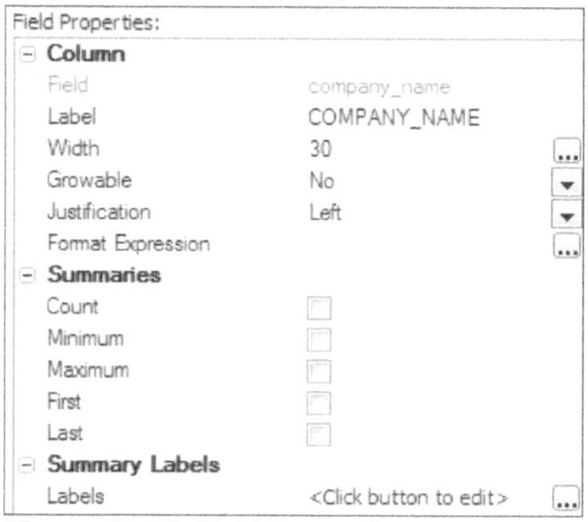

Figure 2-10 Field Properties

The **WIDTH** option is used to adjust how many characters of the field will be displayed on the report. The default value is the field length defined in the table. Clicking the dynamic button at the end of the field opens the dialog box shown in Figure 2-11. The options are used to manually change the column width or have the field(s) automatically sized based on the larger of the label (heading) or field size.

Based on my experiences with other software, the results of using the **SIZE TO FIT** and **SIZE ALL COLUMNS TO FIT** buttons can be mixed.

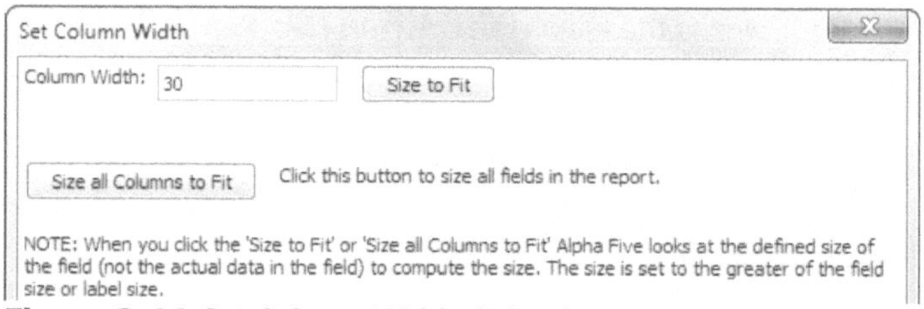

Figure 2-11 Set Column Width dialog box

GROWABLE This option is used to select whether or not the field can expand. This option is most often set to Yes for memo fields.

JUSTIFICATION Is used to select how the data is positioned (left, right, center, etc.) in the column.

FORMAT EXPRESSION Is used to format the data in the column. Clicking the dynamic button opens the Display Format dialog box. The options are used to format the data in the column. [See Chapter 5, Display Format]

The options in the **SUMMARIES SECTION** of the Field Properties dialog box are used to create a summary calculated field for the selected field.

The **SUMMARY LABELS** option is used to customize the label for a summary field.

The **LABELS** option is used to change the default labels for the summary field. Clicking the Dynamic button opens the **EDIT SUMMARY LABELS DIALOG BOX** shown later in Figure 2-28, if the report has at least one summary field.

There will be one entry on this dialog box for each summary type selected in the Summaries section. To change the label, click on the summary at the top of the dialog box. Type the new name in the Label field at the bottom of the dialog box, then click OK once you have changed all of the labels that need to be changed.

2. Change the Company Name field label to Company.

3. Remove the underscore from the following field headings: First Name and Last Name.

4. Change the label of the Postal Code field to `ZIP CODE`.

5. Change the width of the fields in Table 2-4.

Field	Change Width To
Address	30
State	5
Zip Code	10

Table 2-4 Field widths to change

Report Settings Tab

The options on this tab, shown in Figure 2-12, are primarily used to select fonts, font size and colors for different parts of the report.

The **USE LAYOUT TABLES** option is used to select whether the report should be a Free Form report (option not checked) or a Layout Table report (option is checked).

The Dynamic button for the font options opens a dialog box like the one shown in Figure 2-13. The Dynamic button for color options opens the panel shown in Figure 2-14.

The options in the **GROUP SECTION** are used to format the groups on the report.

The options in the **PAGE SECTION** are used to select whether or not the report should have a date and page number. The orientation can also be selected.

6. Change the font size option in the Report section to 9.

7. In the Page section, select the following options: Date, Page Number, Page 1 of N and Landscape orientation, as shown at the bottom of Figure 2-12.

8. Click on the Preview tab. Your report should look like the one shown in Figure 2-15. Figure 2-16 shows the bottom of the report page, which has the page number and date.

9. Click the Save button on the toolbar. Type `aContactsListGenie` as the report name, as shown in Figure 2-17, then click OK.

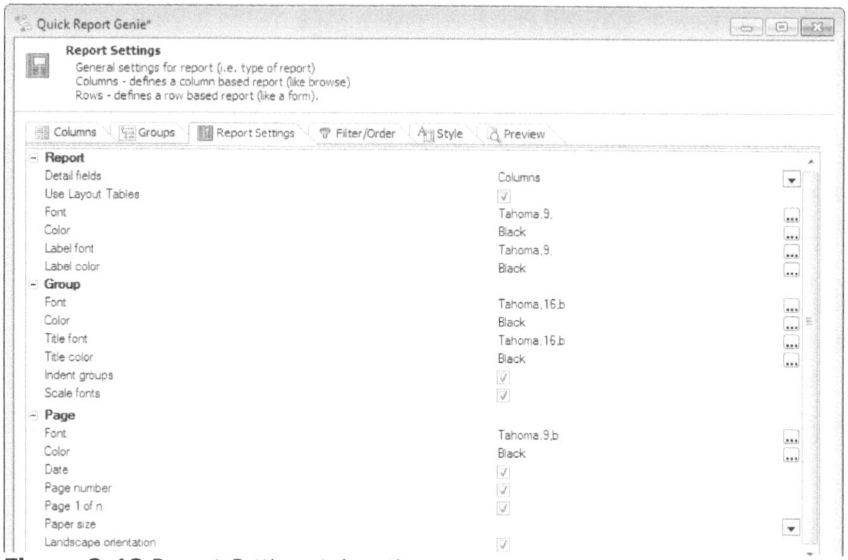

Figure 2-12 Report Settings tab options

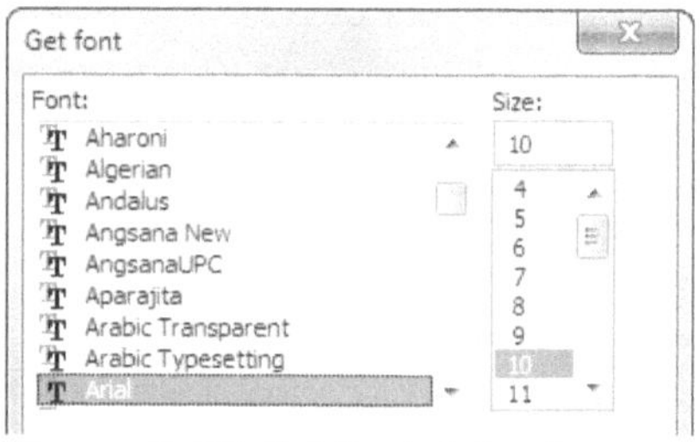

Figure 2-13 Get Font dialog box

Figure 2-14 Color options

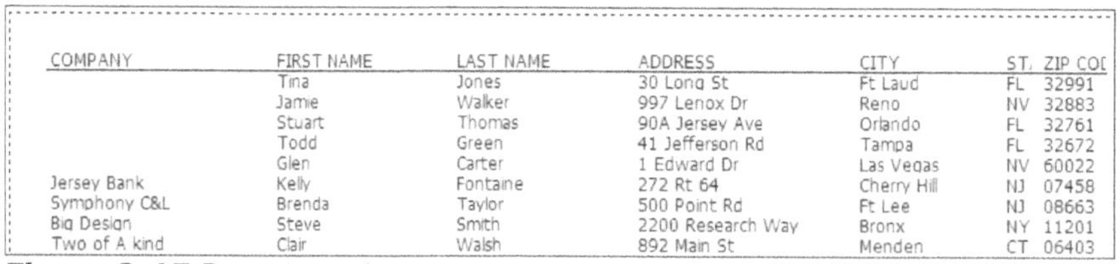

COMPANY	FIRST NAME	LAST NAME	ADDRESS	CITY	ST.	ZIP COD
	Tina	Jones	30 Long St	Ft Laud	FL	32991
	Jamie	Walker	997 Lenox Dr	Reno	NV	32883
	Stuart	Thomas	90A Jersey Ave	Orlando	FL	32761
	Todd	Green	41 Jefferson Rd	Tampa	FL	32672
	Glen	Carter	1 Edward Dr	Las Vegas	NV	60022
Jersey Bank	Kelly	Fontaine	272 Rt 64	Cherry Hill	NJ	07458
Symphony C&L	Brenda	Taylor	500 Point Rd	Ft Lee	NJ	08663
Big Design	Steve	Smith	2200 Research Way	Bronx	NY	11201
Two of A kind	Clair	Walsh	892 Main St	Menden	CT	06403

Figure 2-15 Report preview

Warren	Oneil	89 William Rd	Bogota	NV	32881
May	Vander	30 Long St	Ft Laud	FL	32991

Page 1 of 2 - 06/21/2012

Figure 2-16 Bottom of the report page

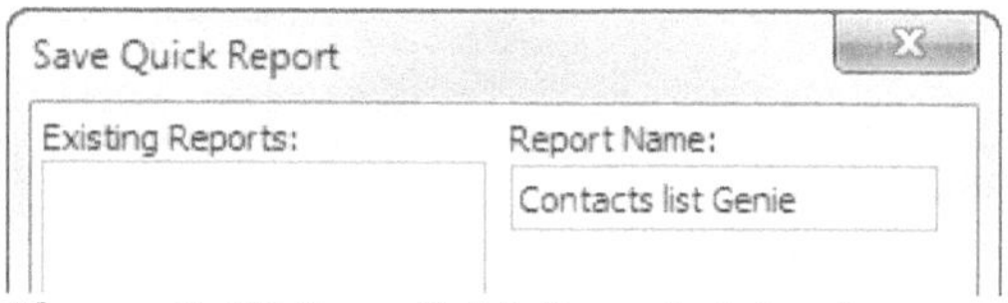

Figure 2-17 Save Quick Report dialog box

Report Genie Preview Tab Toolbar

The preview tab has its own toolbar, as shown in Figure 2-18.

The options are explained in Table 2-5.

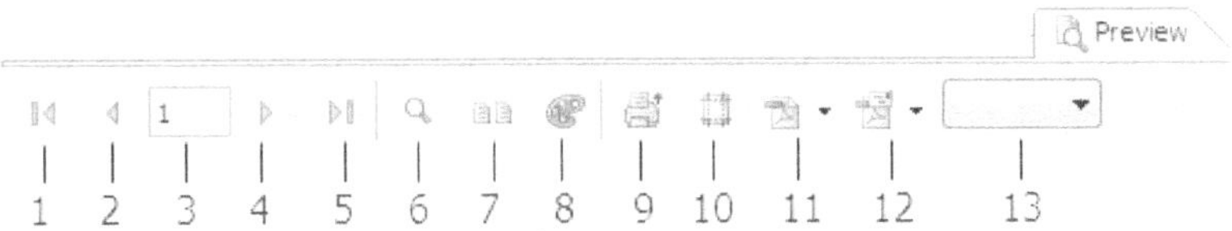

Figure 2-18 Report Genie Preview tab toolbar

Many of these options are also on the Report Editor Preview toolbar that you will learn about in the next chapter.

Button	Description
1	Displays the first page of the report.
2	Displays the previous page of the report.
3	Shows the current page number.
4	Displays the next page of the report.
5	Displays the last page of the report.
6	Enlarges or reduces the size of the report when it is displayed. In addition to clicking this button to change the zoom size, you can also click on the report to enlarge or reduce it.
7	Displays one page of the report The default is to display two pages at the same time, as shown in Figure 2-19.
8	If a report has color, the color will be displayed in gray scale if this option is selected.
9	Opens the Print dialog box. (1)
10	Opens the Print Setup dialog box. (1)
11	Displays the options shown in Figure 2-20. The options are used to save the report in one of the formats shown in the figure. (2)
12	Displays the options shown in Figure 2-20. The options are used to select a format to send the report as an attachment to an email. (2)
13	The options shown in Figure 2-21 are used to select what you want to do with content on the report that over flows.

Table 2-5 Report Genie Preview tab toolbar buttons explained

(1) This option is used to select a printer and the options needed to print the report.
(2) This option does not seem to work. After selecting an option in Figure 2-20, a dialog box should open, like the same options do on the Report Editor Preview toolbar, but that doesn't happen.

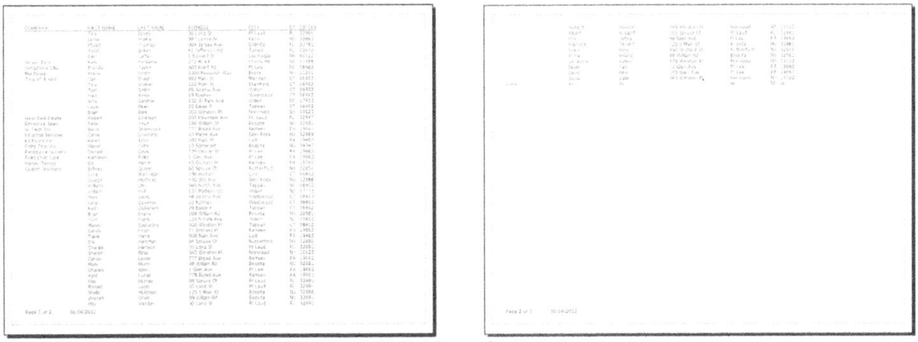

Figure 2-19 Two pages of a report displayed

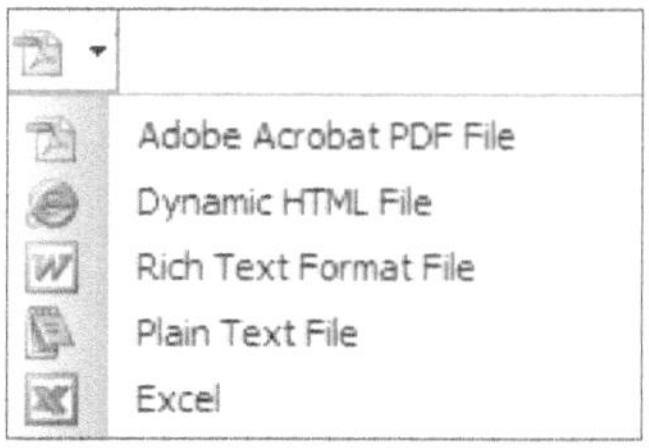

Figure 2-20 Report file options

Figure 2-21 Report overflow options

10. Close the report.

Exercise 2.2: Add A Group To A Report

In this exercise you will learn how to use the options on the Report Genie Groups, Filter/Order and Style tabs. You will create a group for the State field.

1. Open the aContactsListGenie report in design mode. Click the Save As button. Type `aContactsByStateGenie` as the report name, then click OK.

Groups Tab

The options on this tab are used to display records that have the same value or range of values next to each other on the report. Consider the following example:

In the Exercise 2.1 report, at a glance it is hard to tell how many contacts are in CT and how many contacts are in FL. If the report was modified to print all of the records in the same state together, it would be easier to see how many contacts are in each state. This is known as grouping records.

> **Grouping Tips**
> Below are some tips that I follow to help determine if a report needs a group and if so, which field(s) to group on.
>
> ① Reports that retrieve hundreds or thousands of records, probably would be easier to read if there were one or two groups.
> ② If you need to provide a count or subtotal.
> ③ If the report needs to display statistical information.

2. On the Groups tab, add the State field to the Selected Fields list. None of the Group Properties shown on the right side of Figure 2-22 need to be changed.

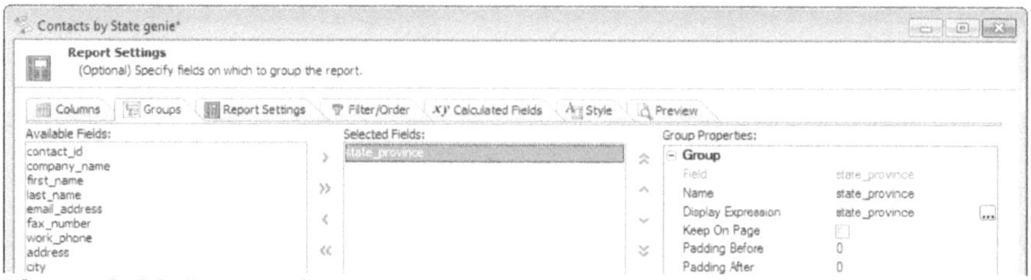

Figure 2-22 Groups tab

The **DISPLAY EXPRESSION** option is the groups title and is automatically placed in the Group Header section.

The **KEEP ON PAGE** option if checked, forces the group to be displayed on the same page, even if that means that the group will start on the next page.

The **PADDING BEFORE** and **PADDING AFTER** options are used to add blank space before or after the groups when printed on the report.

Filter/Order Tab

The options shown in Figure 2-23 are used to select records (filter) that will or will not appear on the report and to sort (order) the records that will appear on the report.

In this exercise only contacts that do not have an email address will be displayed on the report. The records will be sorted by state, then by zip code.

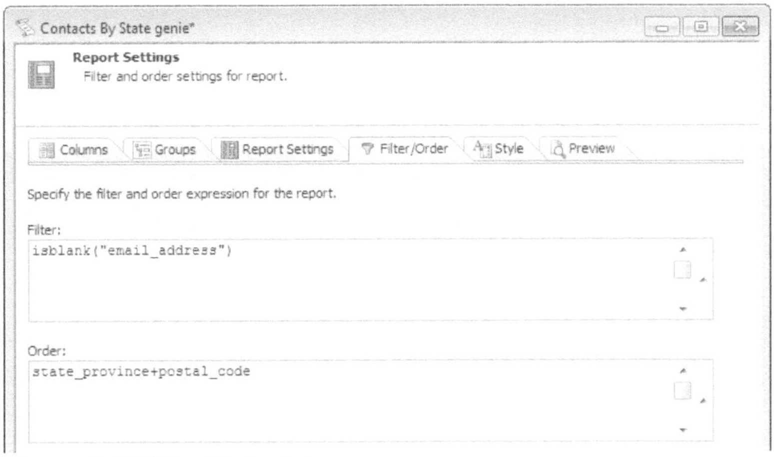

Figure 2-23 Filter/Order tab

Filter Builder

This tool is used to create expressions that will select the records that will appear on the form, browse or report. Most of the time reports do not need to display all of the records in the table or set. Creating a filter is how you select the records that will be displayed. These logical expressions can also be created using the Expression Builder.

By default, the filter expression causes records that evaluate to True to be displayed. Records that evaluate to False are ignored.

To display the records that evaluate to False (instead of True), select the option **EXCLUDE RECORDS THAT SATISFY THIS CONDITION** on the Filter Builder shown later in Figure 2-24.

Create The Filter Criteria

3. On the Filter/Order tab, click the Up arrow button to the right of the scrollbar in the Filter section. The Filter Builder should open.

4. On the Condition 1 tab, select the Email Address field in the first list.

   In the second list, scroll down and select **IS BLANK**.

   You should have the options shown in Figure 2-24.

   Click OK.

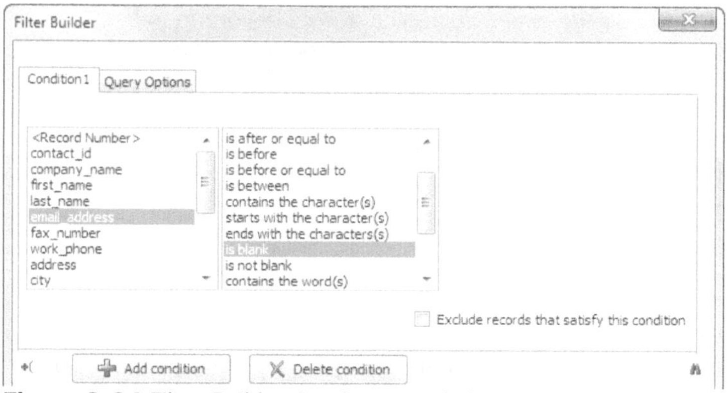

Figure 2-24 Filter Builder Condition 1 tab (Report Genie)

Create The Sort Order

5. On the Filter/Order tab, click the Up arrow button to the right of the scrollbar in the Order section.

6. On the Order By tab, open the **SORT BY** drop-down list and select State.

7. Open the first **THEN, SORT BY** drop-down list and select Postal Code.

   You should have the options shown in Figure 2-25.

   Click OK.

   You should have the expressions shown earlier in Figure 2-23, on the Filter/Data tab.

Figure 2-25 Order Builder (Report Genie)

The binoculars icon in the lower right corner of the Order Builder opens the dialog box shown in Figure 2-26. It displays the expression that was automatically created by the options that you selected on the Order Builder.

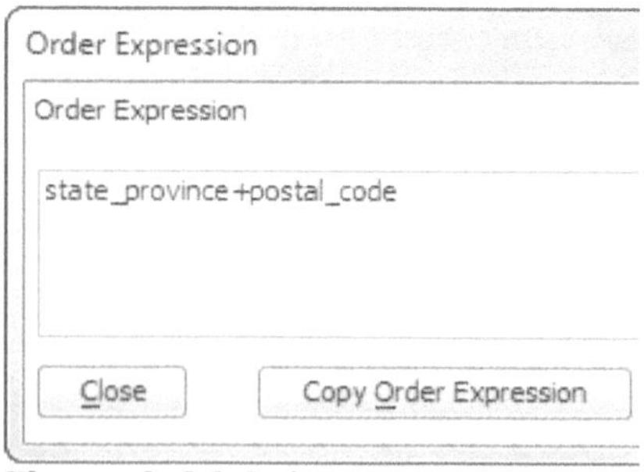

Figure 2-26 Order Expression dialog box

Style Tab

The options on this tab are used to format the report. Borders and color schemes can be applied to the report. The report can also be formatted in the Report Editor.

8. On the Style tab, select the following options: Section Borders, Color alternating rows, Rounded corners and the Blue theme, as shown in Figure 2-27.

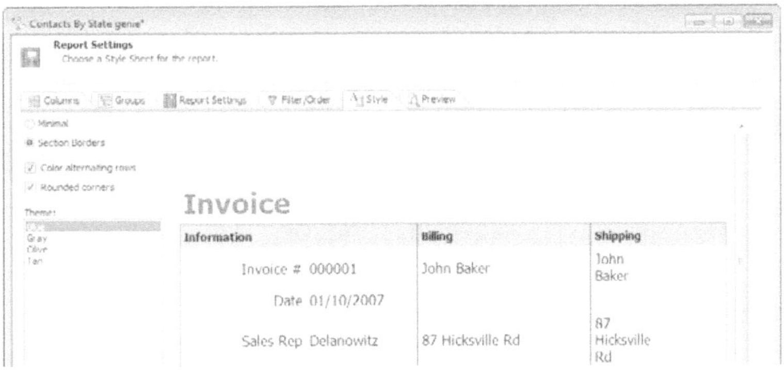

Figure 2-27 Style tab options

Create A Count Of Records Per State Field

It would be helpful if the report displayed how many records are on the report, per state. The report is grouped on the State field, which is the field that the count will be added to.

9. On the Columns tab, click on the State field in the Selected Fields list. In the Field Properties list, check the **COUNT** option.

10. Click the button at the end of the Labels option at the bottom of the Field Properties list. Click on the State field on the Edit summary Labels dialog box.

11. In the Label field at the bottom of the dialog box, type `Contacts in state without an email address`, as shown in Figure 2-28.

    Click OK. The report count will appear at the end of the report.

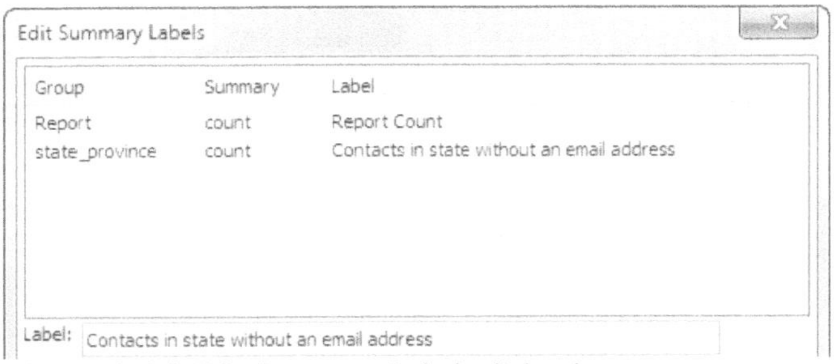

Figure 2-28 Edit Summary Labels dialog box

12. Save the changes.

    Preview the report.

    The first state on the report should look like the one shown in Figure 2-29.

    When you finish viewing the report, close it.

CT

COMPANY	FIRST NAME	LAST NAME	ADDRESS	CITY	ST.	ZIP COI
	Tina	Walker	123 Main St	Stamford	CT	06402
	Louis	Riker	23 Essex Pl	Tappan	CT	06402
	Keith	Dickerson	29 Essex Pl	Tappan	CT	06402
	Marvin	Easterling	300 Winston Pl	Tappan	CT	06402
Two of A Kind	Clair	Walsh	892 Main St	Menden	CT	06403
	Fred	Amos	19 Rodney	Westwood	CT	06403
	June	Brannigan	196 Hudson	Lodi	CT	06403
	Mary	David	48 Jericho Ave	Westwood	CT	06403
	Jane	Downey	22 Rodney	Westwood	CT	06403
	Tom	Smith	45 Jericho Ave	Wilton	CT	06405
Contacts in state without an email address					10	

Figure 2-29 Contacts by state genie report

Quick Report Tool

In addition to using the Quick Report Genie, you can also use the Quick Report tool to create reports. It has similar functionality to the Quick Report Genie. This tool is used to create a new report based on an existing report, including reports created with the Quick Report Genie.

Exercise 2.3: Use The Quick Report Tool

In this exercise you will create a report that displays orders grouped by month.

1. Right-click on the Filter By Month report and select New Report.

2. On the Report Genie, select the Use the Report genie option shown in Figure 2-30, then click OK.

   The Report definition option opens the Free Form report editor.

   The Report Layout table option did not do anything when I tested it.

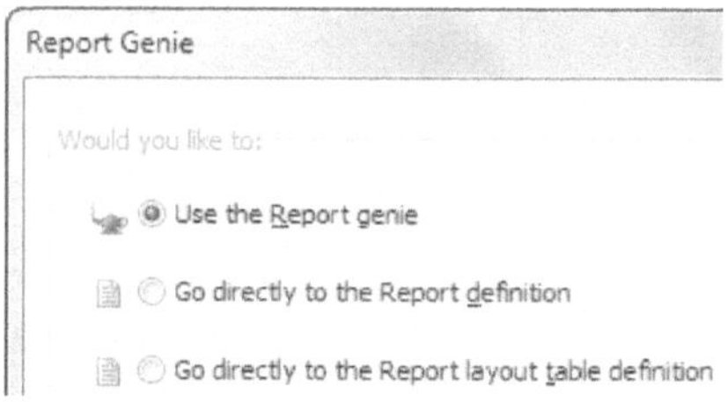

Figure 2-30 Report Genie

Quick Report Dialog Box

The options shown in Figure 2-31 are used to select the title, style and fields for the report. The options are explained in Table 2-6.

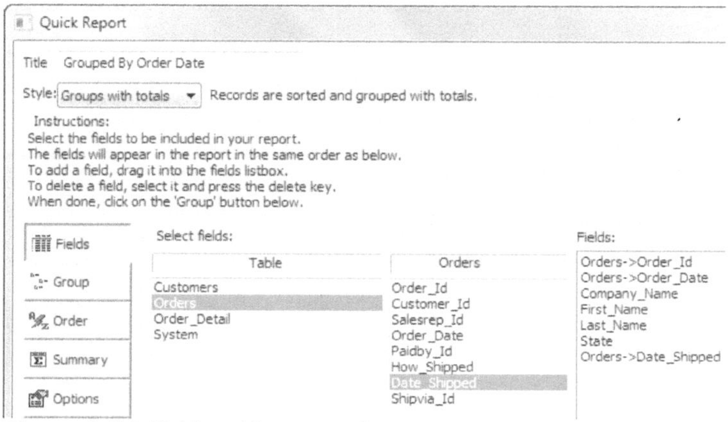

Figure 2-31 Field and layout options

Option	Description
Title	The text that will appear at the top of each page of the report.
Style	[See Style Options below]
Fields	Select the field(s) for the Detail section of the report.
Group	Select the field(s) to group the detail records on.
Order	Select the field(s) to sort the detail records on.
Summary	Select the field(s) to create a total for and the type of summary total value.
Options	Select some formatting for the titles, fields and page.

Table 2-6 Quick Report dialog box options explained

Style Options

The options shown in Figure 2-32 are the types of layouts for the report. They are explained in Table 2-7.

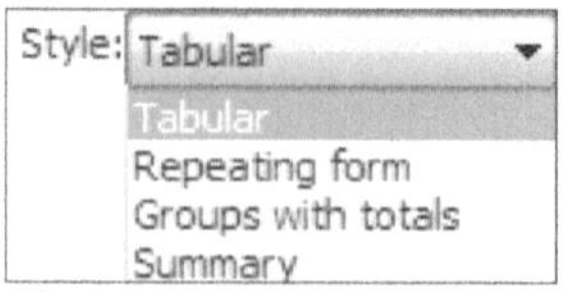

Figure 2-32 Style options

Option	This Style Places The Fields . . .
Tabular	In column format. This is the default option.
Repeating form	Vertically on the report.
Groups with totals	In column format. Groups are created and the records can be sorted.
Summary	In column format. No detail records will print on the report.

Table 2-7 Style options explained

Select The Title, Style And Fields For The Report

1. Type `Grouped by Order Date` in the Title field.

2. Open the Style drop-down list and select Groups with totals.

3. In the Table column, select the Orders table. Drag the following fields in the Orders list to the Fields list: Order ID and Order Date.

4. In the Table column, select the Customers table. Drag the following fields in the Customers list to the Fields list: Company Name, First Name, Last Name and State.

5. In the Table column, select the Orders table. Add the Date Shipped field to the Fields list. You should have the options shown earlier in Figure 2-31.

Select The Group And Order Options

The field(s) that you want to group on must be displayed on the report.

1. Click the Group button.

   Add the Order Date field to the Groups list, as shown in Figure 2-33.

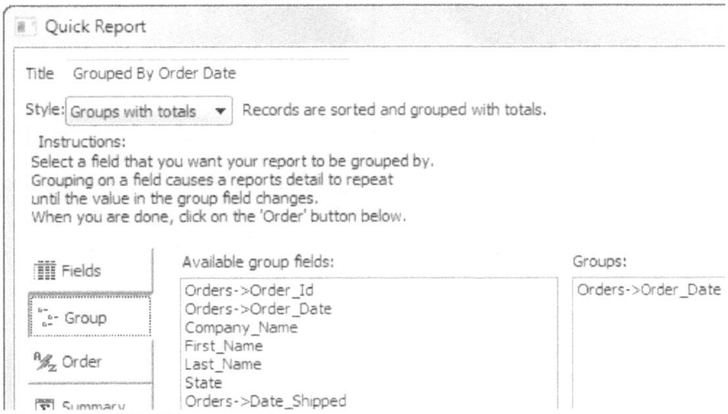

Figure 2-33 Group options

2. Click the Order button.

   Add the State field to the Sort fields list, as shown in Figure 2-34.

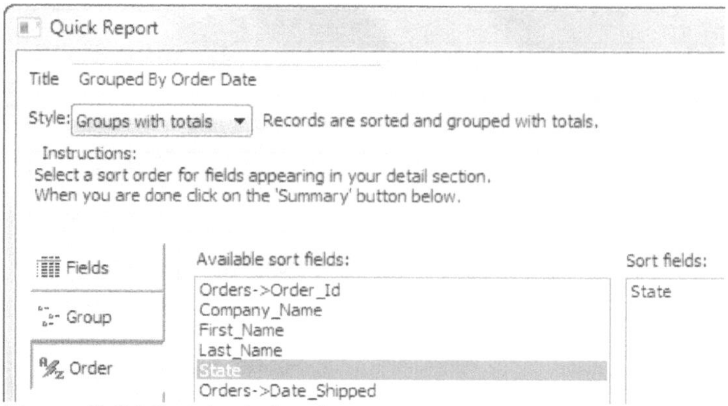

Figure 2-34 Sort (order) options

Select The Summary Options

The summary options provide an easy way to create calculated fields. Summaries cannot be created for fields used to create a group. Fields cannot be added to this screen.

1. Click the Summary button. Open the Summary Operation drop-down list for the Order ID field and select Count.

2. Select the Count summary operation for the State field.

   You should have the options shown in Figure 2-35.

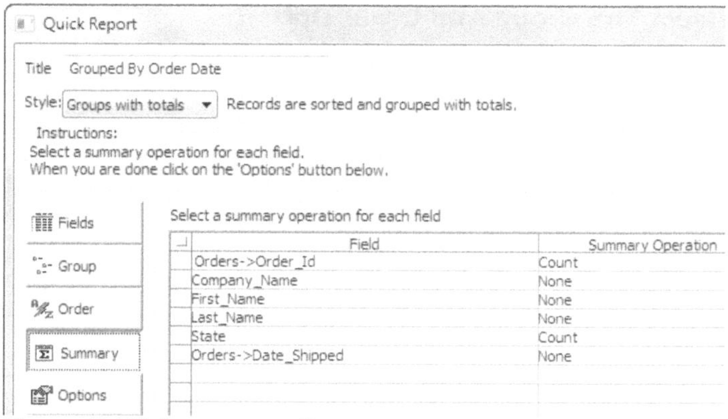

Figure 2-35 Summary options

Select The Other Options

1. Click the Options button.

2. Select the Bold Titles option, then select all three options in the Page section shown in Figure 2-36.

3. Click OK. Report ⇒ Properties ⇒ Band ⇒ Report Properties. On the Page tab, select the Landscape option and Legal paper size option, then click OK.

4. Save the report as `aGroupedByOrderDate`. The report should look like Figure 2-37.

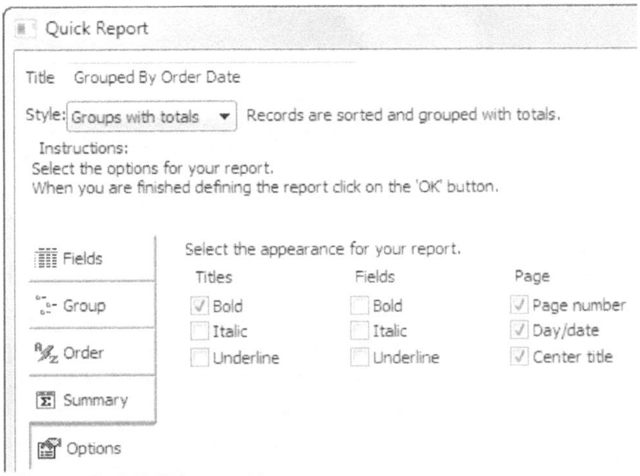

Figure 2-36 Other options

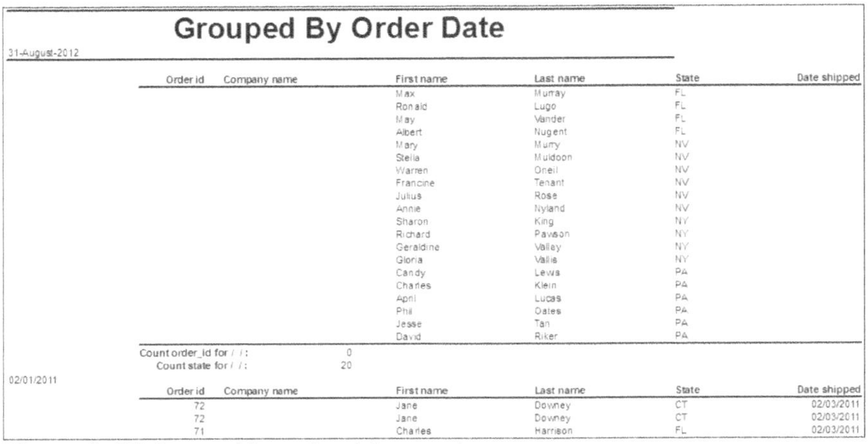

Grouped By Order Date

31-August-2012

Order id	Company name	First name	Last name	State	Date shipped
		Max	Murray	FL	
		Ronald	Lugo	FL	
		May	Vander	FL	
		Albert	Nugent	FL	
		Mary	Murry	NV	
		Stella	Muldoon	NV	
		Warren	Oneil	NV	
		Francine	Tenant	NV	
		Julius	Rose	NV	
		Annie	Nyland	NV	
		Sharon	King	NY	
		Richard	Pawson	NY	
		Geraldine	Valley	NY	
		Gloria	Vallis	NY	
		Candy	Lewis	PA	
		Charles	Klein	PA	
		April	Lucas	PA	
		Phil	Oates	PA	
		Jesse	Tan	PA	
		David	Riker	PA	

Count order_id for / / : 0
Count state for / / : 20

02/01/2011

Order id	Company name	First name	Last name	State	Date shipped
72		Jane	Downey	CT	02/03/2011
72		Jane	Downey	CT	02/03/2011
71		Charles	Harrison	FL	02/03/2011

Figure 2-37 Grouped by order date report

REPORT EDITOR BASICS

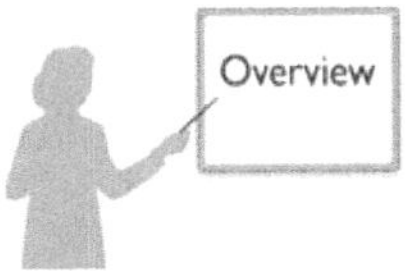

In this chapter, the following report topics are covered:

- ☑ Free Form reports
- ☑ Report Properties
- ☑ Importing Report Layouts

CHAPTER 3

Overview

In the previous chapter, you learned how to create reports using the Quick Report Genie and the Quick Report tool. In this chapter, you will learn the basics of the Report Editor.

Report Editor

Free Form and Layout Table reports can both be initially created and modified using the Report Editor. The main difference is that the editor looks different in design mode depending on which of these report types you are using. Another difference is that the Toolbox is not available for Layout Table reports. Figure 3-1 shows the report editor when a Layout Table report is open. Figure 3-2 shows the report editor when a free form report is open.

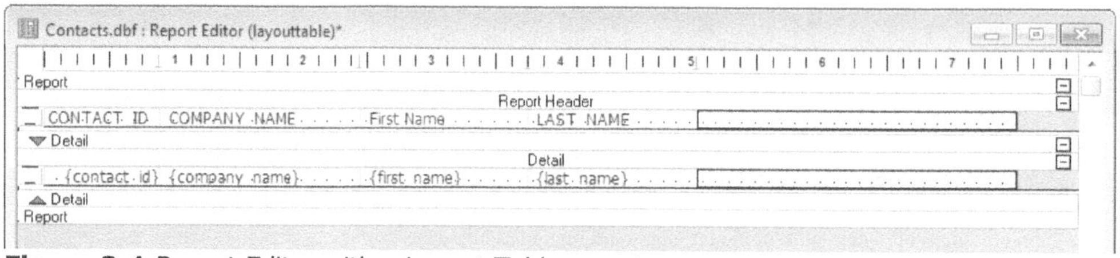

Figure 3-1 Report Editor with a Layout Table report open

Report Workspace

Fortunately, the majority of the report workspace is the same whether a free form or layout table report is open. Figure 3-2 shows the report workspace.

Report Layout Menu

You will see the menu shown in Figure 3-3 when a report is open. The majority of options on the menu are the same as the options for forms. The menu is also used for letters and labels. The menu options specifically for reports are explained in Tables 3-1 to 3-4.

Edit Menu

Select All Option
Usually this option selects all of the objects on the report. For Free Form reports, this option only selects all of the objects in one section of the report.

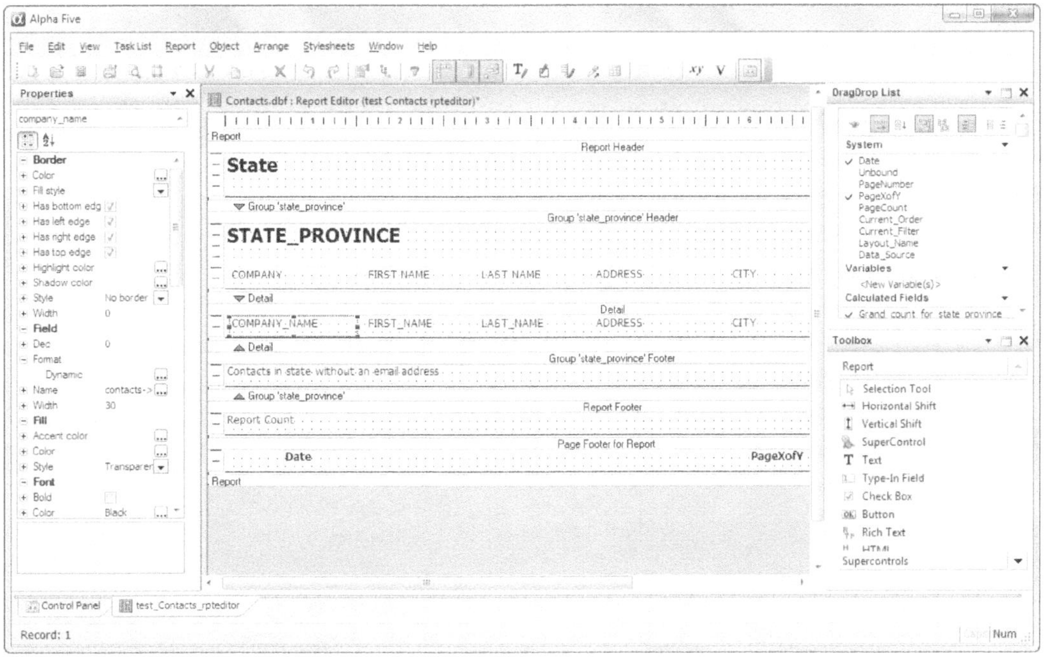

Figure 3-2 Report workspace

Figure 3-3 Report layout menu

View Menu

The options for reports are checked and shown in Figure 3-4.

These options are useful when you do not want to see all of the sections of the report when you are designing it. Table 3-1 explains the checked options.

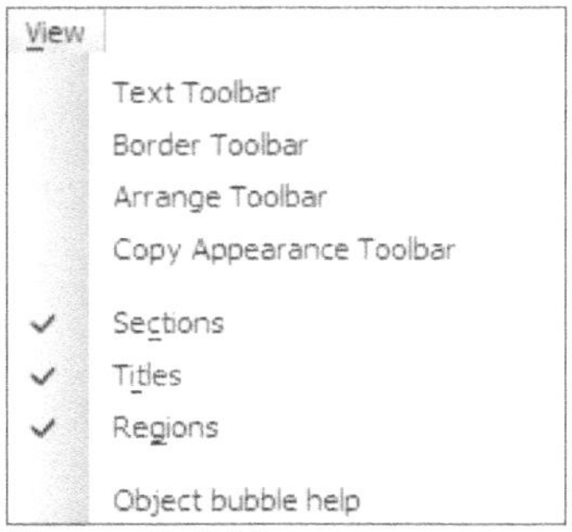

Figure 3-4 View menu

Option	Displays Or Hides . . .
Sections	Report sections (the gray bars with the arrows).
Titles	Header and footer sections (the gray bars with the names in the center of the bar).
Regions	Bands of the report where fields and other objects are added. You can also display or hide a specific region by clicking the plus or minus button on the right side of each band.

Table 3-1 View menu options explained

Report Menu

The Report menu is shown in Figure 3-5.
The options specific to reports are explained in Table 3-2.

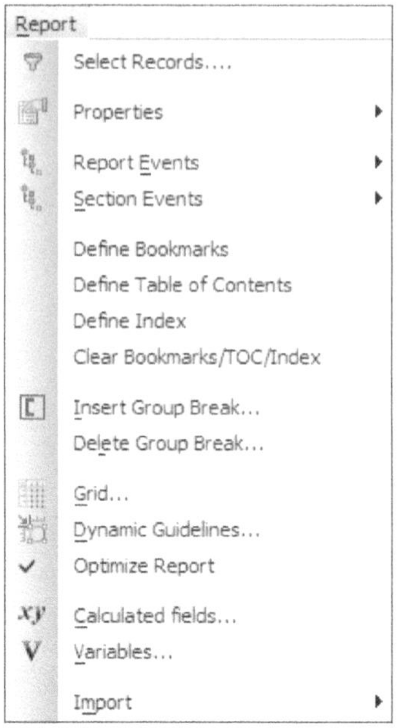

Figure 3-5 Report menu

Option	Description
Select Records	[See Select Records To Print Dialog Box, later in this chapter]
Properties	Displays the submenu shown in Figure 3-6. [See Band Section vs Region Section, later in this chapter] The **LAYOUT TABLE PROPERTIES** option opens the dialog box shown in Figure 3-7 if the open report is a Layout Table report. The options are used to select the layout style, which determines what styles are applied to different sections of the report.
Report Events	Create an event for the selected object. Events are pre-written actions that are available for certain objects or components.
Section Events	Is used to create events (actions) on a section by section basis. The **ON RECORD EVENT** option can be used to update records after the report prints.
Define Bookmarks	Is used to create links that will display a different part of the report.
Define Table of Contents	Is used to create a Table of Contents for the report.
Define Index	Is used to create an index for the report.
Clear Bookmarks/TOC/ Index	Is used to remove a bookmark, Table of Contents or Index entry.
Insert Group Break	Opens the **NEW GROUP PROPERTIES DIALOG BOX**, which is used to create a group on the report.
Delete Group Break	This option is used to delete a group. It is enabled when the report has a group and the section bar of the group that you want to delete is selected in the report layout.
Grid	[See Use The Grid To Align Objects, later in this chapter]

Table 3-2 Report menu options explained

Option	Description
Dynamic Guidelines	[See Using Dynamic Guidelines To Align Objects, later in this chapter]
Optimize Report	Is enabled by default. I could not find or figure out exactly how this option improves the performance of a report.
Import	Is used to open an existing form, browse, report, label or letter as a report. The options available on the Import dialog box that can be opened as a report, were created from the same table or set that the current report is based on.

Table 3-2 Report menu options explained (Continued)

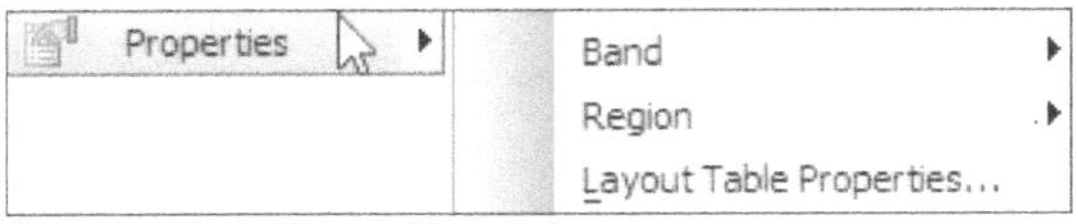

Figure 3-6 Properties submenu

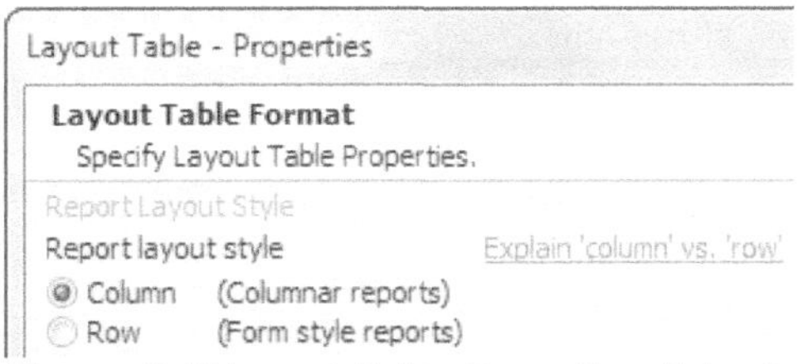

Figure 3-7 Layout Table Properties dialog box

Select Records To Print Dialog Box

The options shown in Figure 3-8 are used to create a filter to select the records to print, as well as, sort the records.

You can also select to have the user prompted when the report is run. If the report was originally created with the Report Genie and had filter or order criteria, that criteria is used by default to select records for the report in the editor. You can change or delete this criteria.

The options are explained in Table 3-3.

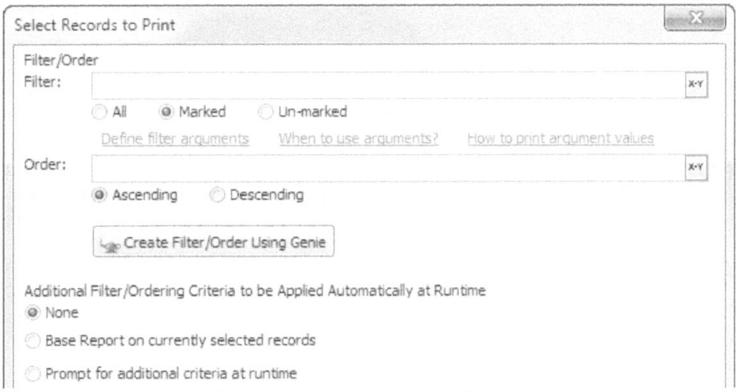

Figure 3-8 Select Records To Print dialog box

Option	Description
Filter	Is used to modify the existing filter expression or create an expression to select the records that will appear on the report.
Record Type	The **ALL, MARKED** and **UNMARKED** options are used to select which types of records will appear on the report.
Define Filter Arguments	This link opens the dialog box shown in Figure 3-9. The options are used to allow the person running the report to select the value(s) for the filter expression.

Table 3-3 Select Records To Print dialog box options explained

Option	Description
Order	Is used to modify the existing order expression or create an expression to order the records in the Detail section of the report.
Ascending	Sorts the records in the Detail section in A to Z or low to high order.
Descending	Sorts the records in the Detail section in Z to A or high to low order.
Create Filter/Order Using Genie button	Opens the dialog box shown in Figure 3-10. (1)
Base report on currently selected records	Select this option to use the order and filter criteria that is currently selected.
Prompt for additional criteria at run time	Opens the **SELECT FILTER DIALOG BOX** to allow the user to select the criteria when they run the report. (1)

Table 3-3 Select Records To Print dialog box options explained (Continued)

(1) The options work the same as the ones used to select records for a form.

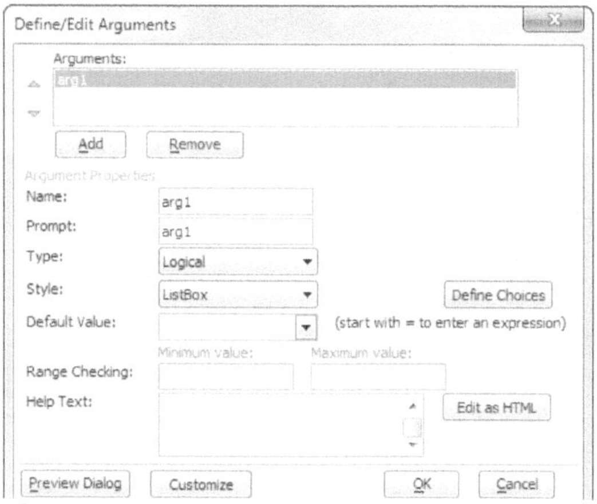

Figure 3-9 Define/Edit Arguments dialog box

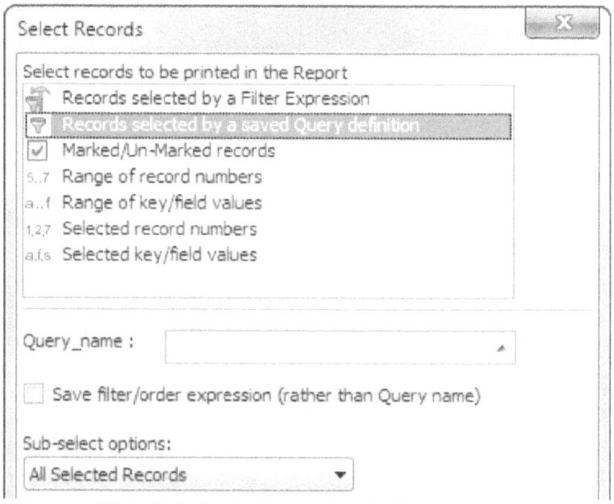

Figure 3-10 Select Records dialog box

Object Menu

The options shown in Figure 3-11 are only enabled when an object or report section bar is selected. The options are explained in Table 3-4.

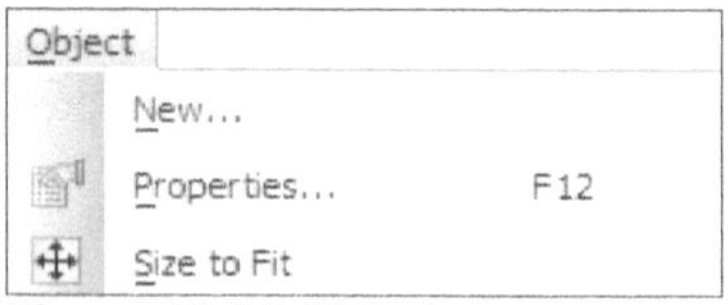

Figure 3-11 Object menu

Option	Description
New	Opens the dialog box shown in Figure 3-12, which is used to select the type of object that you want to add to the report.
Properties	Opens the Properties dialog box for the object that is selected. To display the properties for the entire report, click on the Report bar at the top of the report, then select this option.
Size to Fit	Resizes the objects border to fit the content.

Table 3-4 Object menu options explained

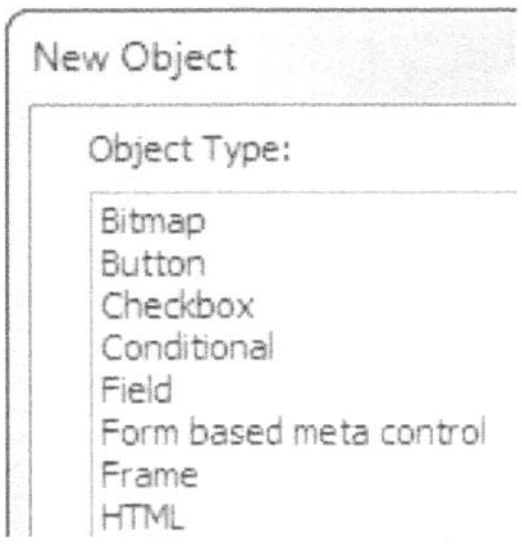

Figure 3-12 New Object dialog box (reports)

Arrange Menu

The options on the menu are shown in Figure 3-13.

AUTO MERGE option [See Chapter 5, Arrange Menu]

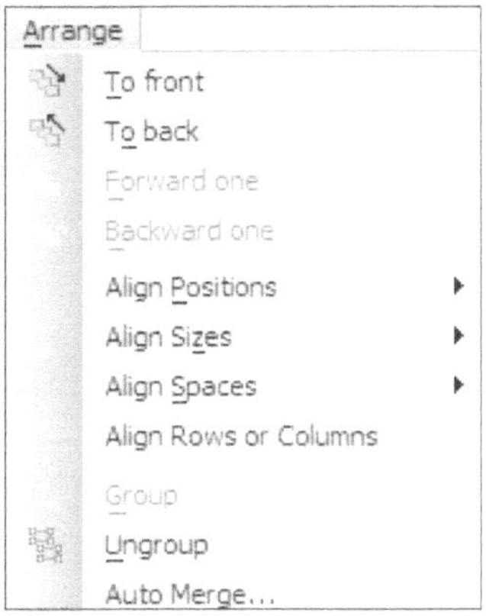

Figure 3-13 Arrange menu

Stylesheets Menu

The **APPLY OR CREATE A STYLESHEET** option opens the Stylesheets dialog box, which is used to apply an existing style sheet to the layout. You can also create a new style sheet, import or export a style sheet from this dialog box.

Panels

Like the Form Editor, the Report Editor has the Properties, Drag Drop List and Toolbox panels. The Toolbox panel for reports has less controls then the one on the Form Editor, but they work the same way. The **SUB-REPORT CONTROL** replaces the Sub-Form control in the Form Editor. The Report Editor has a subset of the Super controls that the Form Editor has.

Report Events

The options shown in Figure 3-14 are on the Report menu. They are used to create actions that you want to happen when the report starts or stops printing. Using these options requires using Xbasic or Action Scripting. The options are explained below.

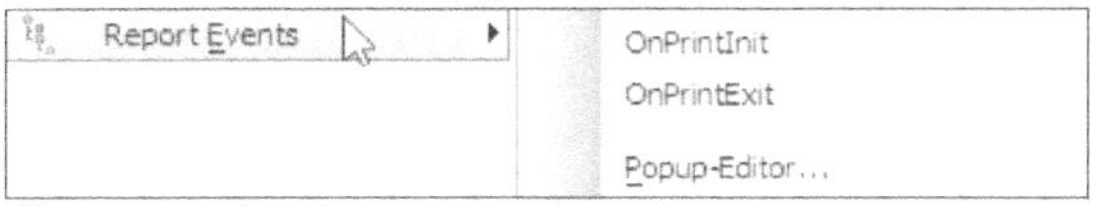

Figure 3-14 Report Events submenu

① **ONPRINTINIT** Use this option when you want the event to happen when the report starts printing.

② **ONPRINTEXIT** Use this option when you want the event to happen when the report has finished printing.

③ **POPUP-EDITOR** Opens the Events for dialog box. Reports do not have fly-over options like forms have, so I'm not sure why this option is here.

Free Form Report Editor Toolbar

The toolbar is shown in Figure 3-15. The buttons specifically for reports are explained in Table 3-5. The last three buttons on the toolbar are not shown. This is the toolbar that you will see when creating or editing a Free Form report. Layout Table reports have a slightly different toolbar.

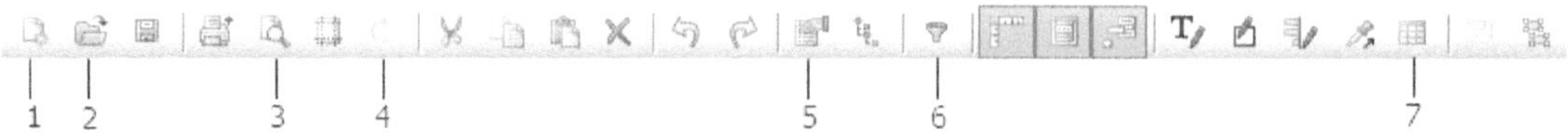

Figure 3-15 Free Form Report Editor toolbar

Button	Is Used To . . .
1	Create a new report.
2	Open an existing report.
3	Preview the report.
4	Refresh an SQL data source.
5	Open the Region or Object Properties dialog box depending on what is selected.
6	[See Table 3-2, Select Records]
7	Display or hide the Layout Table toolbar.

Table 3-5 Free Form Report Editor toolbar buttons explained

Report Design Window Shortcut Menu

The design window has two variations of its shortcut menu.

The shortcut menu shown in Figure 3-16 displays the options when you right-click on a blank space on the design window.

Figure 3-17 shows the design window shortcut menu when an object is selected.

The **CAN SHRINK** option allows the selected object to shrink if it does not need all of the space that has been allocated for it.

Figure 3-16 Design window shortcut menu

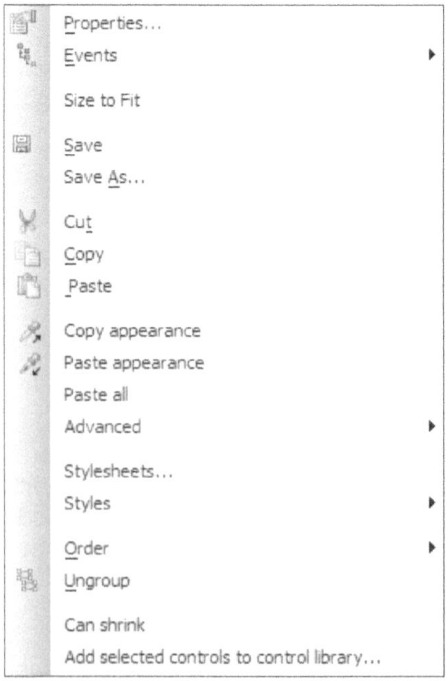

Figure 3-17 Design window shortcut menu when an object is selected

Sections Of A Report

If you have used a tool like Crystal Reports to create reports, you are already familiar with report sections. Alpha Five uses report sections also. In Alpha Five, there are three types of sections: Report, Detail and Group. What is different in Alpha Five is that it supports having multiple header and footer sections in each report type.

In the Report Editor, sections have a dark gray bar. If you are like me and can't really tell light gray from dark gray on the computer screen, the section bars also have a ▼ **OUTLINE BUTTON**, which is used to display and hide the regions that the fields and objects are placed in.

Using this option does not affect the report when it is previewed or printed. The exception is the Report section, which is at the top of the form.

The light gray bars on the layout denote the regions, which is where fields and objects are placed. Figure 3-18 shows the sections and regions of a report. Each section can have more than one region.

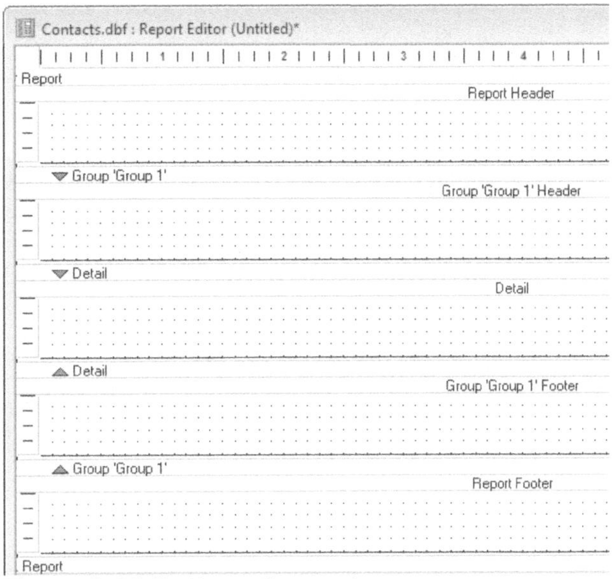

Figure 3-18 Sections of a report

Each section has its own properties that can be customized on a section by section basis. If you place the same calculated field (numbers, totals or amounts) in different sections of the report, it can produce different results.

It is important that you understand how each section of the report functions because they function independently of each other. Keep the following in mind when deciding where to place fields and objects on the report.

① If a report does not need a section, the section can be hidden or deleted so that it does not display blank space on the report.
② If you create a report using the genie, the majority of fields are automatically placed in an appropriate section of the report.
③ All of the report sections except the Group Header and Footer, will automatically appear in the report, whether you use them or not. Grouping is optional.
④ The order of the report sections cannot be changed.
⑤ Sections can be resized vertically as needed.
⑥ Expressions and charts will display different results, depending on which section of the report they are placed in. The expression differences are explained below in each report section.

Section 1: Report Header

This is the first section of the report. A report can only have one Report section. Data fields and other objects placed in this section will only print on the first page of the report. It is quite possible that many of the reports that you create will not have anything in this section. Something that you may want to include in this section of the report is the selection criteria that the report has. If the report needs a cover page, this section can be used for the cover page. If this is what you need to do, add a page break after this section so that the actual report starts on a new page. Expressions are calculated for the entire report.

> If the Report Header section requires more than one page, the information in the Page Header and Footer sections of the report will not print until all of the information in the Report Header section has printed.

Section 2: Page Header

Data fields and other objects placed in this section will appear at the top of every page in the report except the Report Header page if it prints on a page by itself. This is where most people put the report title. Other objects that are commonly placed in this section include the date, page number and headings for the fields in the Detail section of the report. Expressions are calculated at the beginning of every page of the report.

Section 3: Group Header

The group sections are optional. If the report has more than one group, the groups are evaluated from the top of the report to the bottom, in the order that they appear. The Group Header section usually contains the field or expression that was used to create the group. Field headings are automatically placed in the Group Header section instead of the Page Header section when the report has a group.

Data fields and other objects placed in this section will print at the beginning of each group on the report. Each time the data in the field or expression that the group is based on changes, another Group Header and Footer section is dynamically created. This section is always right above the Detail section. If a report is grouped on two or more fields, a new Group Header section will automatically be created for each field or expression that the report is grouped on.

The detail field headings are automatically placed in this section instead of the Page Header section if the report has a group. If all of the groups data does not print on the same page, this section is not printed at the top of the next page. Expressions are calculated one time at the beginning of the group, based on the data in the group, not on all of the data in the report.

Section 4: Detail Header

This section will contain the field headers if the report does not have groups.

> I did not find this to be the case when I created a Free Form report without groups using the report genie or when I created a Free Form report without groups from scratch. When I used the genie the field headings were placed in the Report Header section by default. When I created a Free Form report from scratch, the field headings were placed in the Detail section.

Section 5: Detail

Data fields and other objects placed in this section will print for each record that meets the selection criteria. The data fields and other objects in this section usually have field headings in the Page Header section. This section is the body of the report and is automatically repeated once for each record that will be printed on the report. Expressions are calculated for each record in this section, unless the record does not meet the condition of the expression.

Section 6: Detail Footer

Is used for images or graphics that are used to separate the Detail section from a group.

Section 7: Group Footer

This section is only used if the data is grouped. Data fields and other objects placed in this section will print at the end of each group section on the report. The Group Footer section often includes subtotals and other summary data (like a count or total) for the detail records in the group.
This section is always right below the Detail section. This section will not print at the bottom of a spillover page. Expressions are calculated one time at the end of the group, based on the data in the group, not on all of the data in the report.

Section 8: Report Footer

Data fields and other objects placed in this section will print once at the end of the report. This is usually where grand totals and other types of report summary information is placed. Expressions are calculated once at the end of the report.

Section 9: Page Footer

Data fields and other objects placed in this section will print at the bottom of each page of the report. The Page Footer section is similar to the Page Header section. Page numbers are often placed in this section. The report genie will place the date and page number in this section. Expressions are calculated at the end of every page of the report. This would be useful if the report needs to have totals by page.

Additional Header And Footer Sections

In addition to the header and footer sections discussed above, Alpha Five has additional header and footer sections that are used with page breaks. I have created reports for over 25 years, using a variety of report writing software and this is the first report writer that I have seen use this technique to handle detail or group sections that do not fit on one page. To me, it is more work because you are creating sections with the same information, one for the first page that a detail or group section prints on and another set of report sections for the remaining pages that the detail or group section may print on. These additional header and footer section types are explained below.

① **CONTINUATION HEADERS AND FOOTERS** These sections are used when you want to let the reader know that the section of the report that they are currently looking at started on a previous page. These sections can be set up for different levels of the report. For example, you can set them up for the Detail and Group Header sections. In the Report Editor they appear below the Page Header and above the Page Footer sections, probably because when used, they print instead of the default Page Header and Footer sections.

② **PAGE HEADERS AND FOOTERS** In addition to being used to print at the top and bottom of every page on the report, these sections can also be created for a specific section of the report like a Detail section. Regardless of the number of Page Header and Footer sections that you create, only one will print on each page.

③ **REPEATING GROUP HEADERS AND FOOTERS** These sections are used to print field headings and other objects that are in the Group Header or Footer section.

Section Shortcut Menu

You guessed it. Each section of the report has a shortcut menu similar to the one shown in Figure 3-19. The options are explained in Table 3-6.

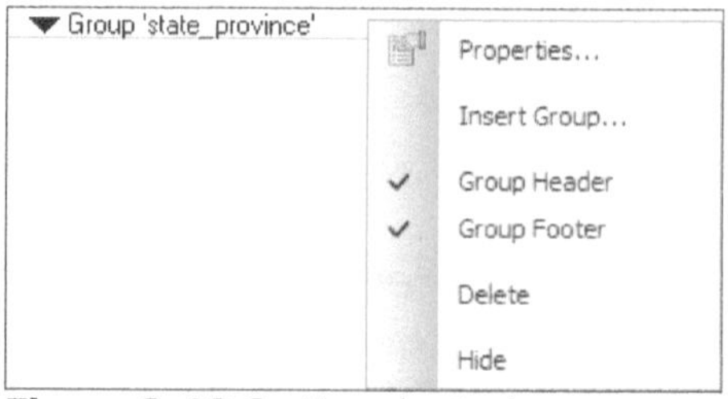

Figure 3-19 Section shortcut menu

Option	Description
Properties	[See Group Properties Dialog Box, later in this chapter]
Insert Group	[See New Group Properties Dialog Box, later in this chapter]
Header/Footer options	Displays or hides the Group Header and Footer sections.
Delete	(2)
Hide	Displays or hides the section.

Table 3-6 Section shortcut menu options explained

(2) Using this option deletes the section and the objects in it without warning. If you do this by mistake, click the Undo button. If you have made changes after selecting this option by mistake and have not saved the changes and want to bring the section back, close the report (do not save it, when prompted) and reopen it. You will loose the other changes that you made, but the section that you removed/deleted by mistake will still be there.

Report Properties

I guess by now you are not surprised that reports have properties. Just like each type of object on a form has a different set of properties, so do the sections on a report.

Report Properties Dialog Box

The options on this dialog box are for the entire report, not a specific band or section of the report. The options are explained in Tables 3-7 to 3-11.

Report Tab

The options shown in Figure 3-20 are general options for the report. They are explained in Table 3-7.

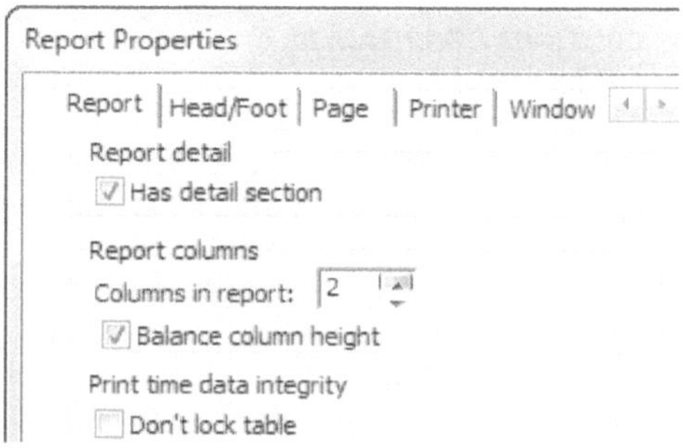

Figure 3-20 Report tab

Option	Description
Has detail section	Displays or hides the Detail section of the report.
Columns in report	Is used to select the number of columns for the detail and group sections of the report. The default is one.
Balance column height	Is only enabled if there are two or more columns in the report. If checked, the height of the columns will be the same when the report is printed.
Don't lock table	If **NOT** checked, the tables that the report is based on will be locked when the report is previewed or printed. This means that no one else can access the tables or any object that uses the tables that the report uses.

Table 3-7 Report tab options explained

Head/Foot Tab

The options shown in Figure 3-21 control the Report Header and Footer sections of the report. The options checked are the defaults. If checked, the report section is displayed on the report, otherwise the report section is hidden.

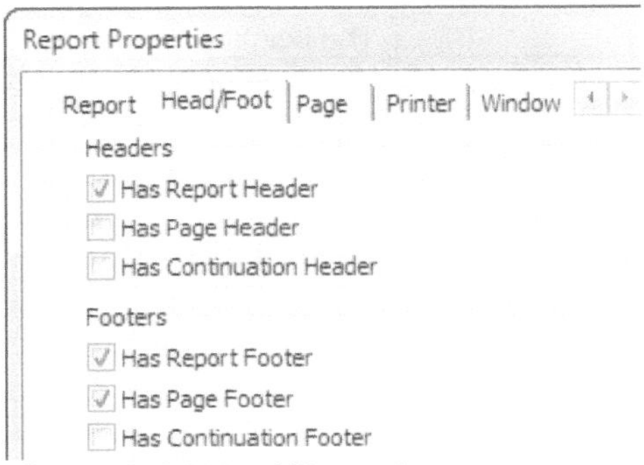

Figure 3-21 Head/Foot tab

Page Tab

The options shown in Figure 3-22 are used to set the margins and orientation for the report, as well as, select what to do if there is an overflow of data. The options are explained in Table 3-8.

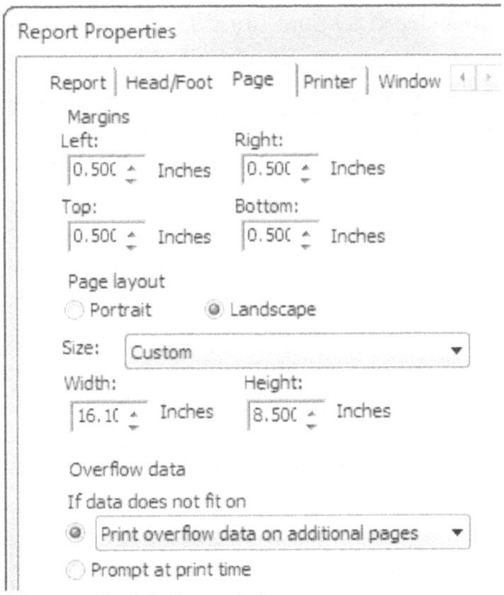

Figure 3-22 Page tab

Option	Is Used To Select . . .
Left margin	How much space should be between the left edge of the paper and where the report starts to print.
Right margin	How much space should be between the right edge of the paper and where the report stops printing.
Top margin	How much space should be between the top edge of the paper and where the report starts to print.
Bottom margin	How much space should be between the bottom edge of the paper and where the report stops printing.
Portrait	How the report should print on the paper. Landscape is useful when there are a lot of fields in the Detail section of the report.
Size	The type of paper.
Width	The width of the page. (3)
Height	The height of the page. (3)
Overflow data	What to do with data that does not fit on the page. The options are explained in Table 3-9. The first three options in the table are in the drop-down list.

Table 3-8 Page tab options explained

(3) This option is only available when the Custom Size option is selected.

Option	Description
Trim	Does not print the data that does not fit on the page.
Shrink	Forces the data to print on the page.
Print overflow	Prints the data that does not fit on the current page, on the next page.
Prompt at print time	Displays a message like the one shown in Figure 3-23. This is the default option, which allows the user select what to do at run-time with the data that does not fit on the page.

Table 3-9 Overflow data print options explained

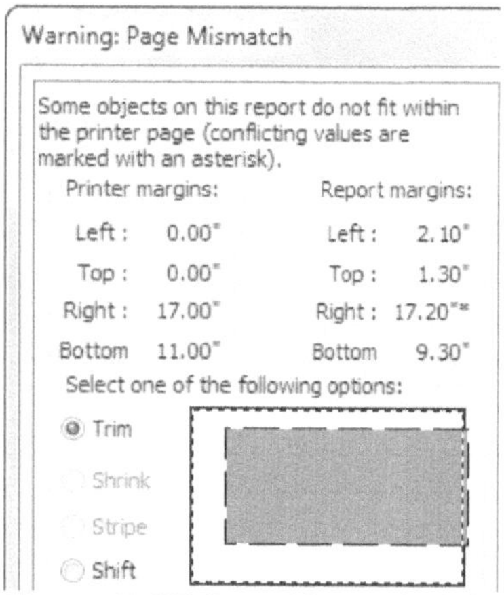

Figure 3-23 Page Mismatch dialog box

Printer Tab

The options shown in Figure 3-24 are used to select and configure the printer. The options are explained in Table 3-10.

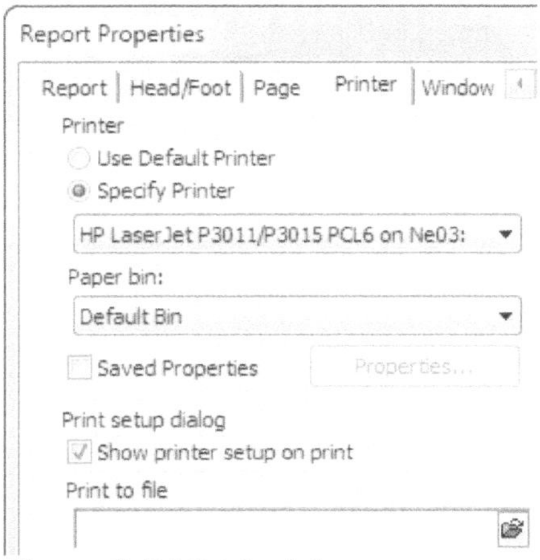

Figure 3-24 Printer tab

Option	Description
Use Default Printer	Uses the default printer connected to your computer.
Specify Printer	Enables the printer drop-down list to select the printer that you want to use.
Paper bin	Is used to select a specific paper tray if the selected printer has more than one paper tray.
Saved Properties	If checked, the options selected on this tab are saved with the report. The saved options can be changed at run time if you create an action script. The **PROPERTIES BUTTON** opens a dialog box that is specific to the selected printer. The options are used to configure the printer for the report.
Show printer setup on print	If checked, the Print dialog box will be displayed after the report is run so that the user can select a printer and options for the printer. If cleared, the report will go straight to the printer.
Print to file	If you want the report to be saved to a file instead of printed on paper, type in the name of the file that you want to create to store the report in.

Table 3-10 Printer tab options explained

Window Tab

The options shown in Figure 3-25 are used to size the Print Preview window. The options are explained in Table 3-11.

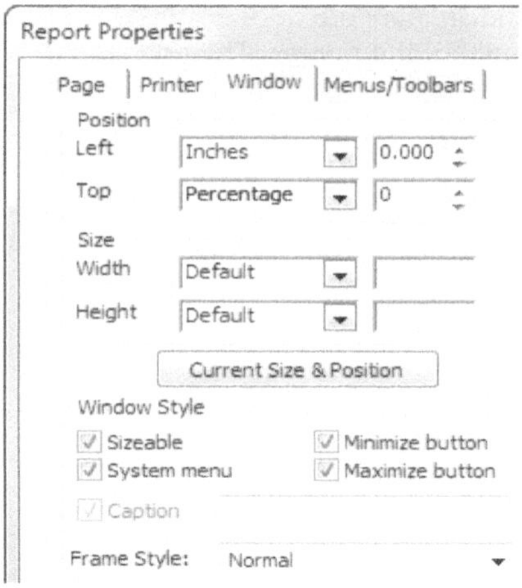

Figure 3-25 Window tab

Option	Description
Position	Sets the left and top position of the preview window. The unit of measurement options are default, percentage and inches.
Size	Sets the width and height of the preview window. The unit of measurement options are default, percentage, inches, use form width and use form height.
Current Size & Position button	Changes the position and size fields (listed above in this table) to the current options of the preview window.
Sizeable	Allows the user to resize the preview window.
System menu	Adds the menu shown in Figure 3-26 to the upper left corner of the preview window.
Minimize button	Adds the minimize button illustrated in Figure 3-27 to the upper right corner of the preview window.
Maximize button	Adds the maximize button illustrated in Figure 3-27 to the upper right corner of the preview window.
Caption	Is enabled when the four Window Style options are not checked. When testing this option, I did not see the text that I entered in this field, displayed anywhere on the preview window. (4)
Frame Style	Is used to select the style of the window. I tried all three options, but did not see a difference in the preview window. (4)

Table 3-11 Window tab options explained

(4) I am not sure that this option works as intended.

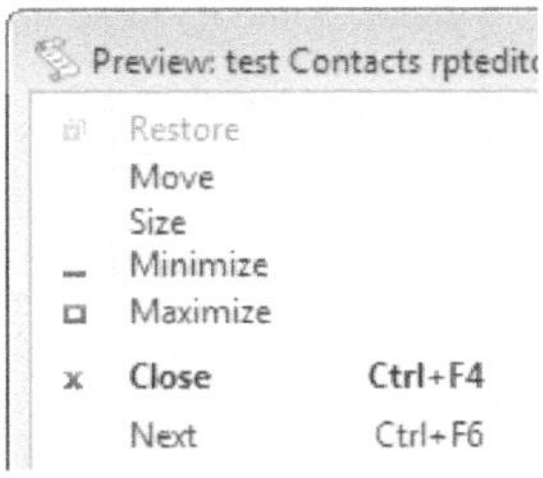

Figure 3-26 System menu

Figure 3-27 Minimize and Maximize buttons illustrated

Menus/Toolbars Tab

The options shown in Figure 3-28 are used to select the menu and toolbar that will appear when the report is previewed.

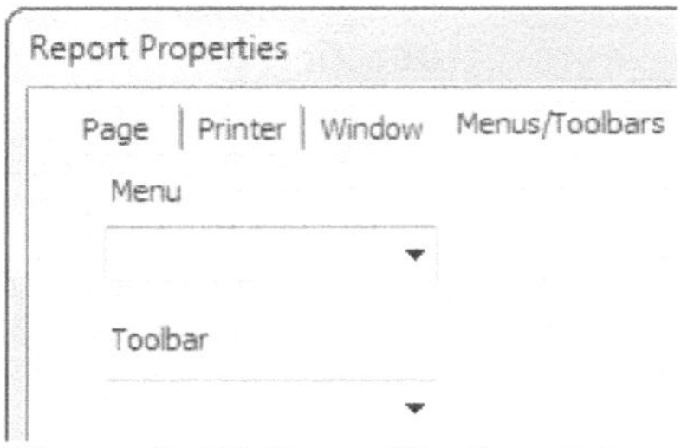

Figure 3-28 Menus/Toolbars tab

Band Section vs Region Section

These are the two sections of the report that are used to configure how the report looks. The bands are the bars with the section names in the layout. Bands are in Free Form and Layout Table report types. The regions are the white space in the report, where fields and other objects are placed. Only Free Form reports have regions. The band and region sections have properties, as explained below.

Band Properties

The previous section covered properties for the report. This section covers the properties for each band of the report shown in Figure 3-29.

The options for each band are explained in Tables 3-12 and 3-13. These options can be accessed by using any of the options listed below.

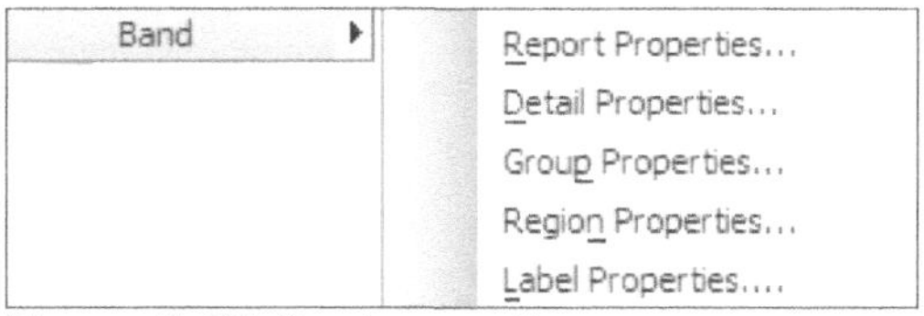

Figure 3-29 Band properties

① Right-clicking on the band in the report layout and selecting Properties.

② Clicking on the band, then press the **F12** key.

③ Selecting the band from the Report menu shown above in Figure 3-29.

Report Band Properties

Selecting the Report Properties option on the submenu shown above in Figure 3-29 opens the Report Properties dialog box. [See Table 3-7]

Detail Band Properties

Selecting the Detail Properties option on the submenu shown above in Figure 3-29 opens the Detail Properties dialog box. The options on this dialog box are explained in the next three sections.

Detail Properties Dialog Box

Region Tab

The options shown in Figure 3-30 are for the Detail section of the report. The options are explained in Table 3-12.

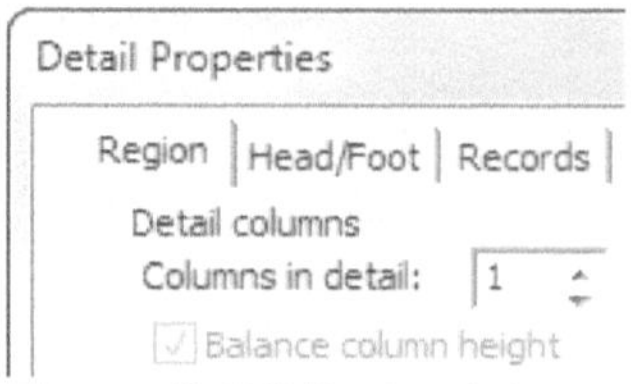

Figure 3-30 Region tab

Option	Description
Columns in detail	This option is used to override the number of columns set by Report and Group level options. If the report already has fields, Alpha Five will not allow you to add more columns than can fit on the page.
Balance column height	[See Table 3-7]

Table 3-12 Region tab options explained (Detail properties)

Head/Foot Tab

The majority of options shown in Figure 3-31 are used to override the same option (on the Report Properties dialog box) set for the report section with the same name.

[See Report Properties Dialog Box, Head/Foot tab, earlier in this chapter]

The other options are explained in Table 3-13.

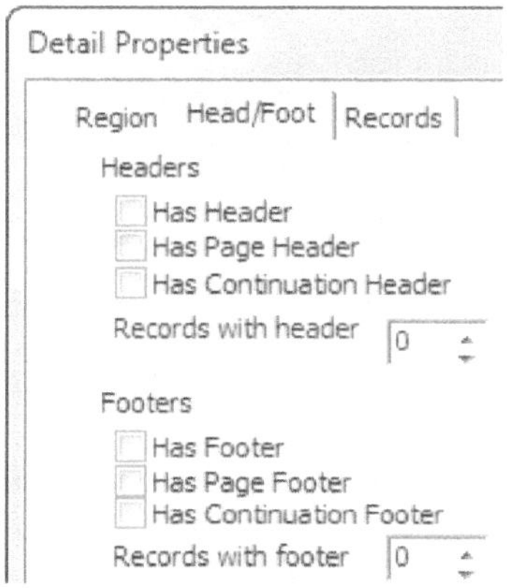

Figure 3-31 Head/Foot tab

Option	Is Used To Set . . .
Records with header	The minimum number of records that have to appear below the header.
Records with footer	The minimum number of records that have to appear above the footer.

Table 3-13 Head/Foot tab options explained (Detail properties)

Records Tab

The options shown in Figure 3-32 are used to select the sort order and filter options for the records in the Detail section. The majority of options were explained earlier in Table 3-3.

The **BASE REPORT ON CURRENT SELECTION OF RECORDS** option is the same as the Base option in Table 3-3.

The **PROMPT FOR CRITERIA AT PRINT TIME** option is the same as the Prompt option in Table 3-3.

The **USE FILTER/ORDER FROM QUERY BUTTON** opens the dialog box shown in Figure 3-33. It is used to select a query that has the order and filter expression that will be used to select the records for the details section.

Figure 3-32 Records tab

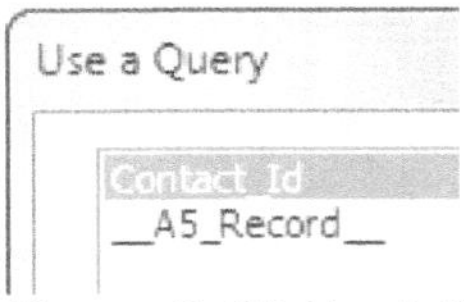

Figure 3-33 Use A Query dialog box

Group Band Properties

Selecting the Group Properties option on the submenu shown earlier in Figure 3-29 opens the dialog box shown in Figure 3-34.

This dialog box shows the groups that have been created for the report.

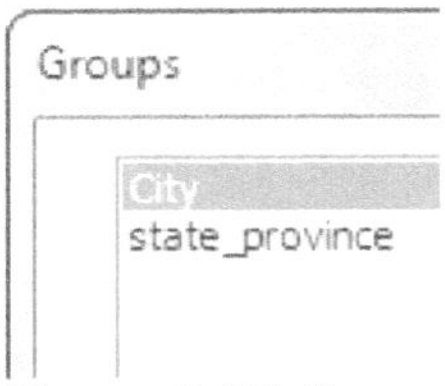

Figure 3-34 Groups dialog box

Group Properties Dialog Box

Group Tab

Once you select the group that you want to change the properties of on the Groups dialog box, click OK.

You will see the dialog box shown in Figure 3-35. The options are explained in Table 3-14.

Figure 3-35 Group tab

Option	Description
Break on change in	Is used to select a field or create an expression that will select the field to group on. To create an expression, open the drop-down list and select **<EXPRESSION>** at the top of the list.
Label	Is the name that will appear on the section bar to denote the group. Each label name must be unique in the report.
Order on break	Forces the groups to display in order based on the value in the field being grouped on.
Use set ordering	Forces the groups to appear in order based on the sort order of the table or set.
Specify order	Create an expression if you do not want to use the Break on change in value to group on.
Ascending	Sorts the groups in A to Z or low to high order.
Descending	Sorts the groups in Z to A or high to low order.

Table 3-14 Group tab options explained

Region Tab

The options shown in Figure 3-36 are for the group section of the report. The options are explained in Table 3-15.

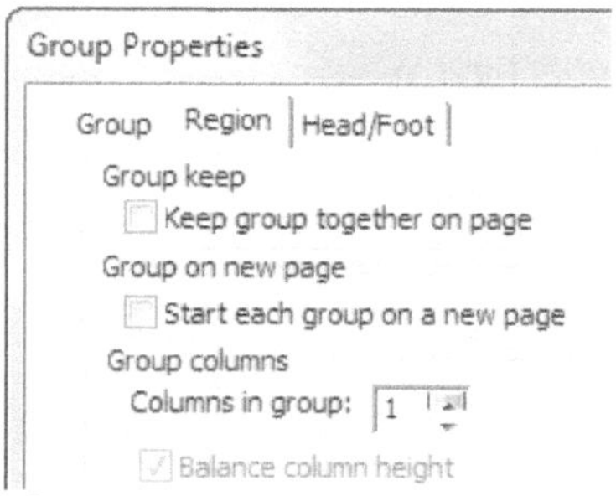

Figure 3-36 Region tab

Option	Description
Keep group together on page	If checked, all detail records in the group are forced to appear on the same page.
Start each group on a new page	If checked, each group will start on a new page of the report.
Columns in group	Overrides the report level setting for columns.
Balance column height	[See Table 3-7]

Table 3-15 Region tab options explained (Group properties)

Head/Foot Tab

The options shown in Figure 3-37 are used to modify the Group Header and Footer sections. The options are explained in Table 3-16.

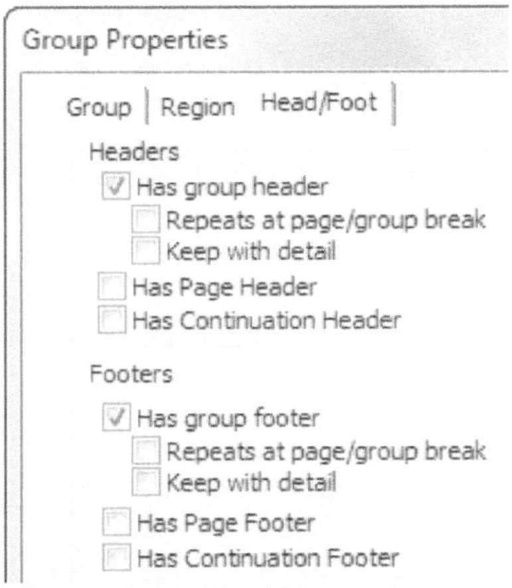

Figure 3-37 Head/Foot tab

Option	Description
Has group header	Displays or hides the Group Header section.
Repeats at page/group break	(Header and Footer sections) If checked, the Group Header or Group Footer section will be repeated at the group and page breaks.
Keep with detail	(In Headers section) If checked, the Group Header section has to be followed by a minimum of one detail record. This option was formerly known as **KEEP WITH FOLLOWING HEADER**.
Has Page Header	Is used to override the report level setting for the Page Header section of the current group.
Has Continuation Header	Is used to override the report level setting for the Continuation Header section of the current group.
Has group footer	Displays or hides the Group Footer section.
Keep with detail	(In Footers section) If checked, the Group Footer section has to come after a minimum of one detail record. This option was formerly known as **KEEP WITH PRIOR FOOTER**.
Has Page Footer	Is used to override the report level setting for the Page Footer section of the current group.
Has Continuation Footer	Is used to override the report level setting for the Continuation Footer section of the current group.

Table 3-16 Head/Foot tab options explained (Group properties)

Region Band Properties

Selecting this option on the Report menu displays the dialog box shown in Figure 3-38. This dialog box displays all of the regions currently on the report.

Select the region that you want to modify, then click OK. The corresponding Region Properties dialog box will open. This is the same as selecting the Region option shown in Figure 3-39.

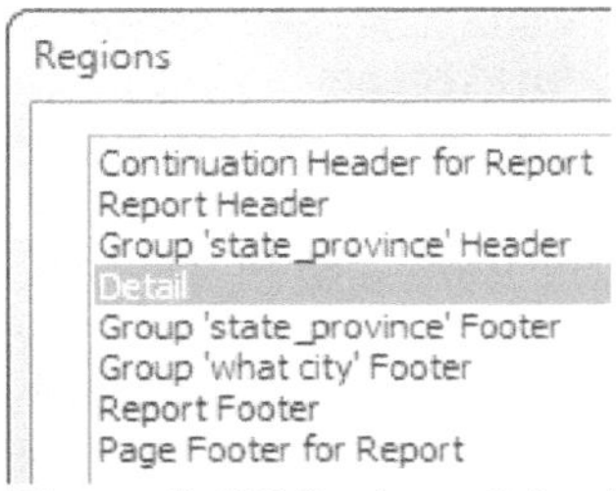

Figure 3-38 Regions dialog box

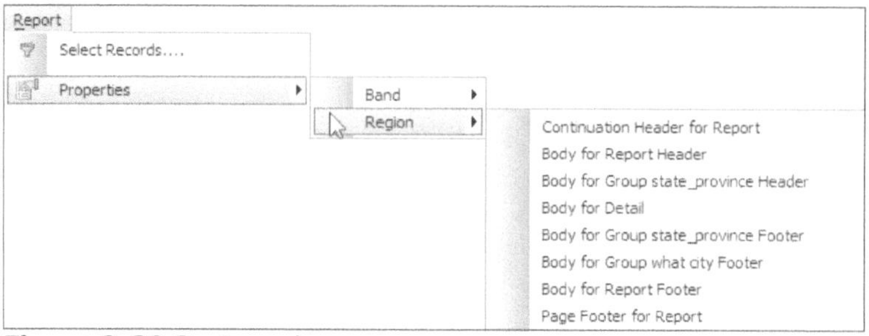

Figure 3-39 Region submenu

Region Properties Dialog Box

The options on this dialog box are used to set options for each region (the sections on the report that have fields and other objects) on the report. There are five tabs on this dialog box. Each region does not use all of the tabs. The options on each tab are explained below.

Backdrop Tab

The options shown in Figure 3-40 are used to change the background of the region.

The options are explained in Table 3-17.

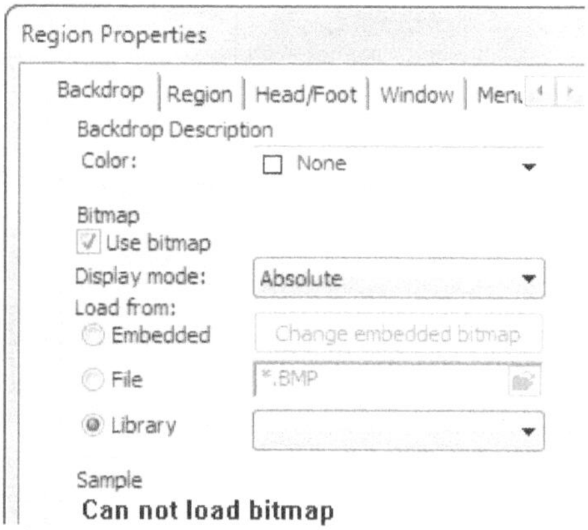

Figure 3-40 Backdrop tab

Option	Description
Color	Is used to select a color for the background.
Use bitmap	Enables the other options in the Bitmap section.
Display mode	Is used to select how the bitmap is displayed in the background. There are four options in the drop-down list: **ABSOLUTE** displays one image pixel for each printer pixel. This option usually is not used for reports. **STRETCH** resizes the image horizontally and vertically to fill the region. This option can distort the image file. **TILE** repeats the image to fill the region. **BEST FIT** resizes the image without distorting it to fill the region.
Embedded	Is used to select an image file, which will be embedded in the report.
File	Is used to select an image file.
Library	Is used to select an icon image file from the images that come with Alpha Five.

Table 3-17 Backdrop tab options explained

Region Tab

The options shown in Figure 3-41 are used to configure how the region is displayed.

The options are explained in Table 3-18.

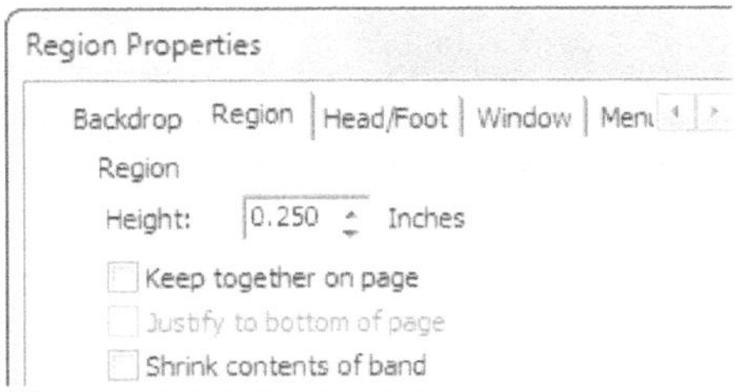

Figure 3-41 Region tab

Option	Description
Height	Is used to select the height of the region.
Keep together on page	If checked, all of the objects in the region will be printed on the same page.
Justify to bottom of page	Is used to determine if the region can be stretched to the bottom of the printed page. This option is not available for the detail Continuation Header and Footer sections.
Shrink contents of band	The region can be shrunk if this option is selected. It is used to suppress blank lines. This option does not apply to Page Header and Footer sections.

Table 3-18 Region tab options explained (Region properties)

Head/Foot Tab

The options shown in Figure 3-42 are used to display and hide header and footer sections.

The options on this tab are the same as the ones on the Report Properties dialog box. [See Table 3-16]

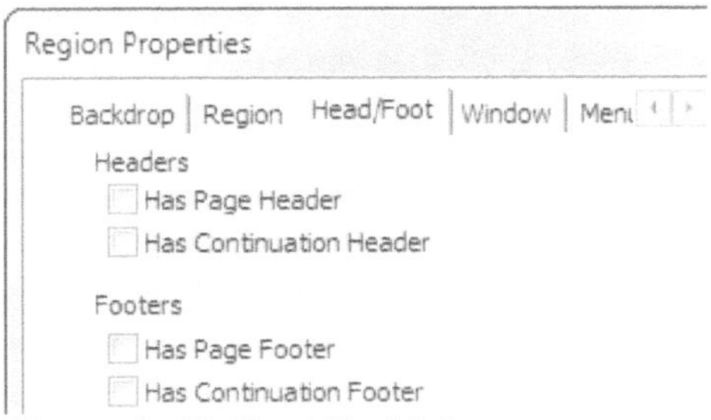

Figure 3-42 Head/Foot tab

Window Tab

The options on this tab are the same as the ones on the Report Properties dialog box. [See Table 3-11]

Menus/Toolbars Tab

The options on this tab are the same as the ones on the Report Properties dialog box. [See Figure 3-28]

Label Band Properties

Selecting this option on the Report menu displays the dialog box shown in Figure 3-43.

Label Properties Dialog Box

The options shown in Figure 3-43 are used to select the direction (flow) that the data will be printed in.

Report ⇒ Properties ⇒ Band ⇒ Label Properties, opens this dialog box.

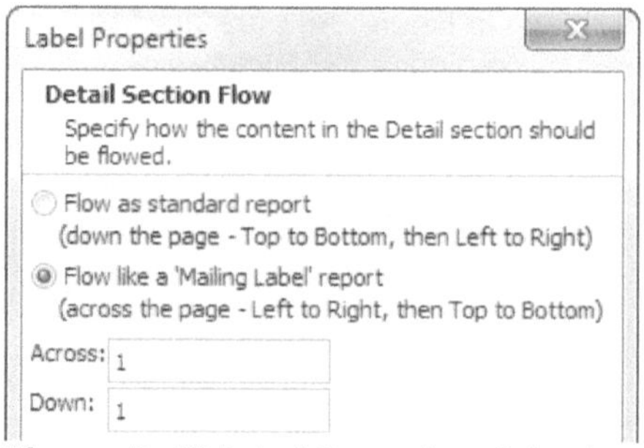

Figure 3-43 Label Properties dialog box

Field Properties Dialog Box

Just like fields on forms have properties, so do fields on a report. Different types of fields and objects on the report have slightly different options. Wouldn't it be cool if you could select an option on this dialog box for a field on a form, that you also apply to any report that uses the field?

Setup Tab

The options shown in Figure 3-44 are used to select general options for a field on the report. Many of the options at the bottom of the tab are better suited for forms then reports.

The options that I think that you would use on a report are explained below.

The **ALLOW GROWTH WHEN PRINTING** option allows the field to expand if needed, so that all of the data in the field will be printed on the report.

The **ALLOW SHRINKING** option allows the data in the field to shrink to fit on the page.

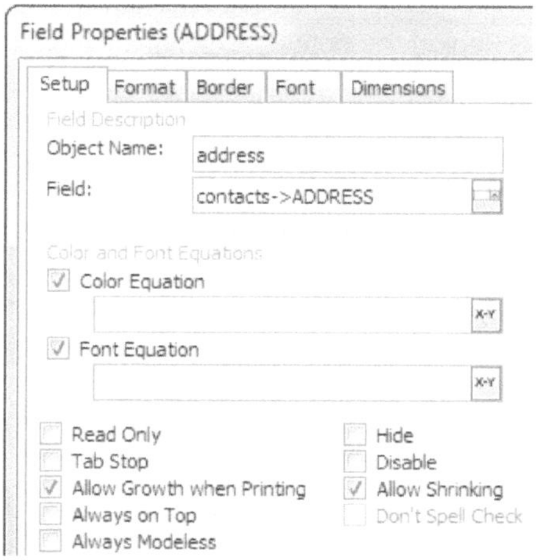

Figure 3-44 Setup tab

Dimensions Tab

The only difference is that reports do not use anchors, like fields do.

New Group Properties Dialog Box

The options on the dialog box shown in Figure 3-45 are used to create a new group. To open this dialog box, right-click on the report section or any section in the report that has a ▼ and select Insert Group. The options are the same as the ones that you learned about earlier in the Group Band Properties section. [See Tables 3-14, 3-15 and 3-16]

The Head/Foot tab has the **KEEP WITH FOLLOWING HEADER** and **KEEP WITH PRIOR FOOTER** options shown in Figure 3-46, instead of the Keep with detail options shown earlier in Figure 3-37. The options have the same functionality.

Figure 3-45 New Group Properties dialog box

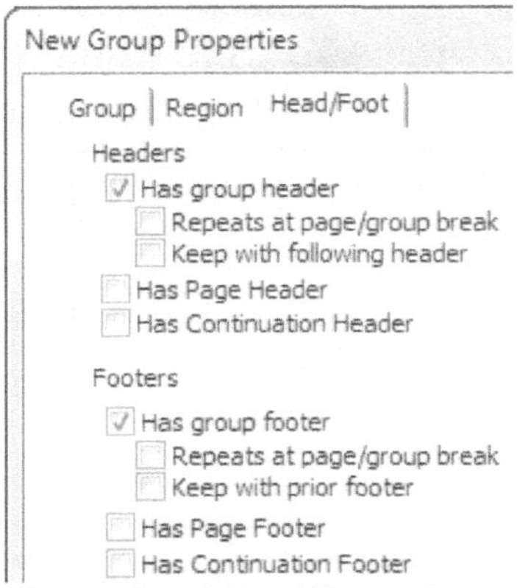

Figure 3-46 Head/Foot tab

Aligning Objects In A Free Form Report

Aligning objects in a Free Form report is similar to aligning objects on a form. In my opinion, it is more crucial to do what I call precision aligning on a report then a form. Many of the alignment options for forms are also available for reports. The most used tools for aligning objects on a report are explained in the next few sections.

Using Rulers To Align Objects

Both rulers can be used to align and move objects. Each ruler has a shortcut menu that has options for aligning objects.

Rows Ruler

When you right-click on the ruler on the left side of the window, all of the objects in the section are selected. You will see the shortcut menu shown in Figure 3-47. The options will align the selected objects on the top, bottom or center of the objects frame.

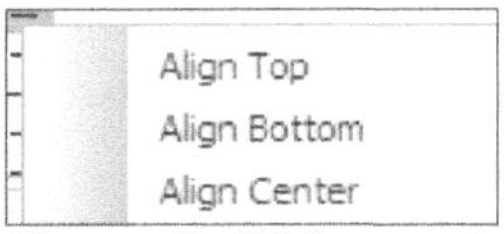

Figure 3-47 Rows ruler shortcut menu

Columns Ruler

When you click on the ruler at the top of the window, objects below the space that you right-clicked on will be selected, as shown in Figure 3-48.

When you right-click on the Columns ruler, you will see the shortcut menu shown in Figure 3-49.

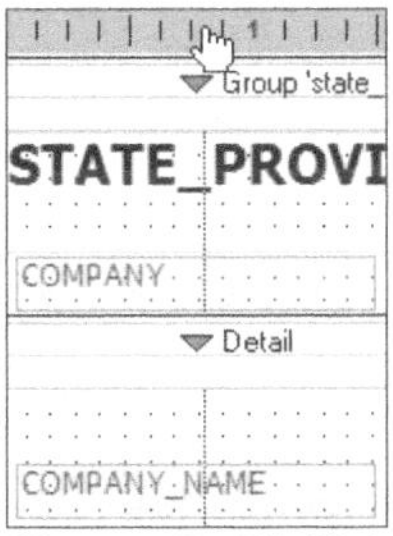

Figure 3-48 Objects selected in different sections

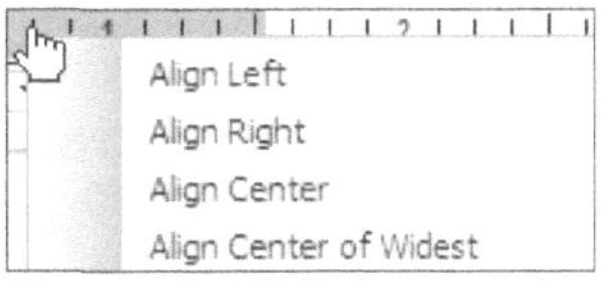

Figure 3-49 Columns ruler shortcut menu

> **Aligning Columns**
> As you saw above in Figure 3-48, objects in each section of the report are selected when you click on the ruler at the top of the window. If you only want to align objects in some sections, but not others, hide the sections that you do not want objects aligned in, then click on the Column ruler.

Using The Grid Option To Align Objects

The Grid option is on the Report menu. It works the same as it does for forms.

Using Dynamic Guidelines To Align Objects

The Dynamic Guidelines option is on the Report menu. In addition to using the guidelines to align objects, guidelines can also be used to size objects. This option works the same as it does for forms.

Importing Report Layouts

This feature is useful if there is a report in one database that you want to use in another database, as is or as the basis for a new report. Layouts that you want to import have to use the **.A5PKG FILE TYPE**. If you need to import a layout, follow the steps below.

1. On the Control Panel, click on the tab of the layout type that you want to import.

2. Right-click on a blank space and select Import Layout.

3. On the dialog box shown in Figure 3-50, navigate to the folder that has the .a5pkg layout package that you want to import.

   Click on the package file, then click the Open button.

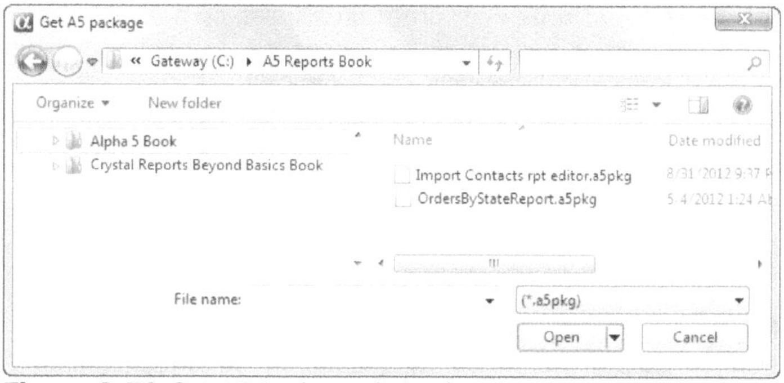

Figure 3-50 Get A5 Package dialog box

Exercise 3.1: Modifying A Report

In this exercise you will modify the Contacts list genie report by opening it in the Report Editor and adding system fields from the Drag Drop List panel to the Report Header section.

Open A Report Created By The Report Genie

Reports that are initially created by the Report Genie can be opened and edited in the Report Editor. As you will see, you will be presented with two options.

Saving A Genie Report As A Free Form Report
During testing, the steps in this section of the exercise worked until I upgraded the software. After the upgrade, I was not able to save the genie report as a free-form report. The genie report would save as a Layout Table report, no matter what options I selected. If you go through the steps in this section of the exercise and find that you have the same issue, (the way to know is if you do not see the Toolbox in the lower right corner of the Report editor), import the Import Contacts report editor package, shown above in Figure 3-50 and use that report instead of the Contacts list genie report in step 1. Save the Import report as `Contacts rpt editor` as instructed in step 4, then start with the steps in the Modify The Report section.

1. Click on the aContactsListGenie report, then click the Design button. You will see the Report Genie.

2. Click the Open in Report Editor button on the toolbar.

   You will see the dialog box shown in Figure 3-51.

   The warning at the bottom of the dialog box is important.

   You can select the report type and whether or not you want to preserve the current report which was created using the genie.

Figure 3-51 Open in Report Editor dialog box

> It may be me, but I find all of the Save options wording confusing. Why not just have these options on the Preview toolbar instead of the Open in Report Editor button: "Save genie report and open as free form report", "Save genie report and open as a layout table report", "Don't save genie report and open as free form report" and "Don't save genie report and open as layout table report".

3. Select the Free Form report option, then click the Save Report As button.

4. Type `aContactsRptEditor` as the report name on the Save Quick Report dialog box, then click OK. The report will open in the editor and the version of the report created with the genie is still intact.

Modify The Report

As you can see, the report does not have a title and some of the field headings were cut off.

1. Right-click on the Report band and select the Page Header option. Make the section longer.

2. Make the Company, First Name and Last Name fields and headings smaller.

3. Move all of the fields left except the Zip Code field.

4. Notice that you cannot see the entire Zip Code heading. Click on the Zip Code heading and make if wide enough to see all of the characters.

> **Help! I Can't Select An Object On The Report**
> If you have trouble selecting an object, follow the steps below.
> 1. Click on the section bar above the object.
> 2. Edit ⇒ Select All.
> 3. Press and hold down the Shift key, then click on every object except the one that you want. It should be the only object in the band that is selected.

> **Unsaved Changes**
> When the report has changes that have not been saved, you will see a * after the report name in the Title bar, as illustrated in Figure 3-52.

Figure 3-52 Unsaved report changes indicator

Add System Fields To The Report

These fields are in the Drag Drop List panel. In this exercise you will add some system fields to the Report Header section.

1. On the Drag Drop List panel toolbar, click the Controls Down button, if it is not already selected. Click the Don't group controls button, then click the Fields with titles button, if it is not already selected. All three buttons should have an orange background.

2. Make the Report Header section longer, then drag the field headings down in the section. Add the following fields from the System section of the Drag Drop List panel to the top of the Report Header section: Current Order, Current Filter and Layout Name, as shown in Figure 3-53.

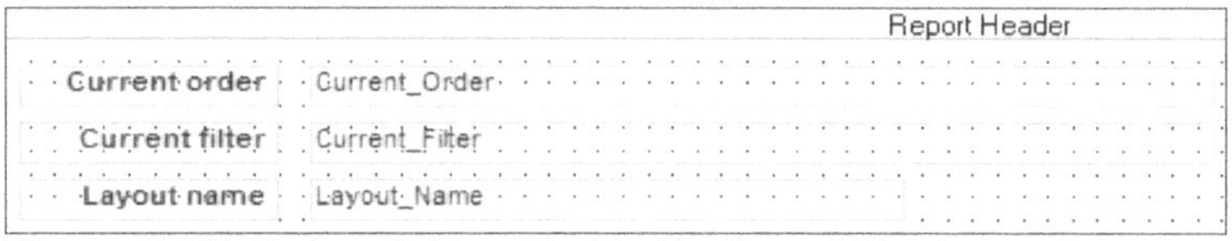

Figure 3-53 System fields added to the Report Header section

Move The Field Headings To Another Section

The field headings are currently in the Report Header section. They need to be in the Page Header section.

1. Select all of the objects in the Report Header section and drag them up to the Page Header section. Make the Report Header section smaller.

2. Save the changes. Now when you preview the report, the field titles will appear at the top of every page. The report should look like the one shown in Figure 3-54.

> **Moving Fields And Headers**
> It would be a real time saver if there was functionality that allowed you to move the field and heading at the same time, even if they are in different sections of the report.

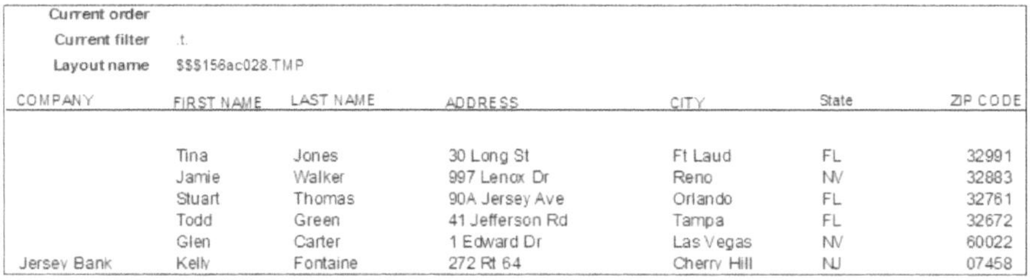

Current order
Current filter .t.
Layout name $$$156ac028.TMP

COMPANY	FIRST NAME	LAST NAME	ADDRESS	CITY	State	ZIP CODE
	Tina	Jones	30 Long St	Ft Laud	FL	32991
	Jamie	Walker	997 Lenox Dr	Reno	NV	32883
	Stuart	Thomas	90A Jersey Ave	Orlando	FL	32761
	Todd	Green	41 Jefferson Rd	Tampa	FL	32672
	Glen	Carter	1 Edward Dr	Las Vegas	NV	60022
Jersey Bank	Kelly	Fontaine	272 Rt 64	Cherry Hill	NJ	07458

Figure 3-54 Modified report

Report Preview Menu

The menu shown in Figure 3-55 has options to preview the report that are not on the preview toolbar. Options on the File menu that are not on the toolbar are explained in Table 3-19.

The options in the table work the same as the options on the Reports shortcut menu on the Control Panel.

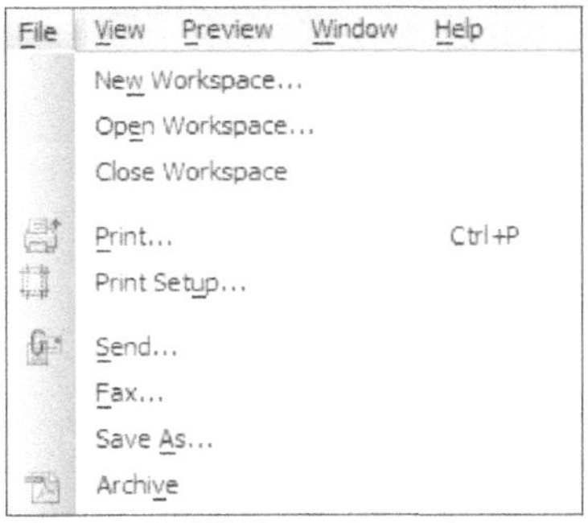

Figure 3-55 Report preview menu

Option	Description
Send	Opens the dialog box shown in Figure 3-56. The options are used to send the report as an **EMAIL ATTACHMENT.** (5)
Fax	Opens the dialog box shown in Figure 3-57. The options are used to send the report as a fax. (5)
Save As	Opens the Save As dialog box, similar to the one shown in Figure 3-56. The difference is that the options are for saving the report as a file. (5)
Archive	This option is similar to the one on the Reports shortcut menu on the Control Panel. The difference is that this option displays the message shown in Figure 3-58. The message lets you know where the archive PDF file was saved.

Table 3-19 File menu options explained

(5) This option works the same as it does for forms.

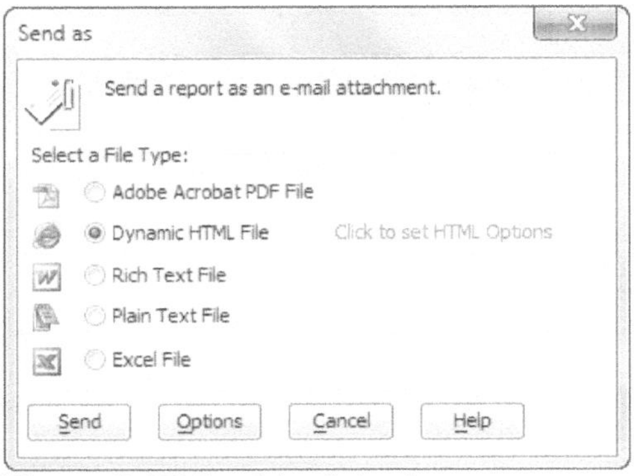

Figure 3-56 Send As dialog box

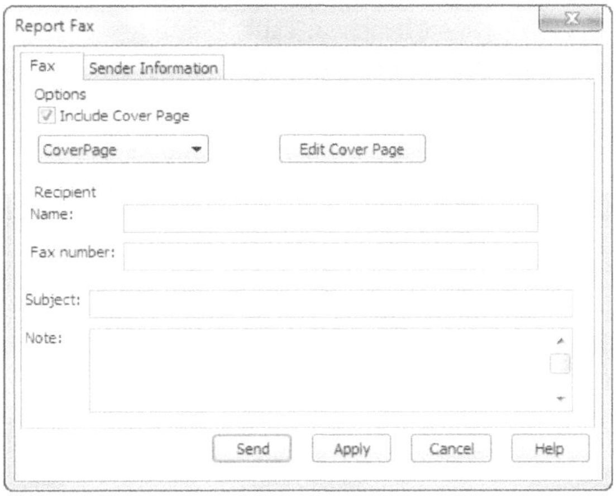

Figure 3-57 Report Fax dialog box

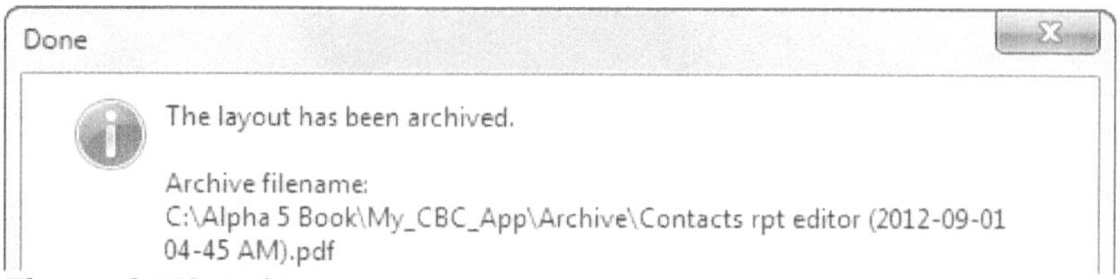

Figure 3-58 Archive message

Report Editor Preview Toolbar

Many of the buttons on this toolbar are the same as the ones on the Report Genie Preview tab toolbar that was covered in Chapter 2. Figure 3-59 shows the toolbar. The options are explained in Table 3-20.

Figure 3-59 Report Editor Preview toolbar

Button	Description
1	[See Chapter 2, Table 2-5, Button 1]
2	[See Chapter 2, Table 2-5, Button 2]
3	[See Chapter 2, Table 2-5, Button 3]
4	[See Chapter 2, Table 2-5, Button 4]
5	[See Chapter 2, Table 2-5, Button 5]
6	[See Chapter 2, Table 2-5, Button 9]
7	[See Chapter 2, Table 2-5, Button 10]
8	[See Chapter 2, Table 2-5, Button 6]
9	[See Chapter 2, Table 2-5, Button 7]
10	[See Chapter 2, Table 2-5, Button 8] When I click this button, a dialog box pops up, then disappears too fast for me to read it.
11	Displays and hides the Bookmark panel.
12	Closes the Preview window.
13	Displays the Control Panel on top of the report.
14	[See Table 3-19, Save As option]
15	[See Table 3-19, Send option]
16	[See Chapter 2, Table 2-5, Button 13]

Table 3-20 Report Editor Preview toolbar buttons explained

ENHANCING REPORTS PART 1

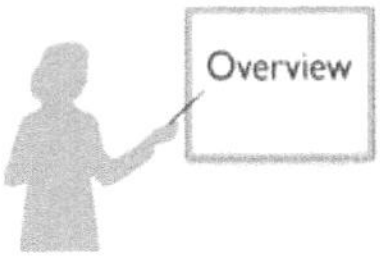

In this chapter you will learn about the following:

- ☑ Creating reports from scratch
- ☑ Creating reports based on a set
- ☑ Restoring a previous version of a report

CHAPTER 4

Overview

In the previous two chapters you learned about the report creation tools. In this chapter you will learn how to create reports from scratch (aka start from a blank free form report). This will help give you a better report writing foundation.

> **Default Placement Of Field Headings In A Free Form Report**
> If you have used other database software, you will probably find what I am about to say interesting. One thing that I noticed when I created a free form report from scratch is that the field headings are automatically placed in the Detail section with the field. I honestly thought that I had done something wrong.
>
> By default in Free Form reports created from scratch, field headings are placed in the Detail section of the report. It would make more sense to have them placed in the Page Header section. Doing that will allow them to be printed at the top of every page in the report, which is usually what you want to have happen.

Exercise 4.1: Create A Report From Scratch

In this exercise you will create the Contact List report from scratch that you created in Exercise 2.1, using the genie.

1. Click the New button on the Reports tab, then select the Contacts data source.

2. Select the Start from a blank free-form report option, then click OK. You should see an empty report in the Report Editor.

Add The Sections And Fields To The Report

As you can see, an empty report does not display all of the sections. I prefer to add the sections to the report before adding the fields, but doing this is optional.

1. Right-click on the Report band, then select the Page Header and Page Footer options.

2. Delete the Report Header section.

3. Make the Page Header and Detail sections longer, then make sure that the **CONTROLS ACROSS**, **DON'T GROUP CONTROLS** and **FIELDS WITH TITLES** buttons on the Drag Drop List toolbar are selected.

> **Resizing Fields And Headers At The Same Time**
> If you know that you want to resize a field and header at the same time, you have to make them a group.

4. Add the following fields to the Detail section: Company Name, First Name, Last Name, Address, City, State Province and Postal Code.

5. Make the State field and header smaller.

6. Change the Postal Code heading to Zip Code, then move the field and heading over to the left.

7. Make the first letter of each word in the remaining headings a capital letter.

8. Select all of the field headings, then drag them up and place them near the bottom of the Page Header section.

9. Move the fields in the Detail section up to the top of the section, then make the section shorter.

10. Click the Save button. Type `aContactsList` as the report name, then click OK. The report layout should look like the one shown in Figure 4-1.

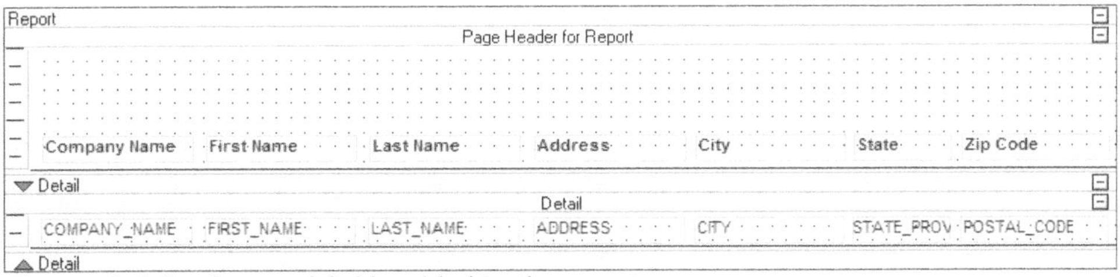

Figure 4-1 Sections and fields added to the report

Add A Title To The Report

In this part of the exercise you will add a text object to the top of the Page Header section.

1. Object ⇒ New. Scroll down the list. Select the Text object type, then click OK.

2. Drag the text object up to the top of the Page Header section.

3. Change the text to `Contact List Report`, then make the text object as wide as the section.

4. Change the horizontal alignment of the text object to Center.

5. Add a border style of your choice to the text object.

6. Change the font size to 14 and bold. Save the changes. Your report layout should look similar to the one shown in Figure 4-2.

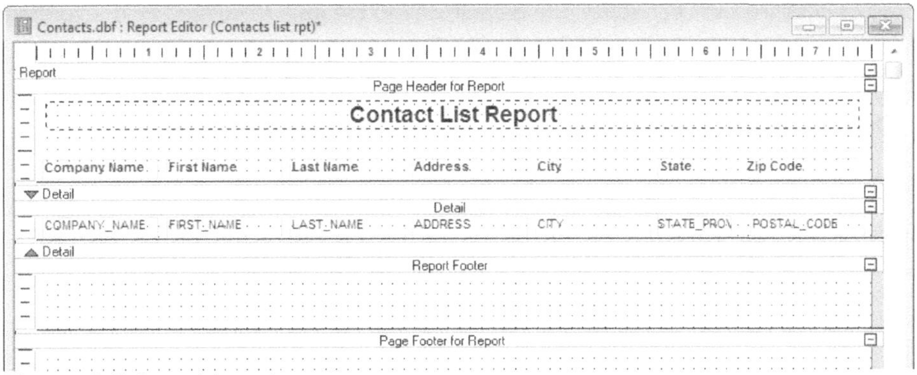

Figure 4-2 Report layout

Add System Fields To The Report

In this part of the exercise you will add the Date and Page Number system fields to the report.

1. Add the Page X of Y system field to the right side of the Page Footer section.
2. Delete the field heading. Move the field up, then make the Page Footer section shorter.
3. Add the Date system field to the Page Header section above and to the right of the State field. Delete the Date field heading, then save the changes.

Add A Group

In this part of the exercise you will create a group for the State field. You will also create a count of the number of contacts in each state.

1. Right-click on the Report band and select **INSERT GROUP**.
2. On the Group tab, select State Province in the first drop-down list.
3. Change the Label to `State`.
4. On the Region tab, check the **START EACH GROUP ON A NEW PAGE** option.
5. On the Head/Foot tab, in the Headers section, select the **REPEATS AT PAGE/GROUP BREAK** option, then click OK.
6. Add the State field to the left side of the Repeating State Group Header section. Accept the Value in the field option. Click the Drop field only (no label) button (second from the left) at the bottom of the dialog box, then click OK.
7. Make the Repeating Group Header section shorter, then save the changes.

Create A Calculated Field

In this part of the exercise you will create a calculated field for the Group Footer section that will provide a count of detail records per state. The easiest way to create a calculated field is to drag a field onto the report and use the **DRAG DROP LIST GENIE**.

1. Make sure that the Drag Drop List Genie button is enabled on the toolbar, then enable the Controls Down option.
2. Drag the State field to the Group Footer section.
3. Select the **COUNT OF THE RECORDS** option on the Drop Fields dialog box.

4. In the Summary field name field type `Contacts In State.`

   The summary expression shown in Figure 4-3 will count the number of detail records for the group.

   Click OK.

   Clicking the **ADVANCED OPTIONS** button opens the dialog box shown in Figure 4-4.

Figure 4-3 Drop Fields options

The options on this dialog box are used to change the default count options. If the Summary Expression field shown above in Figure 4-3 is correct, you will not need to make any changes on this dialog box.

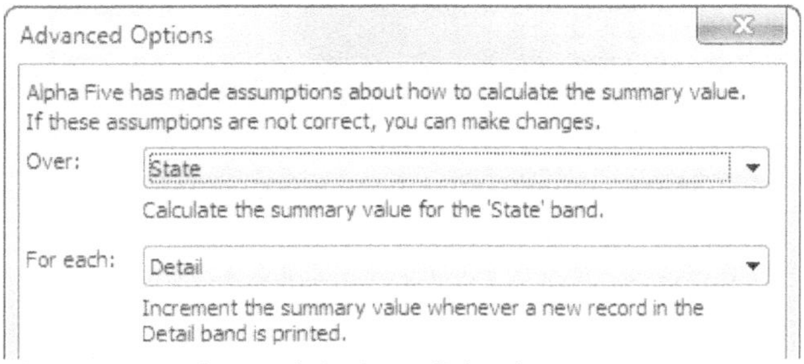

Figure 4-4 Advanced Options dialog box

If you type a name in the Summary field name field on the Drop Fields dialog box, then open the Advanced Options dialog box, the name that you typed in the Summary field name field, goes back to what it was. I don't think that should happen, but I wanted to let you know the work around that I use is to enter the Summary field name last.

The Drop Fields Dialog Box Cannot Be Re-Opened
Before you close this dialog box, make sure that you have selected the correct options for the calculated field that you are creating because you cannot reopen this dialog box. If you find that you need to change the expression, open the Field Properties dialog box for the calculated field and change the expression on the Setup tab.

5. Change the horizontal alignment of the Summary field to left. Move the field and label to the left in the Group Footer section. Save the changes.

Create A Grand Total For The Report

Grand totals (or **RUNNING TOTALS**, as they are also known) are usually placed in the Report Footer section. In other report writing software packages, if there is a group total field already on the report for the same field, more than likely you can use it in the Report Footer section to calculate the grand total. Sadly, Alpha Five does not seem to support this functionality.

> **Creating A Grand/Running Total Field**
> This type of calculated field is very popular. The **CALCULATE RUNNING VALUE** option on the Drop Fields dialog box will create it for you. You do not need to select this option on the Drop Fields dialog box if the grand total field is placed in the Report Footer section.

1. Enable the Field Genie, then drag the State field to the Report Footer section.
2. Select the Count of the records option.
3. In the Summary field name field, type `Total # of contacts on report`, then click OK to close the dialog box.
4. Save the changes, then preview the report.

   The first page of the report should look similar to the one shown in Figure 4-5.

   The bottom of the last page of the report should look like the one shown in Figure 4-6.

Contact List Report

06/24/2012

Company Name	First Name	Last Name	Address	City	State	Zip Code
CT						
Two of A kind	Clair	Walsh	892 Main St	Menden	CT	06403
	Tina	Walker	123 Main St	Stamford	CT	06402
	Tom	Smith	45 Jericho Ave	Wilton	CT	06405
	Fred	Amos	19 Rodney	Westwood	CT	06403
	Louis	Riker	23 Essex Pl	Tappan	CT	06402
	June	Brannigan	196 Hudson	Lodi	CT	06403
	Mary	David	48 Jericho Ave	Westwood	CT	06403
	Jane	Downey	22 Rodney	Westwood	CT	06403
	Keith	Dickerson	29 Essex Pl	Tappan	CT	06402
	Marvin	Easterling	300 Winston Pl	Tappan	CT	06402
Contacts In State 10						
	Tina	Jones	30 Long St	Ft Laud	FL	32991
	Stuart	Thomas	90A Jersey Ave	Orlando	FL	32761

Figure 4-5 First page of the Contact List report

Contact List Report

06/24/2012

Company Name	First Name	Last Name	Address	City	State	Zip Code
	Frank	Harris	800 Main Ave	Lodi	PA	19463
	Candy	Lewis	777 Broad Ave	Ramsey	PA	19001
	Charles	Klein	1 Glen Ave	Ft Lee	PA	19863
	April	Lucas	779 Borad Ave	Ramsey	PA	19001
	Phil	Oates	98 Glen Ave	Ft Lee	PA	19863
	Jesse	Tan	12 Glen Ave	Ft Lee	PA	19863
	David	Riker	173 Glen Ave	Ft Lee	PA	19863
Contacts In State 13						
Total # of contacts on report 59						

Page 3 of 3

Figure 4-6 Last page of the Contact List report

Exercise 4.2: Create Group Totals

In the previous exercise you learned how to create a count of contacts per state. In this exercise you will learn how to create a total amount of orders by state. This report will be based on data in a set, instead of a single table.

1. Click the New button on the Reports tab. Select the Customers Orders and details set.
2. Select the Free Form report option, then click OK.

3. Add the Page Header section, then click the Contacts Across button.

4. Add the following fields to the Detail section from the Orders table: Order ID and Order Date.

5. Add the following fields to the Detail section from the Customers table: First and Last Name, City and State.

6. Move all of the field headers up to the Page Header section, then make the Page Header section shorter. Move all of the fields in the Detail section up, then make the Detail section shorter.

7. Save the report as `aGroupTotals`.

Change The Record Sort Order

In this part of the exercise you will sort the records on the Order Date field.

1. Right-click on the Detail section bar and select Properties. On the Detail Properties dialog box Records tab, click the button at the end of the Order expression field.

2. On the Expression Builder, click the **CREATE ORDER USING GENIE BUTTON**. Open the Sort by drop-down list and select the Order Date field, as shown in Figure 4-7. Click OK twice to close both dialog boxes.

   Notice that this version of the dialog box has the **QUERY RECORDS AT WHICH LEVEL** option and **CHANGE LEVELS BUTTON**.

   The Order Builder in the Report Genie does not have these options. [See Chapter 2, Figure 2-25]

   Clicking the Change Levels button opens the Select Level dialog box. It is used to select the table that you want to use to query records in.

Figure 4-7 Order Builder

3. You should see the order expression shown in Figure 4-8.

   Click OK.

   Save the changes.

   You do not have to use the genie to create the sort order. I just wanted to show you another way to do it.

Figure 4-8 Records tab sort order

Create The Groups

1. Right-click on the Report band, then select Insert Group. Select Customer ID from the drop-down list, then click OK.

2. Hide the Customer ID Group Header section. Delete the Report Header and Customer ID Group Footer sections.

3. Create a group for the State field, then add the State field to the State Group Header section. Accept the Value in the field option, then click OK.

4. Delete the State field header, then move the State field to the upper left corner of the section.

5. Enable the Field Genie and Controls Down options, then drag the Price field to the State Group Footer section. Select the Total of the field option. Change the Summary field name to `Total amount of sales for state`, then click OK.

6. Open the Field Properties dialog box for the Total amount field. Left align the Total field, then select the third option in the Format Style drop-down list.

7. Move the Total amount field and header to the far left of the section. Save the changes. The top of the first page of the report should look like the one shown in Figure 4-9.

The total for CT should look like the one shown in Figure 4-10.

On my report, the total is on page 3.

Order id	Order date	First Name	Last name	City	State
CT					
6	02/03/2011	Clair	Walsh	Menden	CT
57	03/15/2011	Clair	Walsh	Menden	CT
48	02/06/2011	Tina	Walker	Stamford	CT
58	03/15/2011	Tina	Walker	Stamford	CT
58	03/15/2011	Tina	Walker	Stamford	CT

Figure 4-9 First page of the report

109	06/12/2011	Marvin	Eastering	Tappan	CT
Total amount of sales per state	$3,708.35				

Figure 4-10 Totals for CT

Exercise 4.3: Copy Objects From One Report To Another

In this exercise you will copy objects, in this case the System fields, from one report to another. Just pretend that you customized some of the System fields <smile>.

1. Open the aContactsRptEditor report. Select both fields in the Page Footer section.

2. Edit ⇒ Copy. Close the report.

3. Open the Group Totals report if it is not already open, then add a Page Footer section.

4. Right-click in the Page Footer section and select Paste. Save the changes. When you preview the report, you will see that the fields that you pasted into the report work as if they were added from the Drag Drop List panel.

Exercise 4.4: Filter Records Displayed On The Report

In Exercise 4.2 you learned how to sort the records in the Detail section. Using a filter allows you to prevent records from being displayed on the report. More than likely, you will create at least one filter for a report. In this exercise you will create a filter that only displays orders for a specific month.

1. Save the aGroupTotals report as `aFilterByMonth`.

2. Click the **SELECT RECORDS** button on the toolbar.

3. Click the button at the end of the Filter field on the Select Records to Print dialog box. Notice the word (Logical) in the Title bar of the Expression Builder. That lets you know the type of expression that you are going to create. Click the Create Filter Using Genie button.

4. Open the drop-down list and select the Orders table, then click on the Order Date field. In the middle column (the one with the operators), click on the **IS BETWEEN** operator. In the third column, click on the button before the word And.

5. Click the button at the end of the first Value field. The dates shown in Figure 4-11 are from the Order Date field in the Orders table. Scroll down the list and click on the date 3/2/2011, then click the Insert button. You should see the date that you just selected, as shown in Figure 4-12. Click OK.

   The options on the Value dialog box are used to get the data for the filter. If this application was going into production, you would have selected the **SPECIFY AN ARGUMENT** option because that would allow the person running the report to select the date range that they want. Doing this makes the report much more flexible.

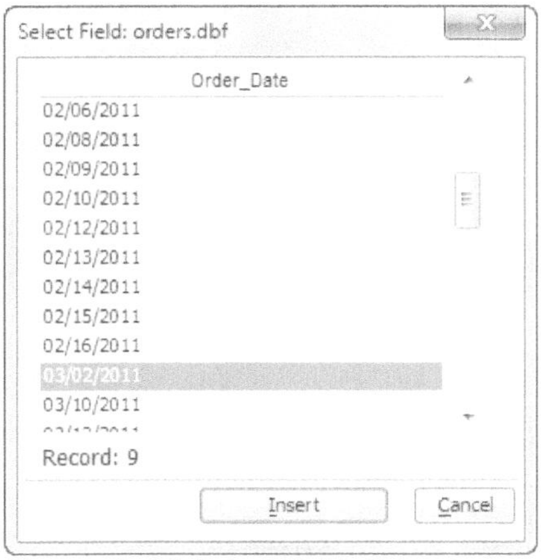

Figure 4-11 Select Field dialog box

Figure 4-12 Value dialog box

6. Click the first button in the last column. Select the **SPECIFY A VALUE NOW** option on the Value dialog box. This option is used when the value that you want to use is not in the field that the filter is based on.

7. Type `03/31/2011`, as shown in Figure 4-13, then click OK. You should have the options shown in Figure 4-14. Click OK. Your expression should look like the one shown in Figure 4-15. Click OK.

   You can type the values in the fields on the Filter Builder shown in Figure 4-14, instead of selecting them on this dialog box.

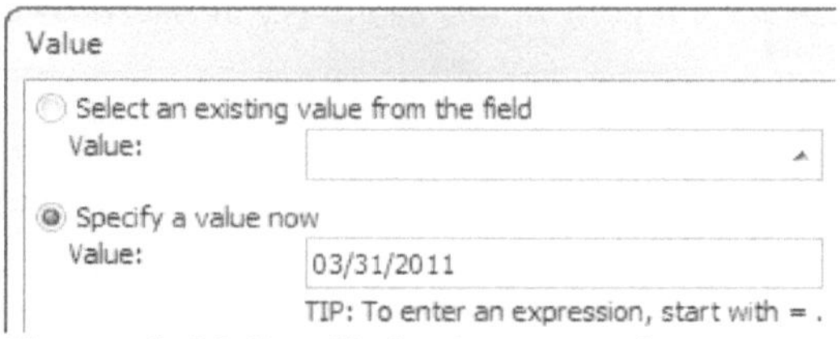

Figure 4-13 Specified value entered

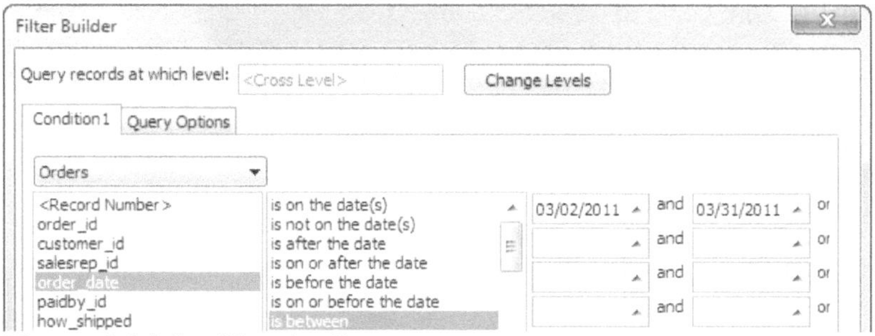

Figure 4-14 Conditional options

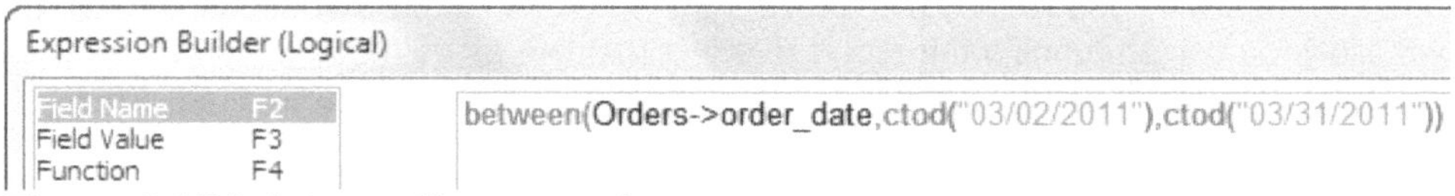

Figure 4-15 Is between filter expression

8. The filter criteria should be in the Filter field shown in Figure 4-16. This criteria will only display orders with an order date between 3/2/2011 and 3/31/2011. Click OK.

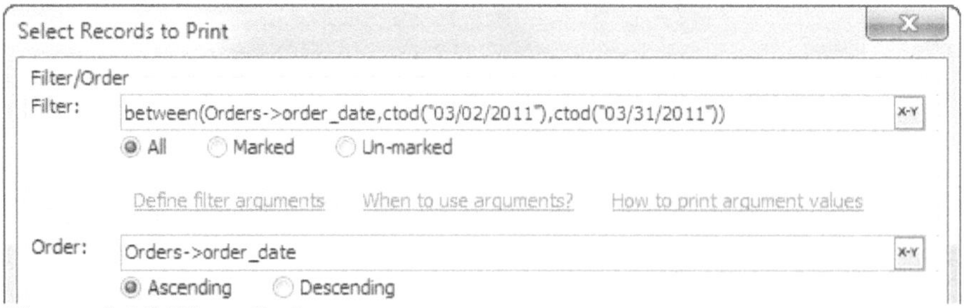

Figure 4-16 Filter criteria

> **Expression Builder**
> If you see the message shown in Figure 4-17, it means that something is wrong with the expression. If you can, you can fix it on the Expression Builder shown earlier in Figure 4-15. If you can't and need to use the Filter Builder genie shown earlier in Figure 4-14, you have to delete the expression in the Expression Builder for the Create Filter Using Genie button to be enabled (appear) on the Expression Builder.

Figure 4-17 Filter Expression error message

9. Save the changes.

   When you preview the report you will only see orders with an order date between 3/2/2011 and 3/31/2011, as shown in Figure 4-18.

   Compare this to the report shown earlier in Figure 4-7.

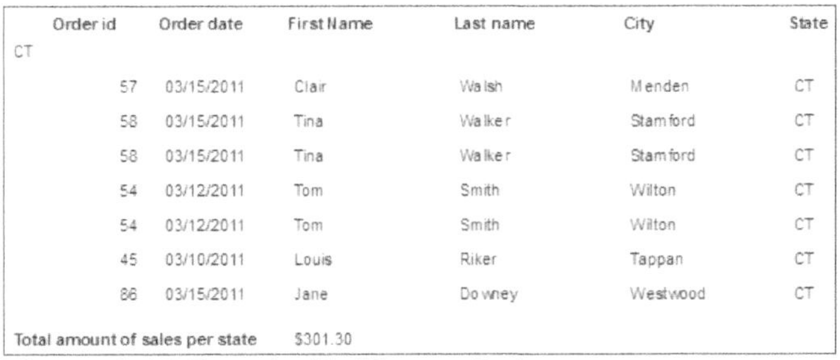

Order id	Order date	First Name	Last name	City	State
CT					
57	03/15/2011	Clair	Walsh	Menden	CT
58	03/15/2011	Tina	Walker	Stamford	CT
58	03/15/2011	Tina	Walker	Stamford	CT
54	03/12/2011	Tom	Smith	Wilton	CT
54	03/12/2011	Tom	Smith	Wilton	CT
45	03/10/2011	Louis	Riker	Tappan	CT
86	03/15/2011	Jane	Downey	Westwood	CT
Total amount of sales per state		$301.30			

Figure 4-18 Report with filter applied

Combining Text And Fields

In the reports that you have created with totals, you used a text object for the heading of the total field. If you had trouble either getting the text object and total field to line up or getting the two fields to be close together, the next exercise will show you how to combine these fields using a formula, which means that you will not have to align the field and text object.

Another common use of combining text and fields is with the **DATE() FUNCTION**. Table 4-1 explains some of the more common date format options. Table 4-2 provides examples for the date 6/1/11.

Character	Description
d	Day of the month in numeric format without a leading zero.
dd	Day of the month in numeric format with a leading zero if necessary.
Weekday	Name of the day spelled out.
M	Month in numeric format without a leading zero.
MM	Month in numeric format with a leading zero if necessary.
Month	Name of the month spelled out.
y or yy	Last two digits of the year.
yyyy	Four digit year.

Table 4-1 Mask character options explained

This Mask . . .	Displays
dd, MM, yy	01, 06, 11
Month dd yyyy	June 01 2011
Weekday Month d, yyyy	Wednesday June 1, 2011
M, d, yy	6, 1, 11

Table 4-2 Mask examples

Exercise 4.5: Combine Text With The Date Function

In this exercise you will learn how to display text with a date field as one field. This is done by creating a calculated field and using a date function.

There are several Date and Time functions that you can use to change how a date is displayed. The reports that you have created so far that displayed a date, displayed it in this format 6/24/12. There may be times when you want to print or display dates in other formats. You will learn how to display dates in these formats: June 24, 2012 and Sunday June 24, 2012.

1. Save the aContactList report as `aChangeDateDisplay`.

2. Make the Page Header section longer, then move the field headings down.

Create The Month Day Year Expression

1. Drag the <New Calculated Field> option in the Drag Drop List panel to the Page Header section.

2. On the Define Calculated/Summary Field dialog box, type `layout_mmddyy` as the Expression name.

You can type the expression in step 3 below in the Expression field on the Define Calculated/Summary Field dialog box or click the XY button and type it in on the Expression Builder. The advantage of using the Expression Builder is that it lets you know if the expression is correct. It will also show the result of the expression.

3. Type the following in the Expression field: `"Report Printed - " + mdy(date())`. You will see the result illustrated in Figure 4-19 on either dialog box. Click OK.

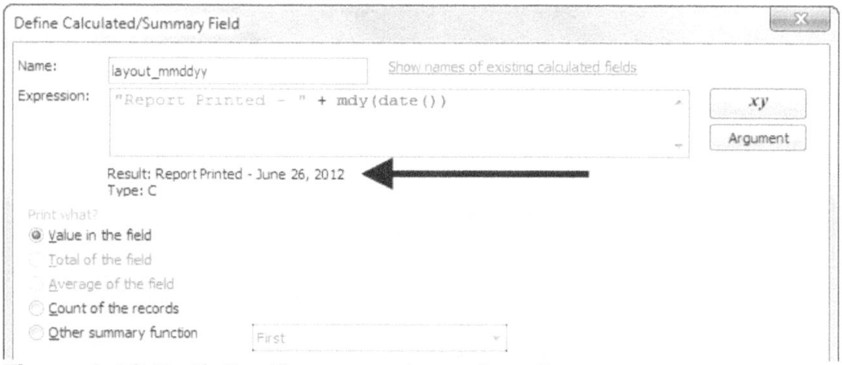

Figure 4-19 Month Day Year expression and result

4. Delete the calculated field heading. Move the field so that it is below the report title. Make the field wider, then save the changes.

Create The Weekday Expression

1. Drag the <New Calculated Field> option to the Page Header section.

2. Type `layout_weekday` as the Expression name.

3. Type the following expression.
   `"Report Printed - "+ CDOW(date()) + ", " + mdy(date()).`
   You will see the result illustrated in Figure 4-20 on either dialog box. Click OK.

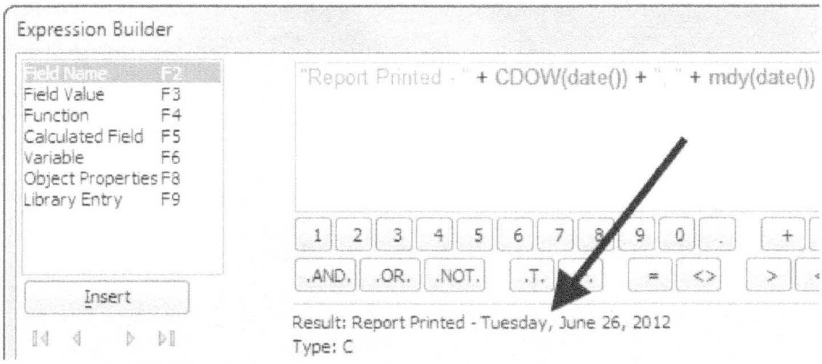

Figure 4-20 Weekday expression and result

4. Delete the field heading. Move the field so that it is below the other calculated field. Make the field wider. Save the changes. The Page Header section of the report should look like the one shown in Figure 4-21.

Figure 4-21 Report with combined text and date calculated fields

Deleting Calculated Fields

You may create calculated fields that are no longer needed on the report. When I tried to delete a calculated field from the Drag Drop List panel, I was surprised to find out that there is no "Delete" option on the shortcut menu. If you need to delete a calculated field, follow the steps below.

1. Click the Calculated Fields button on the toolbar.

2. On the dialog box shown in Figure 4-22, highlight the calculated field that you want to delete.

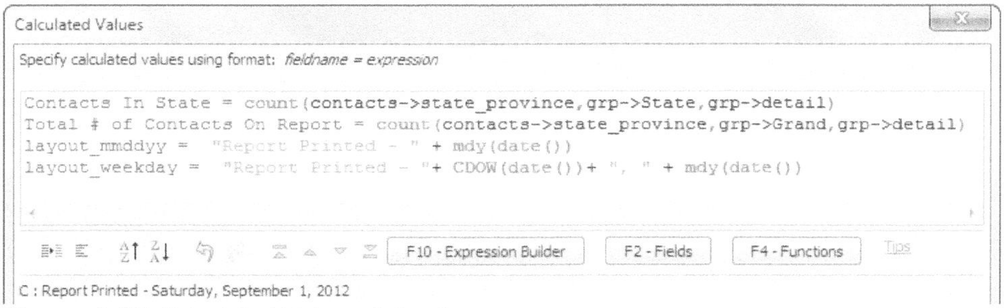

Figure 4-22 Calculated Values dialog box

3. Press the Delete key, then click OK.

   If the calculated field that you are trying to delete is on the report, you will see the dialog box shown in Figure 4-23.

   This dialog box lets you know that the field(s) that you are trying to delete are on the report.

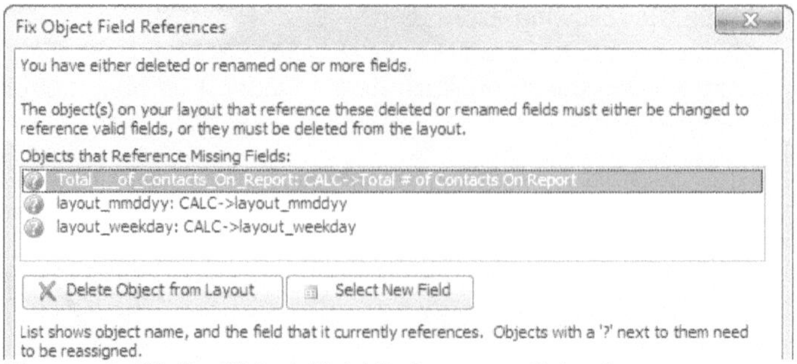

Figure 4-23 Fix Object Field References dialog box

4. If you want to delete a field, select it, then click the **DELETE OBJECT FROM LAYOUT** button.

5. Delete the calculated field from the report layout, then save the changes.

Restoring Report Layouts

Each time that you save a report, another copy is saved in a back up folder. There may be a time when you need to restore a prior version of a report layout. For example, in the previous section you learned how to delete a calculated field from a report. If you decide that you want the calculated field back, to use with a different report, you could restore the original report with a new name, get the formula, then delete the report. To restore a previous version of a report, follow the steps below.

1. Right-click on the report that you want to restore, then select Restore Prior version.

2. On the dialog box shown in Figure 4-24, select the Backup (prior version) that you want to restore.

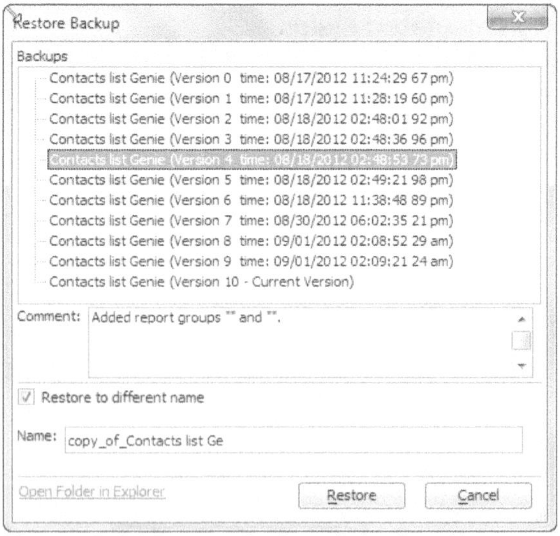

Figure 4-24 Restore Backup dialog box (for reports)

3. If you want to restore the report with a different name, select the option, then type in the new name.

4. Click OK and a previous version will be restored.

INTRODUCTION TO LAYOUT TABLE REPORTS

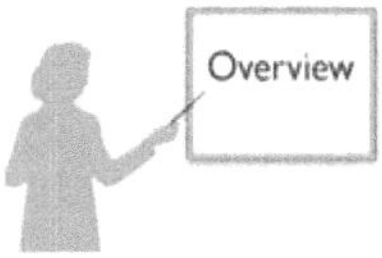

As the title of this chapter indicates, you will learn how to create Layout Table reports.

Overview

Layout Table Reports were added to Alpha Five in version 11. All of the report chapters up to this point only used the report editor for Free Form reports. Like Free Form reports that can be created from a report that was created with the genie, so can Layout Table reports. What you will notice about Layout Table reports is that the data is in columns and rows. The data is actually locked into cells, which is what makes this report type more ideal for exporting data to Excel. You can apply properties to multiple cells at the same time.

If you create a Layout Table report from scratch, field headings are automatically added to the Page Header section, if this section is added to the report and the Report Header section is deleted before fields are added to the report. If not, field headers are added to the Report Header section. This is different then the free form reports created from scratch, where you have to manually move the field headers to the Page Header section.

Exercise 5.1: Use A Genie Report In The Layout Table Report Editor

As you have already created reports using the genie, that step can be skipped. In this exercise you will open a report that was created with the genie, then save it in Layout Table format. Then you will modify it in the Report Editor.

1. Open the aContactsByStateGenie report in design mode, then click the Open in Report Editor button.

2. The Layout Table report option should be selected. Click the Save Report As button.

3. Type `aContactsByStateLayout` as the report name, then click OK.

Layout Table Report Editor

Figure 5-1 shows the report and Layout Table Report Editor workspace. Compare this layout to the free form version of the same report shown in Chapter 3, Figure 3-2. As you can see, the majority of the editor looks like the Free Form report editor. The differences are discussed in the next few sections.

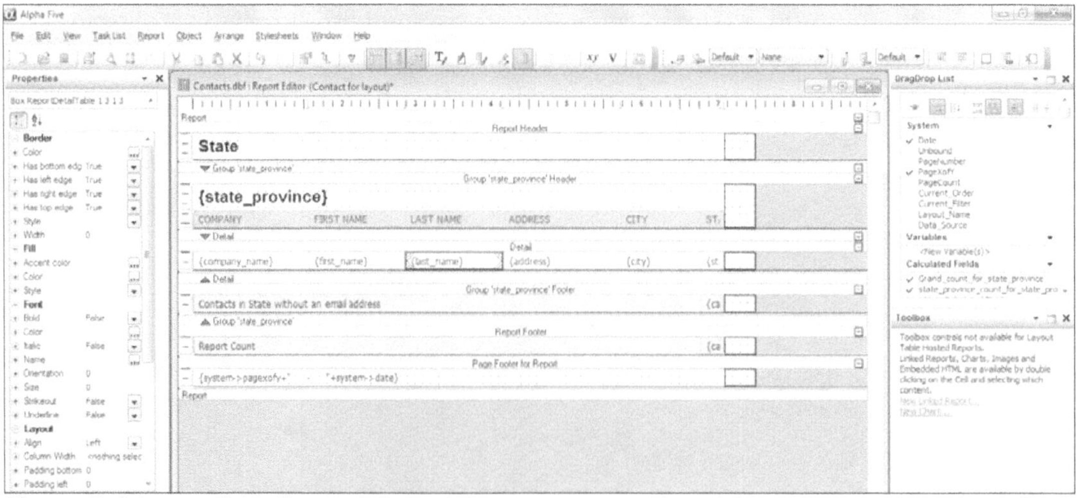

Figure 5-1 Layout Table Report Editor

The brackets around a field indicate a value.

Layout Menu

The layout menu for the Layout Table report editor has the same options as the Free Form Report Editor. [See Chapter 3, Report Layout Menu] The differences are explained below.

Object Menu

The Properties option opens the Edit Layout Table dialog box.

Arrange Menu

The following options on this menu are not enabled for a Layout Table report: Align Positions, Align Sizes, Align Spaces, Group, Ungroup.

The **AUTO MERGE** option is only enabled when a Layout Table type report is open. It displays the dialog box shown in Figure 5-2.

The options are used to merge rows or columns of data.

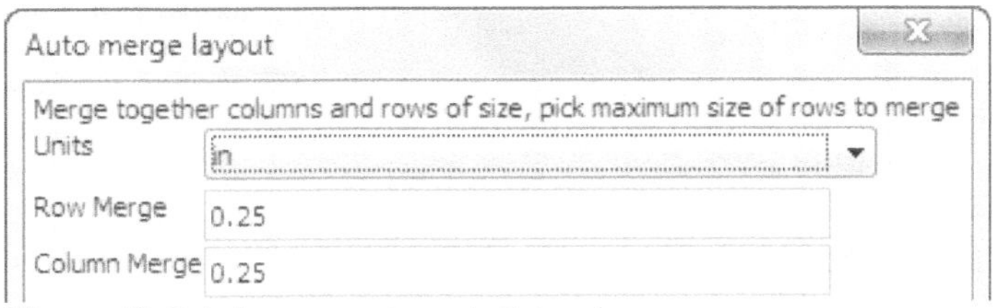

Figure 5-2 Auto merge layout dialog box

Stylesheets Menu

Selecting the Apply or create a Stylesheet option opens the dialog box shown in Figure 5-3.

These are the same options that are on the Report Genie Style tab. The difference is that you can create a new style sheet and edit style sheets that you have created.

This is different from the Free Form report layout which opens the same dialog box as forms.

The **CUSTOM** option and **EDIT STYLE SHEET** button are only available after you have created a style sheet.

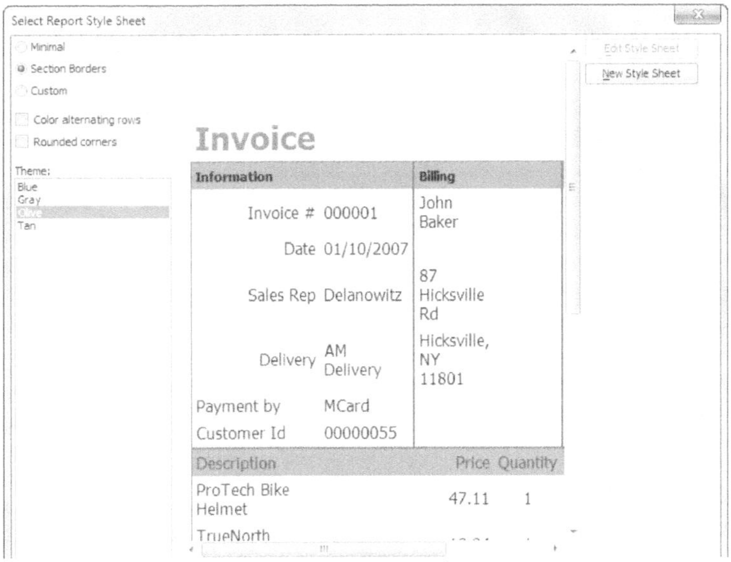

Figure 5-3 Select Report Style Sheet dialog box

The **NEW STYLE SHEET** button opens the dialog box shown in Figure 5-4. The options are used to create your own style sheet.

After I upgraded, the dialog box shown in Figure 5-4 did not open when I clicked the New Stylesheet button. Instead, another copy of the dialog box shown above in Figure 5-3 opened.

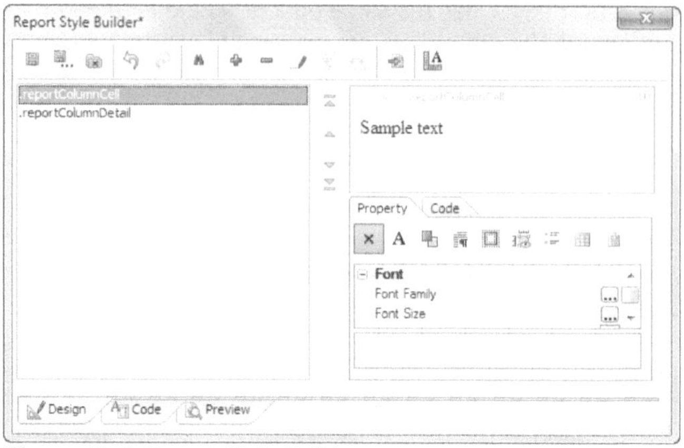

Figure 5-4 Report Style Builder

Layout Table Report Editor Toolbar

In addition to the differences discussed in Chapter 2, the Layout Table report editor has its own toolbar, as shown in Figure 5-5. The buttons that are different from the Free Form report editor toolbar are explained in Table 5-1.

Figure 5-5 Layout Table report editor toolbar

Button	Description
1	Opens the Edit Layout Table dialog box. [See Figure 5-12] (1)
2	Displays a warning message if the selected object does not have any events.
3	Displays or hides the Layout Table toolbar, shown in Figure 5-6.

Table 5-1 Layout Table report editor toolbar buttons explained

(1) After I upgraded, the Region Properties dialog box opened instead of the Edit Layout Table dialog box.

Layout Table Toolbar

The toolbar shown in Figure 5-6 is specifically for Layout Table reports. The buttons are explained in Table 5-2.

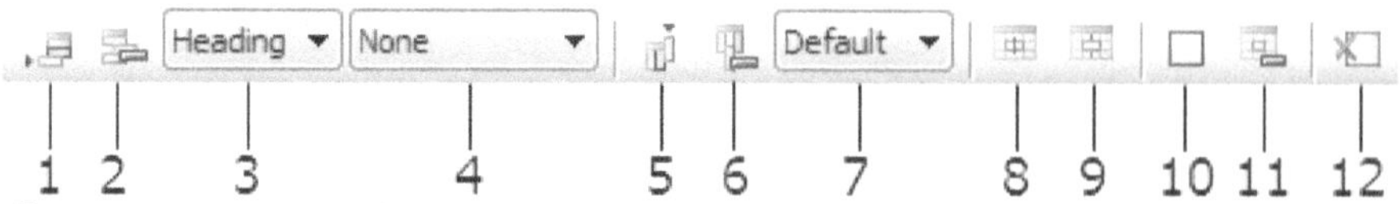

Figure 5-6 Layout Table toolbar

Button	Description
1	Adds a row below the selected row in the same report section. If there is more than one row in a section, they can be swapped.
2	Deletes the selected row.
3	Selects how the row will be formatted based on the style sheet. (2)
4	Selects the Page Break setting for the row. The options are None (the default), Before, After, Before-Sheet and After-Sheet. The last two options create a new sheet in the Excel workbook and place the data there.
5	Adds a column after the selected column in all sections.
6	Deletes the selected column.
7	Selects how the column will be formatted based on the style sheet. (2)
8	Splits a cell that has already been merged.
9	Merges the selected cells.
10	Adds a box around the selected cell.
11	Removes the box from the selected cell.
12	Opens the dialog box shown in Figure 5-7, which is used to modify style options that have been applied to the report.

Table 5-2 Layout Table toolbar buttons explained

(2) The Style sheet formatting options are Default, Heading and Total.

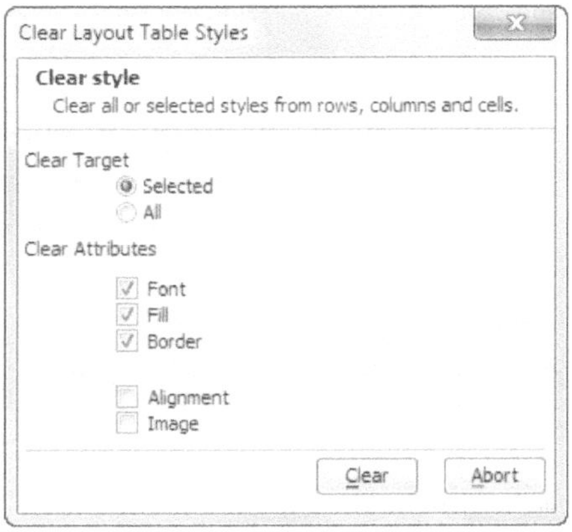

Figure 5-7 Clear Layout Table Styles dialog box

Layout Table Report Ruler Shortcut Menu

Layout Table reports have different ruler and shortcut menu options then Free Form reports, as shown in Figures 5-8 and 5-9.

The options are explained in Tables 5-3 and 5-4.

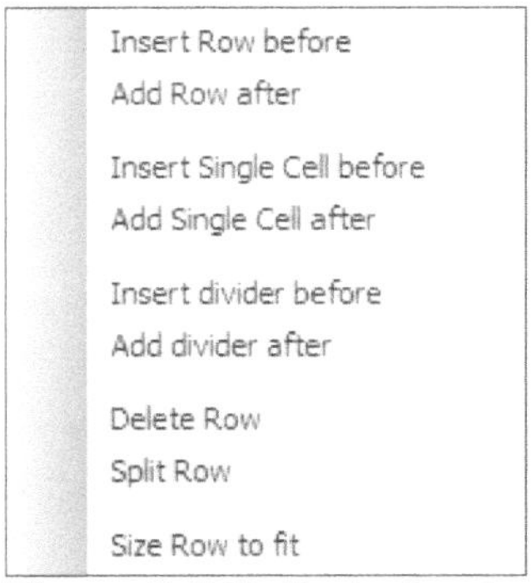

Figure 5-8 Vertical ruler shortcut menu

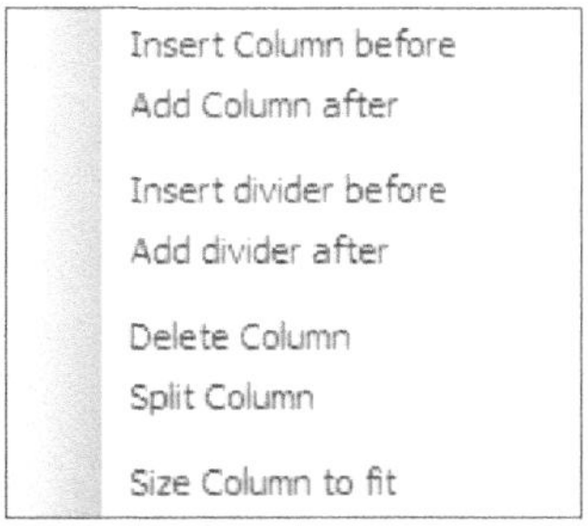

Figure 5-9 Horizontal ruler shortcut menu

Vertical Ruler Shortcut Menu Options

Option	Description
Insert row before	Adds a row above the selected row that has the same number of cells.
Add row after	Adds a row below the selected row that has the same number of cells.
Insert single cell before	Adds a row with one cell above the selected cell.
Add single cell after	Adds a row with one cell below the selected cell.
Insert divider before	Adds vertical space before the selected row.
Add divider after	Adds vertical space after the selected row.
Delete row	Deletes the selected row.
Split row	Divides the selected row into two rows.
Size row to fit	Resizes the row to fit the size of the contents that it will display.

Table 5-3 Vertical ruler shortcut menu options explained

Horizontal Ruler Shortcut Menu Options

Option	Description
Insert column before	Adds a column to the left of the selected column.
Add column after	Adds a column to the right of the selected column.
Insert divider before	Adds column space before the selected row.
Add divider after	Adds column space after the selected row.
Delete column	Deletes the selected column.
Split column	Divides the selected column.
Size column to fit	Resizes the column to fit the size of the contents that it will display.

Table 5-4 Horizontal ruler shortcut menu options explained

Layout Table Report Design Window Shortcut Menu

Unlike the Free Form report layout workspace that has two shortcut menus in the design window, the Layout Table report workspace only has the one shown in Figure 5-10. The options are explained in Table 5-5.

In addition to right-clicking to display the shortcut menu, you can click on the arrow in the upper right corner of a cell, as illustrated.

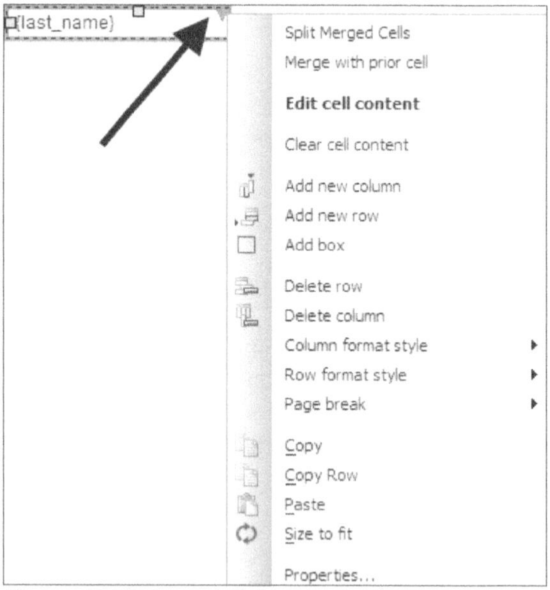

Figure 5-10 Layout Table shortcut menu

Option	Description
Split merged cells	This option is only available when the selected cell has already been merged. It is used to split the selected cell into two cells.
Merge with prior cell	Removes the selected cell. The cell to the left becomes the size of both cells. The data in the selected cell is removed.
Merge selected cells	(Not shown in figure) The option is only available if two or more cells are selected.
Edit cell content	[See Cell Contents Dialog Box, later in this chapter]
Clear cell content	Removes the field from the selected cell.
Add new column	[See Table 5-2, Button 5]
Add new row	[See Table 5-2, Button 1]
Add box	[See Table 5-2, Button 10]
Delete row	Deletes the selected row.
Delete column	[See Table 5-2, Button 6]
Column format style	[See Table 5-2, Button 7] In addition to these options, there is also a **ID COLUMN** format style.
Row format style	[See Table 5-2, Button 3]
Page break	[See Table 5-2, Button 4]
Copy Row	Copies the cells in one row to the Windows clipboard so that they can be pasted in another row.
Properties	Displays the dialog box shown in Figure 5-11.

Table 5-5 Layout Table shortcut menu options explained

This dialog box currently does not have a real purpose that I could find. It just lets you know that you have to use the Properties panel to change the properties.

The **SHOW PANEL BUTTON** is only enabled when the Properties panel is not displayed in the report workspace.

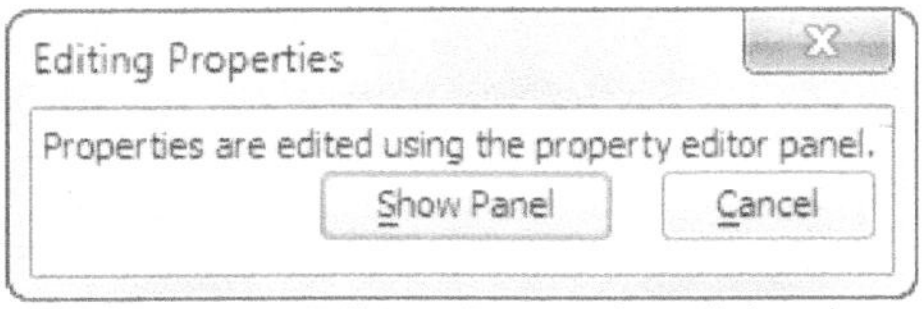

Figure 5-11 Editing Properties dialog box

Edit Layout Table Dialog Box

The options shown in Figure 5-12 are used to change the properties of the selected object.

To open this dialog box, click on the object that you want to change, then click the Properties button on the toolbar.

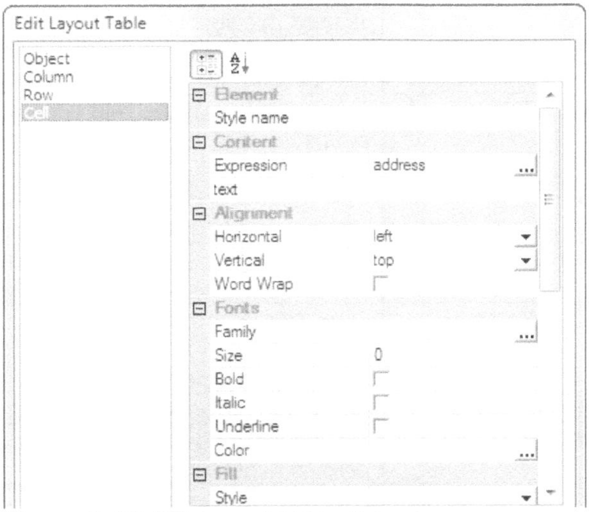

Figure 5-12 Edit Layout Table dialog box

Cell Contents Dialog Box

The options shown in Figure 5-13 are used to edit the contents of a cell.

The easiest way to open this dialog box is to double-click on the cell that you want to edit.

By default, the option selected on the dialog box (static text, field, expression, etc.) when this dialog box is opened, depends on the object that is selected. The options are explained in Table 5-6.

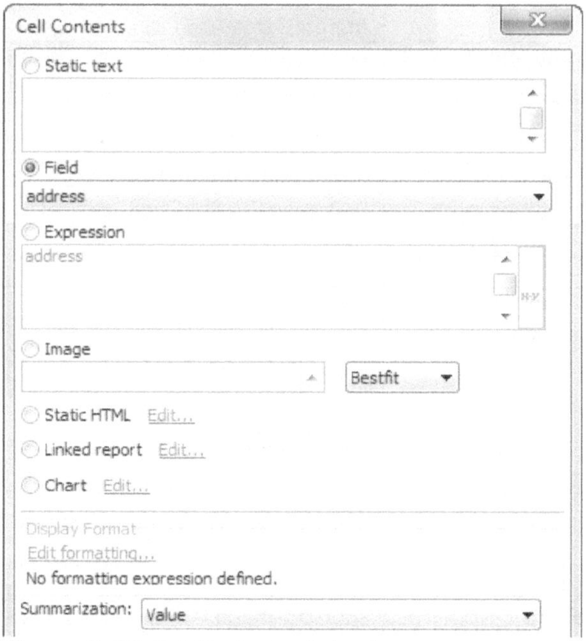

Figure 5-13 Cell Contents dialog box

Option	Description
Static text	This is one way to format the text. If you want to change the color or font size, select the Static HTML option below. (3)
Dynamic text builder link	Opens the dialog box shown in Figure 5-15. This dialog box works the same as the Color Equation Genie.
Field	Is used to select a different field or change the formatting of a field.
Expression	Is used to change the expression. Clicking the Edit button at the end of this field opens the dialog box shown in Figure 5-15.
Image	Is used to select an image by using the dialog box shown in Figure 5-16. The options shown in Figure 5-17 are used to select how the image is displayed in the cell.
Static HTML	Is used to format the cells contents in HTML format. Clicking the Edit link opens the dialog box shown in Figure 5-18. This option use to open the HTML Editor.
Linked report	The Edit link opens the **EDIT LINKED REPORT DIALOG BOX**, which is used to create a link to a report. [See Chapter 7, Figure 7-61]
Chart	The Edit link opens the **GRAPH DATA DIALOG BOX**. It is used to format charts. [See Chapter 10, Graph Data Dialog Box]
Embedded Layout Table	Displays the options shown in Figure 5-19. The options are used to select the number of rows and columns for an embedded table that will be added to the selected cell.
Edit Formatting link	Opens the dialog box shown later in Figure 5-20. (4)
Justify cell	The options in the drop-down list are used to select the alignment of the cells contents. (4)

Table 5-6 Cell Contents dialog box options explained

(3) **Static Text Formatting Options**
Using the HTML Editor to change static text will not allow the cell to use the Cell Contents dialog box. The **EDIT CELL CONTENT** option on the shortcut menu will change to Edit HTML, as illustrated in Figure 5-14. From that point on, you will only be able to use the HTML Editor for the cell.

If you need to format the text in a cell, but do not want it formatted in HTML, use the floating Text toolbar. Using this method to format the cell, still lets you use the Cell Contents dialog box.

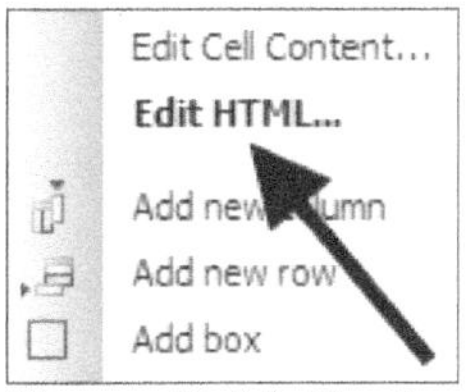

Figure 5-14 Shortcut menu with Edit HTML option illustrated

(4) This option is only available when the field or expression option is selected. [See Display Format, later in this chapter]

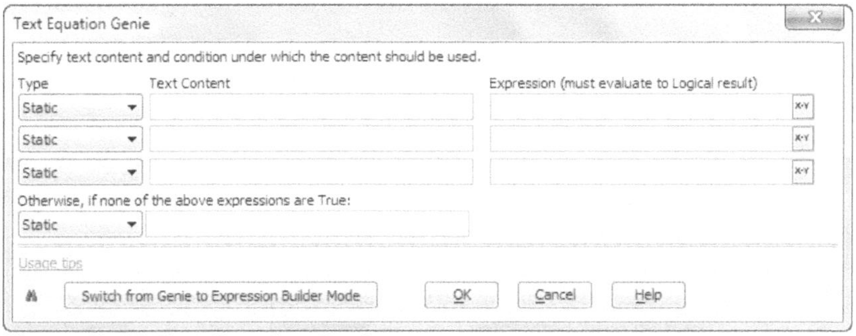

Figure 5-15 Text Equation Genie

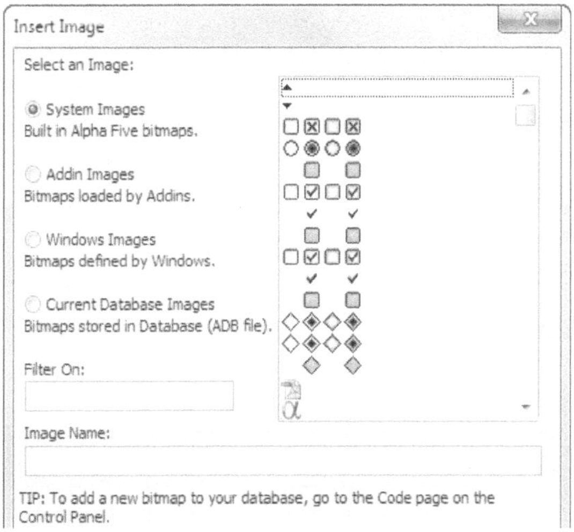

Figure 5-16 Insert Image dialog box

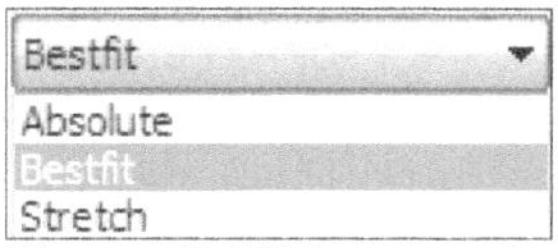

Figure 5-17 Image sizing options

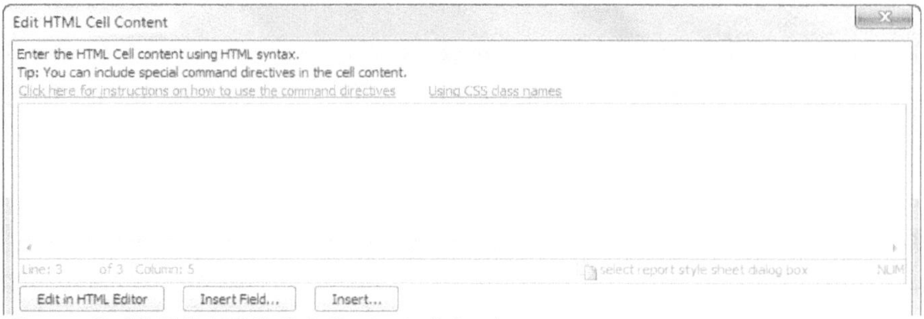

Figure 5-18 Edit HTML Cell Content dialog box

Figure 5-19 Embedded Layout Table options

Display Format

This option is available when a field or expression option on the Field Properties panel or the Cell Contents dialog box is selected.

The options on the dialog box shown in Figure 5-20 are used to format the data in the field or cell.

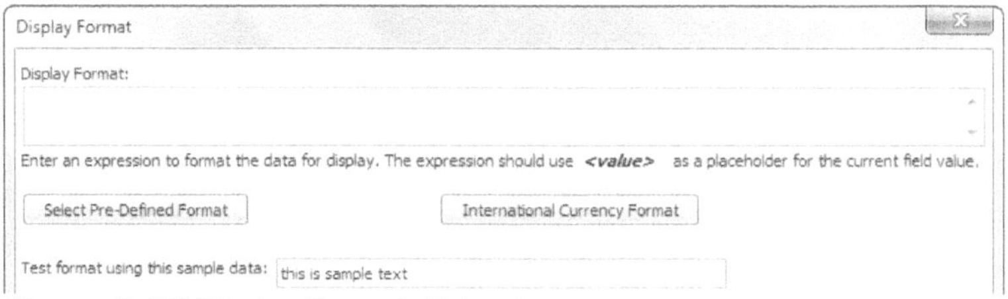

Figure 5-20 Display Format dialog box

The values displayed when the **SELECT PRE-DEFINED FORMAT BUTTON** is clicked, depends on the value in the field or cell. If the field or cell contains numeric data, the values shown in Figure 5-21 are available. If the field or cell contains text, the values shown in Figure 5-22 are available.

The **INTERNATIONAL CURRENCY FORMAT BUTTON** opens the dialog box shown in Figure 5-23. The options are used to format text and currency.

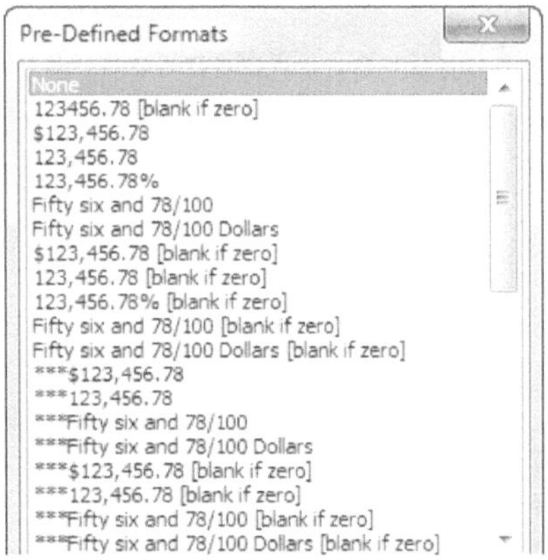

Figure 5-21 Pre-defined numeric formats

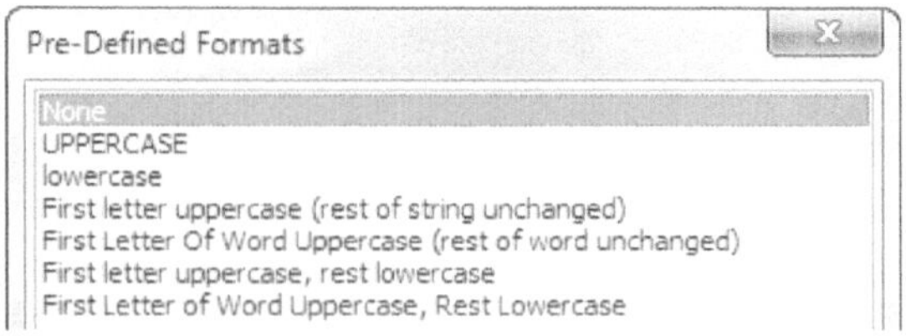

Figure 5-22 Pre-defined text formats

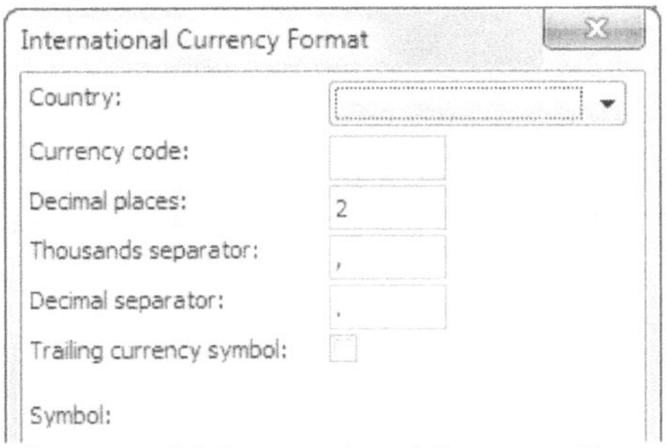

Figure 5-23 International Currency Format dialog box

Summarization

This option, shown earlier at the bottom of Figure 5-13, is only available if the Field or Expression option on the Cell Contents dialog box is selected. The options in the drop-down list shown in Figure 5-24 are used to select what will be displayed in the cell. The options vary, depending on the type of data that is in the cell. Once the summarization type is selected, the fields shown in Figure 5-25 are displayed.

The **CONVERT SUMMARY CALCULATION TO A NAMED CALCULATED FIELD LINK** opens the dialog box shown in Figure 5-26, which is used to enter a name for the calculated field. Saving the calculated field allows you to use it in other calculations. The calculated fields are automatically added to the Drag Drop List panel. This option works the same as the options on the Advanced Options dialog box. [See Chapter 4, Figure 4-4]

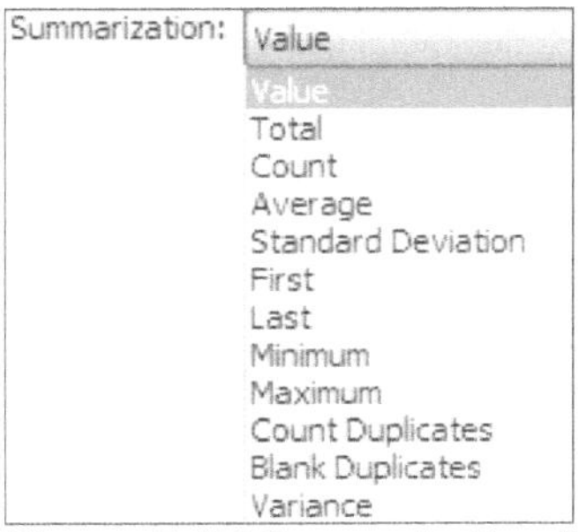

Figure 5-24 Summarization field drop-down list options

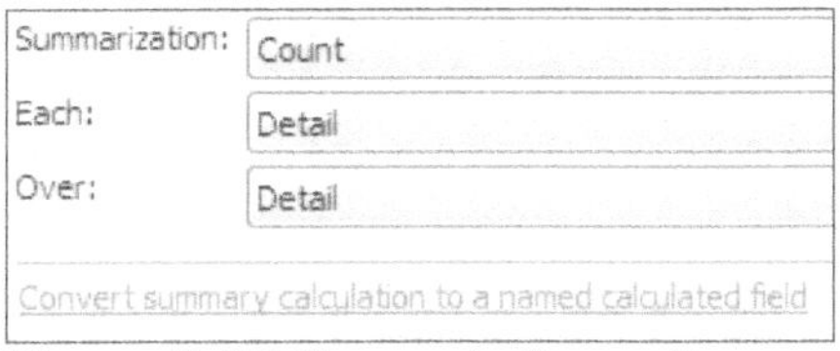

Figure 5-25 Summarization options

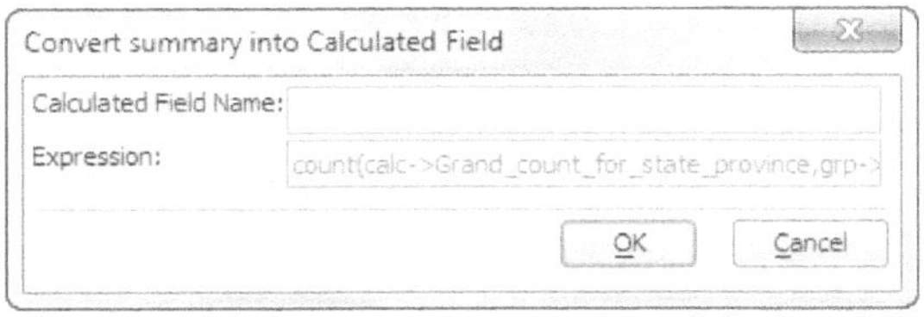

Figure 5-26 Convert summary into Calculated Field dialog box

> **Floating Toolbars**
> The Text, Border and Copy Appearance floating toolbars are the only toolbars available for Layout Table reports.

Exercise 5.2: Modify A Layout Table Report

If you previewed the Contacts by state layout report, you would see that the Zip Code field is not displayed, as shown in Figure 5-27.

In this exercise you will modify this report to display the Zip Code field, add the Note field and merge cells.

COMPANY	FIRST NAME	LAST NAME	ADDRESS	CITY	ST.
	Tina	Walker	123 Main St	Stamford	CT
	Louis	Riker	23 Essex Pl	Tappan	CT
	Keith	Dickerson	29 Essex Pl	Tappan	CT
	Marvin	Easterling	300 Winston Pl	Tappan	CT
Two of A kind	Clair	Walsh	892 Main St	Menden	CT
	Fred	Amos	19 Rodney	Westwood	CT
	June	Brannigan	196 Hudson	Lodi	CT
	Mary	David	48 Jericho Ave	Westwood	CT
	Jane	Downey	22 Rodney	Westwood	CT
	Tom	Smith	45 Jericho Ave	Wilton	CT
Contacts in State without an email address					10

Figure 5-27 Report with fields cut off

1. Open the aContactsByStateLayout report.
2. File ⇒ Print Setup. Change the Orientation to landscape, then click OK.
3. Look on the ruler. Around the 7 inch mark, you should see two blue vertical lines. Drag the last one to the right, to the 7.5 inch mark.
4. Save the report as `aModifiedContactsLayout`.

CREATING LETTERS, LABELS AND ENVELOPES

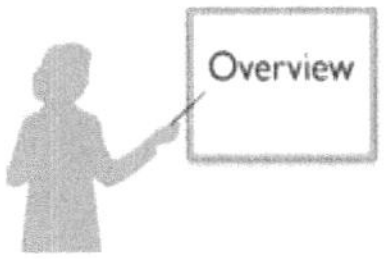

In this chapter you will learn how to create form letters, labels and envelopes.

CHAPTER 6

Overview

In the previous two chapters you learned how to create a variety of reports. In some circles, form letters and labels are considered types of reports. Letters use the Rich Text format instead of objects. The Letter Editor is very similar to the Report Editor. Like the Report Editor, the Letter Editor has region properties.

Exercise 6.1: Use The Form Letter Genie

In this exercise you will create a basic letter using the Form Letter Genie.

1. Click on the Letters tab, then click the New button.

2. Select the Contacts table, then click OK.

   You will see the dialog box shown in Figure 6-1.

   The **USE THE LETTER GENIE** option opens the genie to walk you through creating the form letter.

   The **GO DIRECTLY TO THE LETTER DEFINITION** option opens the Letter Editor so that the letter can be created from scratch.

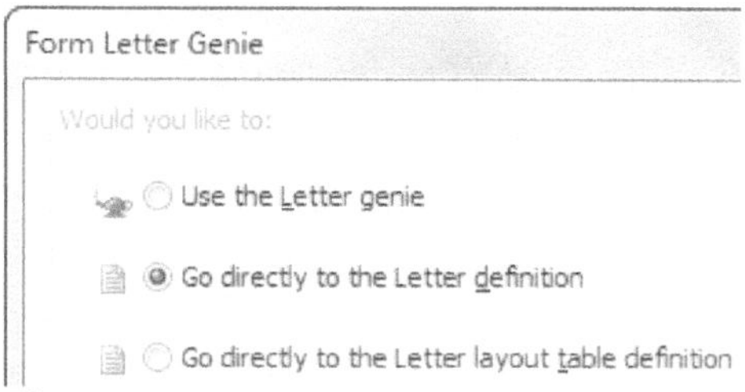

Figure 6-1 Form Letter Genie

The **GO DIRECTLY TO THE LETTER LAYOUT TABLE DEFINITION** option does not open anything.

3. Select the Use the Letter genie option, then click OK. The options shown in Figure 6-2 are used to set up the letterhead portion of the form letter.

   Type your name and address in the box at the bottom of the dialog box, then click Next.

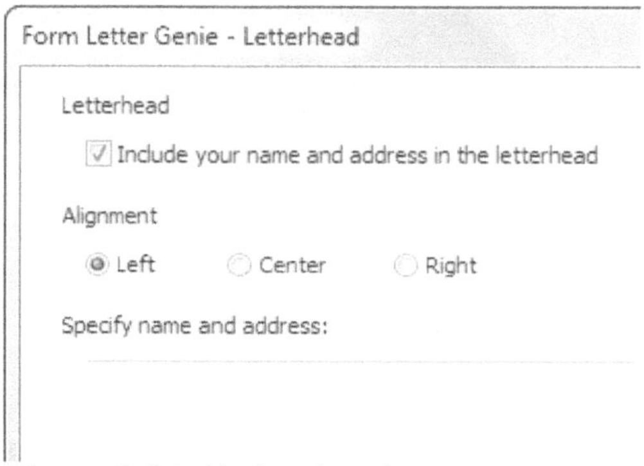

Figure 6-2 Letterhead genie screen

The options on the Addressee screen are used to create the address information for who the letter is for.

The >> next to the first row in the label section lets you know what row you are working on. To move to a different row, just click in the row.

4. Click on the First Name field in the list then click the arrow button. Press the space bar, then add the Last Name field to the same row.

5. Click in the next row, then add the Company Name field.

6. Add the remaining fields, as shown in Figure 6-3.

   Don't forget to add a comma after the City field.

   Click Next.

   The **SEE EXAMPLE** button will let you view how the address information will appear on the report.

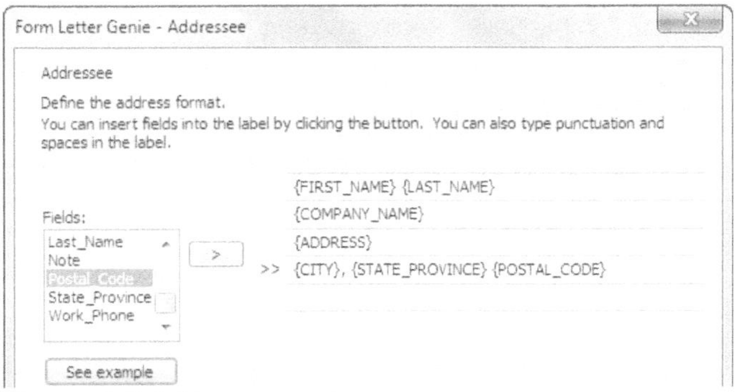

Figure 6-3 Addressee genie screen

The options on the Salutation screen are used to set up a greeting. Doing this is optional. If you use a field, you should make sure that every record that will print has data in the field, otherwise your letter may look a bit strange.

7. In the first drop-down list select the First Name field, as shown in Figure 6-4, then click Next.

   The option illustrated is used to create an expression that will display part of the salutation.

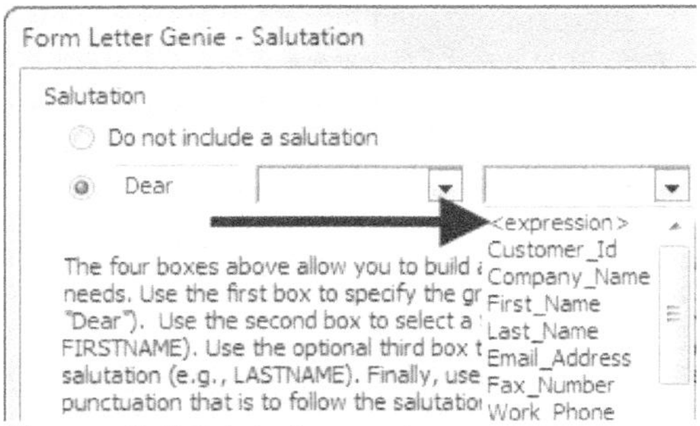

Figure 6-4 Salutation genie screen

8. On the Date screen, open the drop-down list and select the format shown at the bottom of Figure 6-5.

   Click Next.

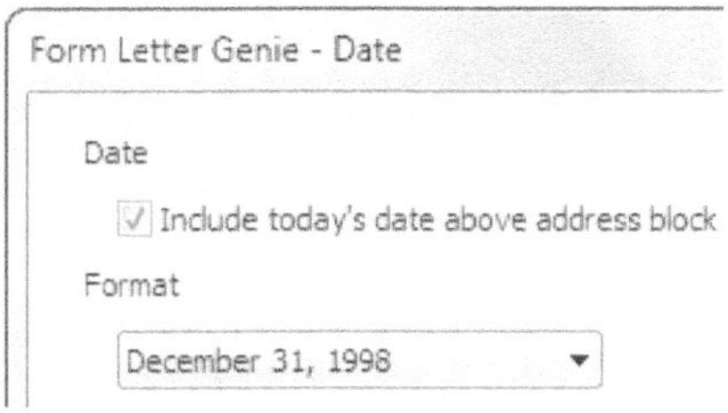

Figure 6-5 Date genie screen

9. On the Close screen, type your name three lines below the word Sincerely, as shown in Figure 6-6.

   Click Next.

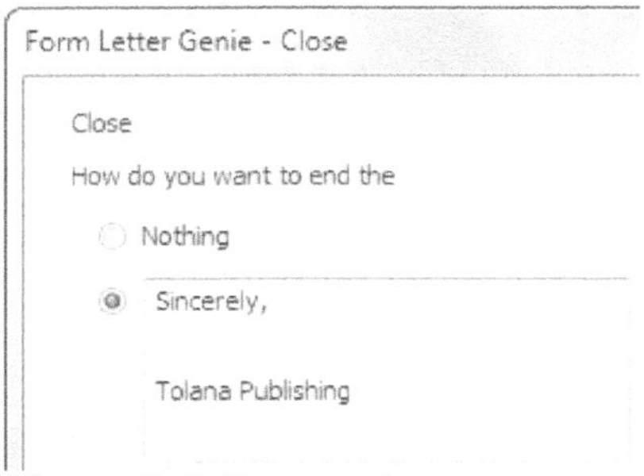

Figure 6-6 Close genie screen

The options on the Select Records screen are used to select which records will be printed on the form letter. The options are explained below.

① **ALL RECORDS** prints a letter for every record.

② **CURRENTLY SELECTED RECORDS** prints a letter for every record retrieved from a query or filter.

③ **MARKED RECORDS OR UNMARKED RECORDS** selects records that have or have not been tagged.

④ **FILTER CRITERIA** selects records that meet the filter expression or saved query.

10. Select the last option. Open the Specify filter drop-down list and select Expression, then click the button at the end of the field below.

    Create an expression to only display contacts in FL, NV or PA.

    The expression should look like the one shown in Figure 6-7.

    Click Next.

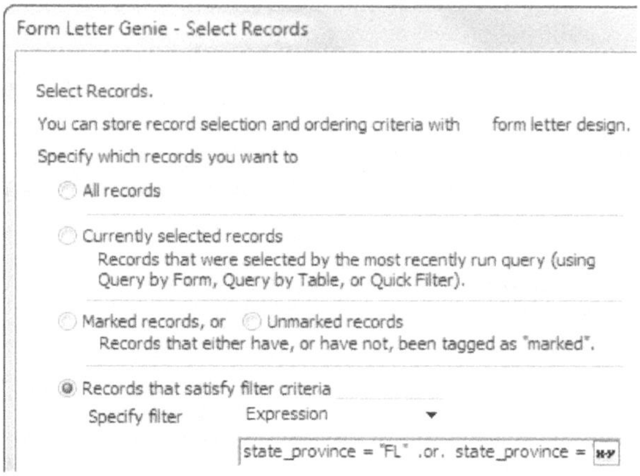

Figure 6-7 Select Records genie screen

The options on the Record Order screen are used to select (sort) the records that will be printed.

11. Open the Order drop-down list and select the State_Province field.

    Open the next drop-down list and select City, as shown in Figure 6-8.

    Click Next.

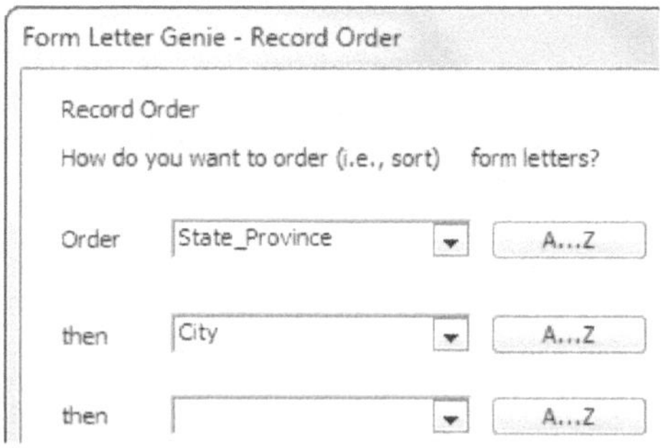

Figure 6-8 Record Order screen

The options shown in Figure 6-9 are used to select what you want to do after the form letter is created. The first option opens the form letter in the Letter Editor. The second option displays the form letter in the preview window with data.

If you want to review any of the options that you selected, review them before clicking the Finish button on this screen.

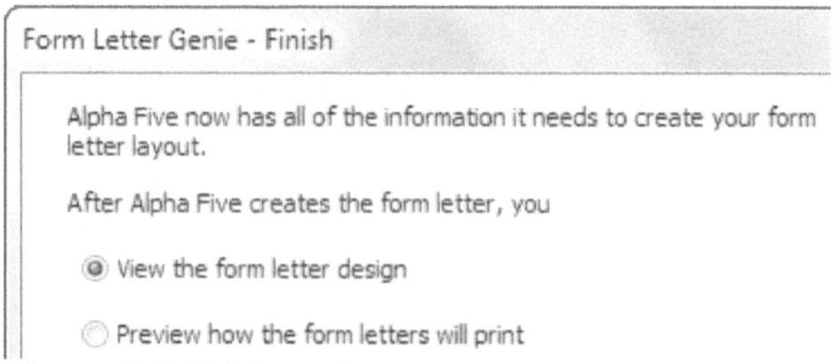

Figure 6-9 Finish genie screen

12. Select the first option, then click the Finish button.

    You will see the letter in the editor shown in Figure 6-10.

    Save the letter as `aMyGenieFormLetter`.

    On your own, you would type in the body of the letter.

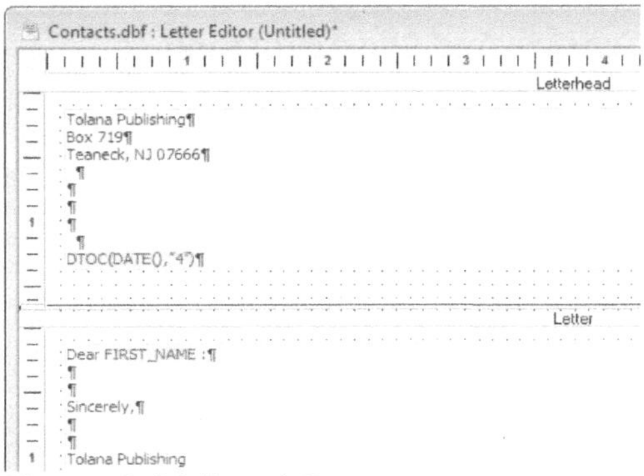

Figure 6-10 Form letter

13. Preview the letter. The first letter should look like the one shown in Figure 6-11.

Figure 6-11 Preview of letter

Using The Letter Editor

As you saw earlier in Figure 6-10, the Letter Editor has the two sections explained below:

① The **LETTERHEAD SECTION** contains the sender and addressee information. By default, this section does not display all of the information. To view the rest of the section, drag the Letter section bar down, then make the Rich Text field in the Letterhead section longer, as shown in Figure 6-12.

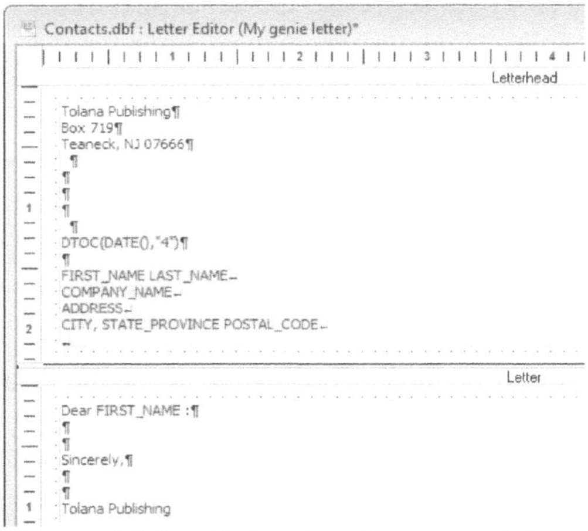

Figure 6-12 Letterhead section expanded

② The **LETTER SECTION** contains the body of the letter. Double-click in the section to create the body of the letter.

Letterhead Toolbar And Shortcut Menu

The options on the menu, toolbar and shortcut menu are the same as the ones for reports.

Letter Properties

There are four ways to open the Region Properties dialog box shown later in Figure 6-13.

① Right-click on the Letterhead or Letter section bar and select Properties.
② Right-click on a blank space in the editor and select Properties.
③ Letter ⇒ Properties.
④ Object ⇒ Properties.

Region Properties Dialog Box

I am not sure why this dialog box is not named Letter Properties. Many of the tabs on this dialog box are the same as the ones on the Report Properties, Detail Properties and Region Properties dialog boxes. The options that are unique to letters are explained below.

Backdrop Tab

[See Chapter 3, Region Properties Dialog Box, Backdrop Tab]

Letter Tab

The options shown in Figure 6-13 are used to select the header and footer sections for the letter. The options are explained in Table 6-1.

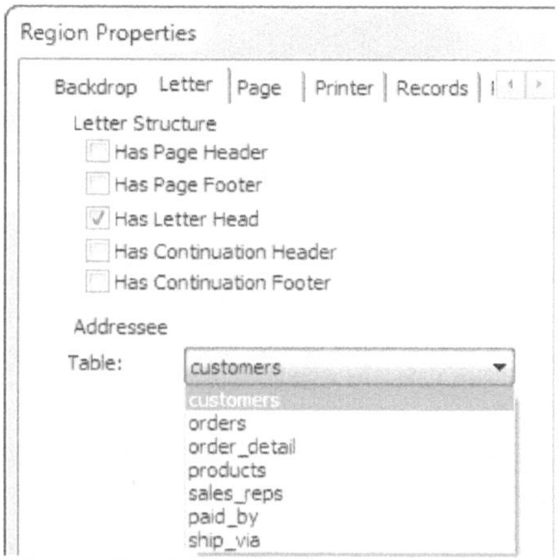

Figure 6-13 Letter tab

Option	Description
Has Letter Head	This option is enabled by default. It displays the Letterhead section shown earlier in Figure 6-12. (1)
Has Continuation Header	(1) (2)
Has Continuation Footer	This section prints after the Letter section and before the Page Footer section. (2)
Table	Displays the name of the table(s) that can be used for the letter.

Table 6-1 Letter tab options explained

(1) This section appears after the Page Header section and before the Letter section.
(2) This section starts printing on Page 2 to the end of the document.

Page Tab

[See Chapter 3, Report Properties Dialog Box, Page Tab]

Printer Tab

[See Chapter 3, Report Properties Dialog Box, Printer Tab]

Records Tab

[See Chapter 3, Detail Properties Dialog Box, Records Tab]

Region Tab

[See Chapter 3, Region Properties Dialog Box, Region Tab]

Window Tab

[See Chapter 3, Report Properties Dialog Box, Window Tab]

Menus/Toolbars Tab

[See Chapter 3, Report Properties Dialog Box, Menus/Toolbars Tab]

Creating Labels

The Label Genie will walk you through creating a variety of label styles.

Exercise 6.2: Create A Label Layout

In this exercise you will create labels for the contacts in the database.

1. On the Labels tab, click the New button.

2. On the New Label dialog box, select the Contacts table, then click OK.

3. On the dialog box shown in Figure 6-14, you can create a label or envelope.

   Select the Label genie option, then click OK.

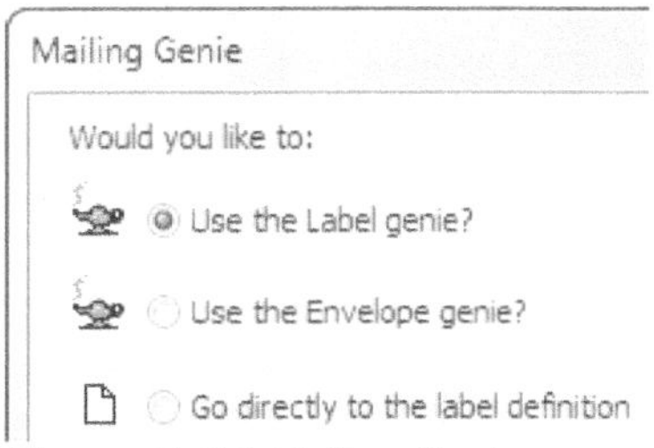

Figure 6-14 Mailing Genie

Mailing Label Genie

The options on the screen shown in Figure 6-15 are used to select the printer type that the labels will be printed on and the label size.

If the label size that you need is not in the list, select the **CUSTOM** option, then click Next. The options shown in Figure 6-16 are used to create a custom size label.

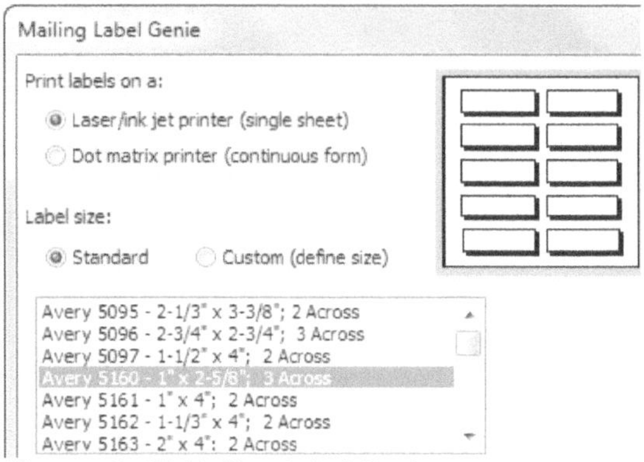

Figure 6-15 Mailing Label Genie

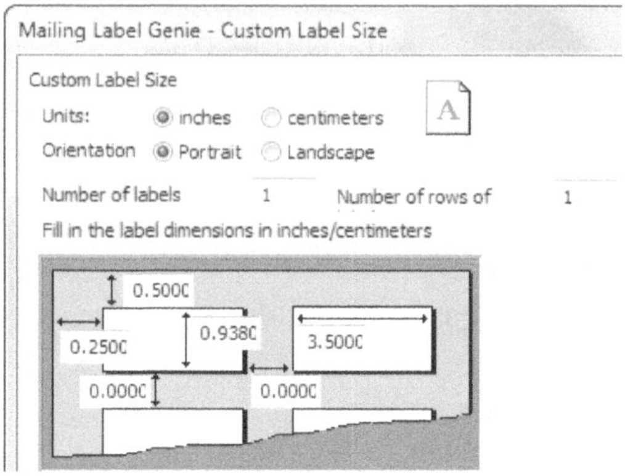

Figure 6-16 Custom Label Size genie screen

4. Select the Avery 5160 label size shown above in Figure 6-15, then click Next.

5. On the Layout screen, add the following fields: Company Name, First Name, Last Name, Address, City, State_Province and Postal Code. Add spaces and commas as needed.

6. Check the **INCLUDE DELIVERY POINT BAR CODE ON MAILING LABEL** option.

   Your screen should look like the one shown in Figure 6-17.

   Click Next.

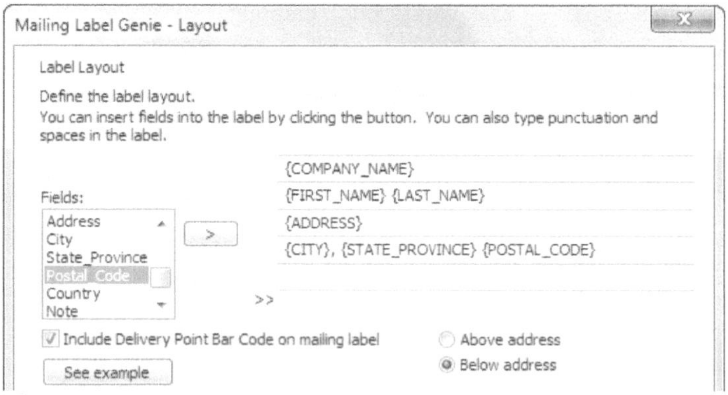

Figure 6-17 Layout genie screen

The options shown in Figure 6-18 are only available when the Delivery Point Bar Code option on the screen shown above in Figure 6-17 is selected. These options are used to create the bar code. If you do bulk mailings, adding a bar code to the mailing label will save you money.

7. Select the options shown above in Figure 6-18, then click Next.

8. If the default font options shown in Figure 6-19 are not what you need, select what you need, then click Next.

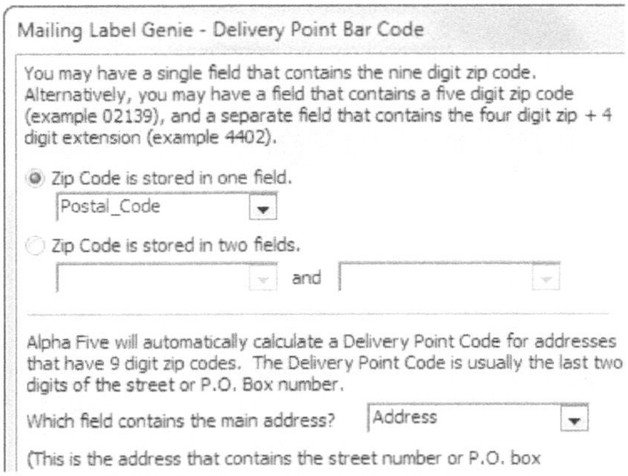

Figure 6-18 Delivery Point Bar Code genie screen

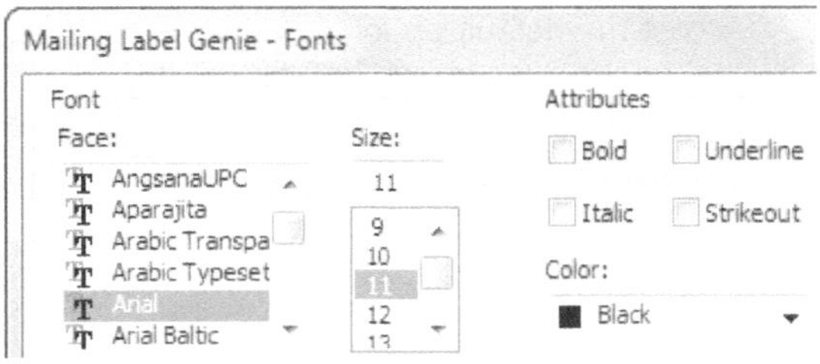

Figure 6-19 Fonts genie screen

9. The option shown in Figure 6-20 is used to select how many copies of each address you want to print. In this exercise accept the default, then click Next.

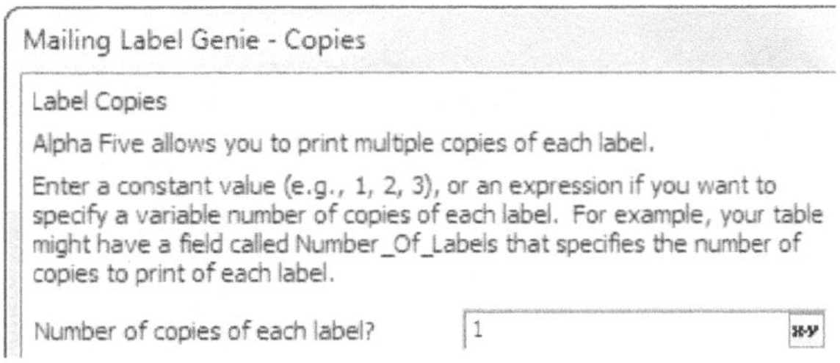

Figure 6-20 Copies genie screen

The options on the screen shown in Figure 6-21 are the same as the ones for the form letter shown earlier in Figure 6-7.

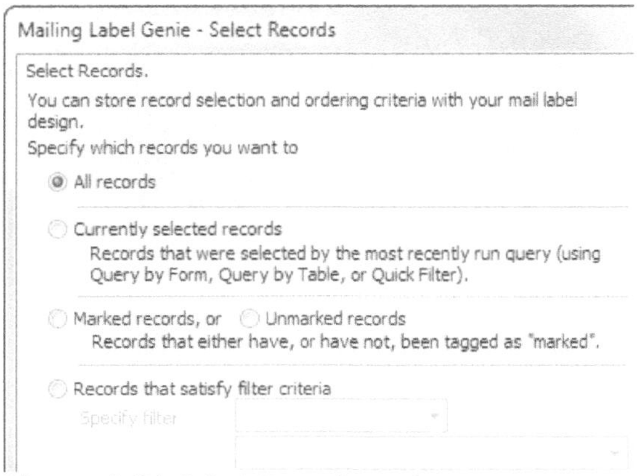

Figure 6-21 Select Records genie screen

10. Accept the default Select Records option, then click Next.

11. Sort the records by the Postal Code field, as shown in Figure 6-22, then click Next.

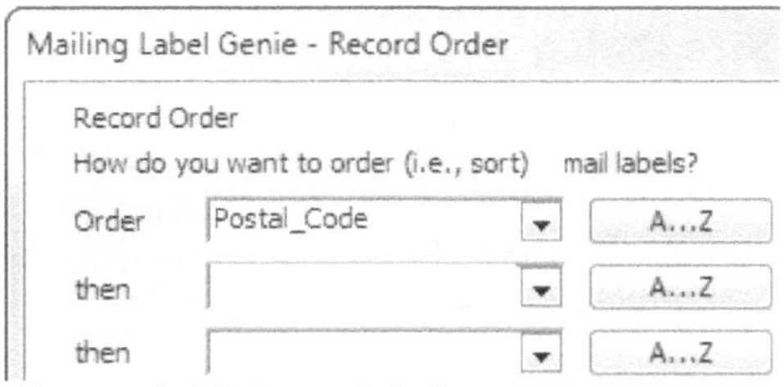

Figure 6-22 Record Order genie screen

12. Accept the default option to view the mailing label, as shown in Figure 6-23, then click Finish.

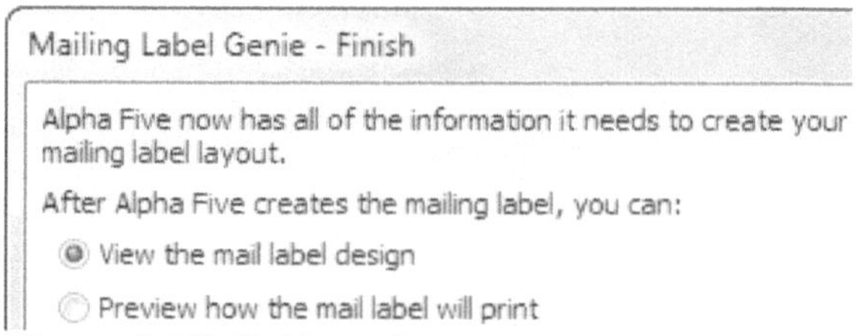

Figure 6-23 Finish genie screen

13. Save the label as `aContactsMailingLabel`. The label layout should look like the one shown in Figure 6-24. When you preview the labels, they should look like the ones shown in Figure 6-25.

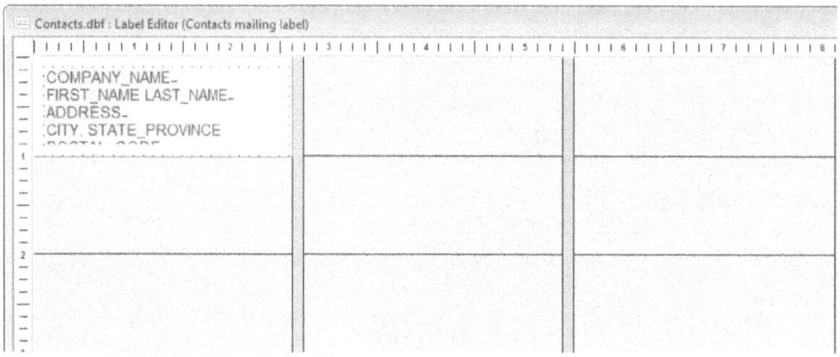

Figure 6-24 Mailing label layout

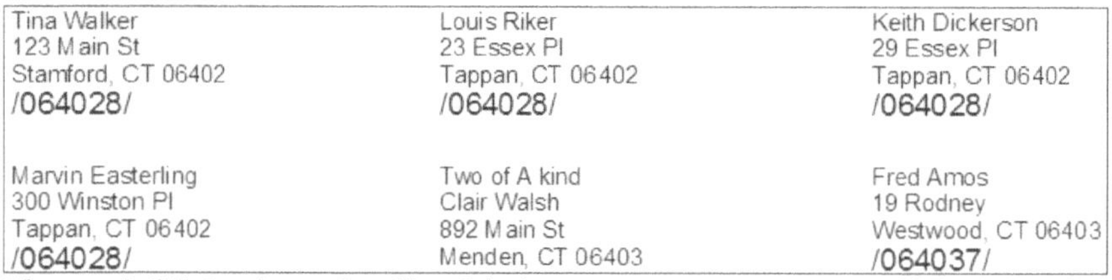

Figure 6-25 Preview of mailing labels

Label Editor Workspace

The label editor workspace is almost identical to the letter workspace. The differences are explained below.

Label Menu

The Size and Properties options on this menu in the workspace are explained below.

Label Size Dialog Box

Selecting the Size option on the Label menu opens the dialog box shown in Figure 6-26. The options are used to change the current label options, save a custom label size with the current label layout, create a custom label size, copy a label layout to a new layout, rename or delete a custom label size. This is the same dialog box that is opened when the **GO DIRECTLY TO THE LABEL DEFINITION** option is selected on the Mailing Genie. [See Figure 6-14]

Figure 6-26 Label Size dialog box

Label Properties Dialog Box

Selecting the Properties option on the Label menu opens the dialog box shown in Figure 6-27.

The options on the Label tab are used to select how many copies of each label to print.

Figure 6-27 Label Properties dialog box

Creating Envelopes

The Envelope Genie will walk you through creating a variety of envelope styles.

Exercise 6.3: Create An Envelope Layout

In this exercise you will create a layout for envelopes.

1. On the Labels tab, click the New button.
2. On the New Label dialog box, select the Customers table, then click OK.
3. On the Mailing Genie, select the **USE THE ENVELOPE GENIE** option, then click OK.

Envelope Genie

The options shown in Figure 6-28 are used to select an existing envelope size or create a custom envelope size. Selecting the **CUSTOM** option displays the screen shown in Figure 6-29. Notice on your screen that the Back button is not enabled. Make sure that you select the correct table or set.

4. Accept the default options shown in Figure 6-28, then click Next.

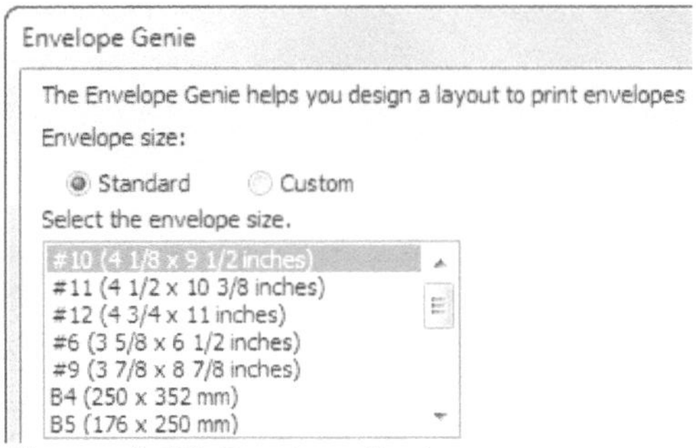

Figure 6-28 Envelope Genie

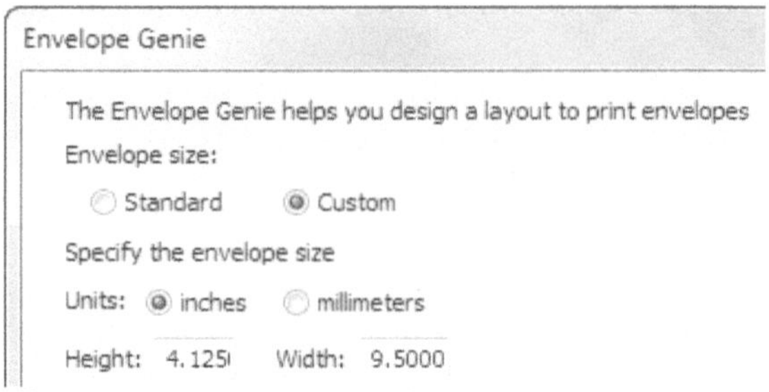

Figure 6-29 Custom envelope options

The options shown in Figure 6-30 are used to select how your printer needs the envelopes fed.

The **FACE-DOWN** option means that your printer requires the front of the envelope to be placed down in the printer tray.

The options shown in Figure 6-31 are used to select how envelopes have to be aligned in the printer.

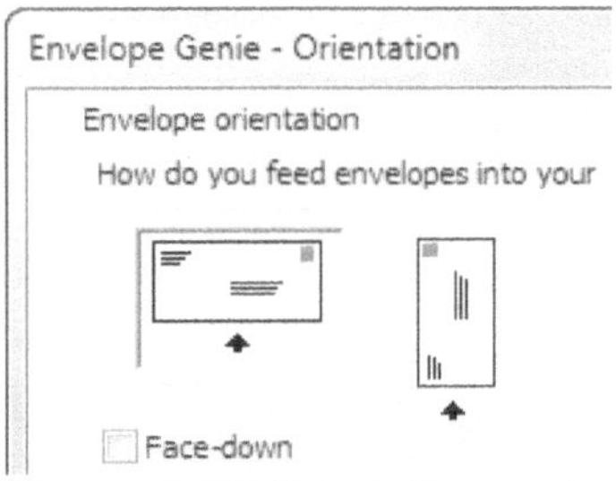

Figure 6-30 Orientation genie screen

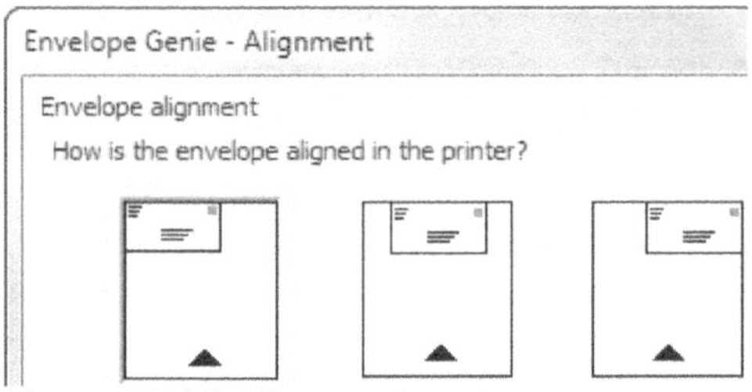

Figure 6-31 Alignment genie screen

5. Accept the defaults on the Orientation screen, then click Next.
   Accept the defaults on the Alignment screen, then click Next.

6. On the Layout screen, add the fields shown in Figure 6-32, including spaces and a comma, then click Next.

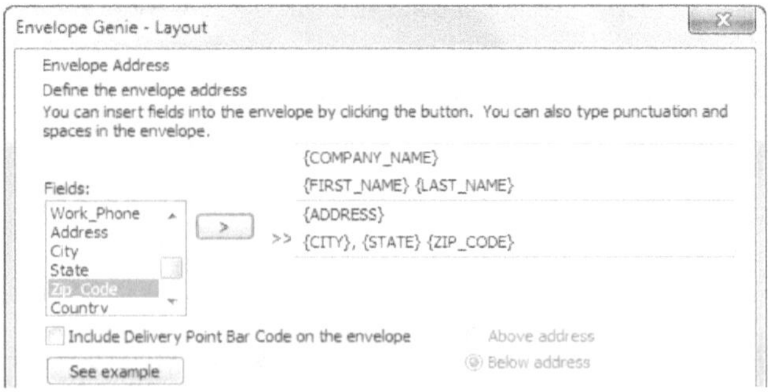

Figure 6-32 Fields selected to print on envelope

The options shown in Figure 6-33 are used if the envelopes that you are going to use do not have your return address pre-printed on them. If your envelopes are pre-printed, clear the check mark on this dialog box.

The options shown in Figure 6-34 are used to select the font, size and formatting of what will be printed on the envelope.

Figure 6-33 Return Address genie screen

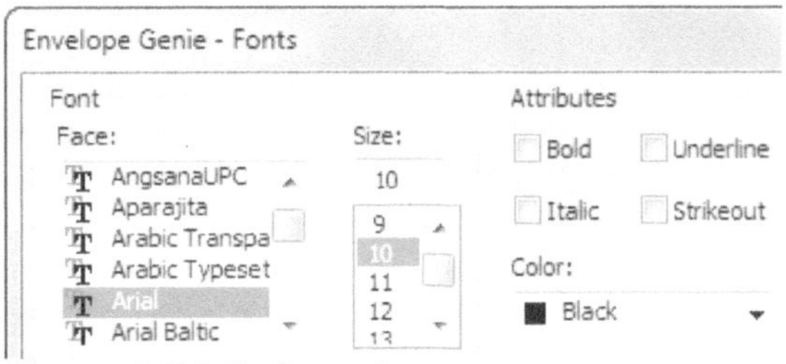

Figure 6-34 Fonts genie screen

7. On the Return Address screen type in the return address that you want to use on the envelope, then click Next. On the Fonts screen, select the font options that you need, then click Next.

8. On the screen shown in Figure 6-35, select the number of copies that you want to print, then click Next. You can also create an expression to determine how many copies of an envelope to print. The options on the Select Records screen are the same as the options for letters. [See Figure 6-7]

   Click Next.

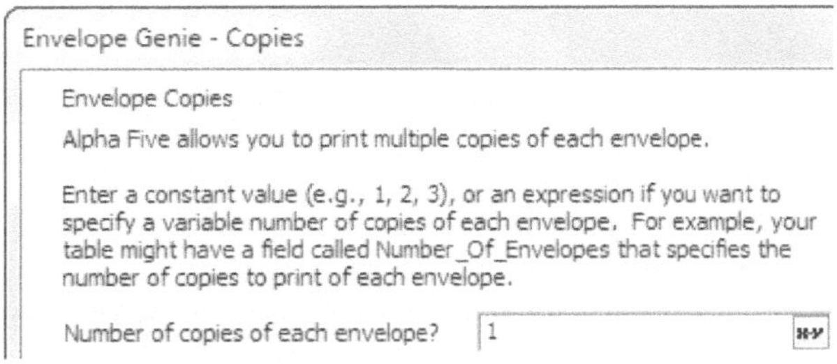

Figure 6-35 Copies genie screen

9. If it does not matter the order that the envelopes print in, click Next on the Record Order screen. For this exercise, click Next.

10. On the Finish screen, select the option to view the envelope, then click Finish.

11. Save the layout as `aCustomersEnvelope`.

Envelope Workspace

As shown in Figure 6-36, envelopes use the Label Editors features and tools.

Figure 6-36 Envelope layout

ENHANCING REPORTS PART 2

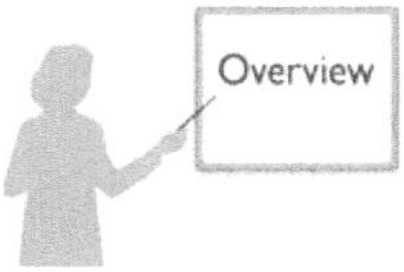

In this chapter you will learn techniques including the following, that will help make reports look professional.

- ☑ Using header and footer report sections
- ☑ Suppressing fields
- ☑ Alternating background row color
- ☑ Creating filters
- ☑ Conditionally format data displayed on a report
- ☑ Creating groups

CHAPTER 7

Overview

This chapter covers features that can make reports look more visually appealing. Reports are an important part of an application because they allow people to see the data in a variety of ways. For some, reports are a large part of their decision making process. Knowing this means that a lot of care must be taken to ensure that the data is presented in an easy to understand way and more importantly in my opinion, the data presented must be accurate.

Report Headers And Footers

By default, reports have the Report Header section, which only prints at the top of the first page of the report and the Report Footer section, which only prints at the bottom of the last page of the report.

Continuation Header And Footer Sections

The most important thing to remember about these sections are that there can be more than one continuation header and footer section on the same page. Table 7-1 explains the types of continuation header and footer sections.

Section	This Section Prints . . .
Report section header	On every page except the first page.
Report section footer	On every page except the last page.
Edit region header	Only if the edit region continues from the previous page.
Edit region footer	Only if the edit region continues onto the next page.
Detail section header	On every page except when every edit region in the Detail section printed on the previous page, meaning part of the edit region does not print on the current page.
Detail section footer	On every page except pages where every edit region in the Detail section is printed without being continued on another page.
Group section header	On every page if there is a Group Header section, except pages that the Group Footer section was the last section to print on the previous page.
Group section footer	On every page if there is a Group Footer section, except pages that the Group Footer section is the last section to print on the page.

Table 7-1 Continuation header and footer sections explained

Exercise 7.1: Create A Continuation Footer

One of the most popular uses for a continuation footer is to let the person reading the report know if there is more information on the next page about the group that prints at the bottom of the current page.

1. Save the aGroupedByOrderDate report as `aContinuationFooter`.

2. Right-click on the Group Order Date footer section bar (above the Report Footer section) and select Properties.

3. On the Head/Foot tab, select the **HAS CONTINUATION FOOTER** option.

4. Add a Text control to the Continuation Footer for Group section. Line it up with the State field in the Detail section. Double-click in the Text control and type `*Order Date continued on next page*`, as illustrated in Figure 7-1. Resize the continuation section so that it is the same size as the Text control. When you view the bottom of the second page, you will see the content that you added to the Continuation footer section, as displayed in Figure 7-2.

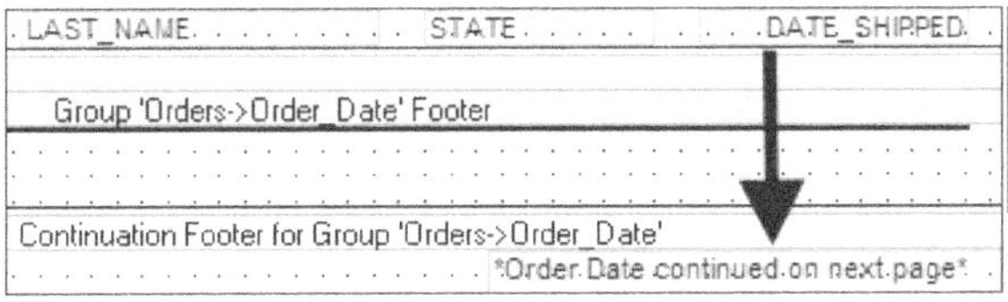

Figure 7-1 Continuation Footer section

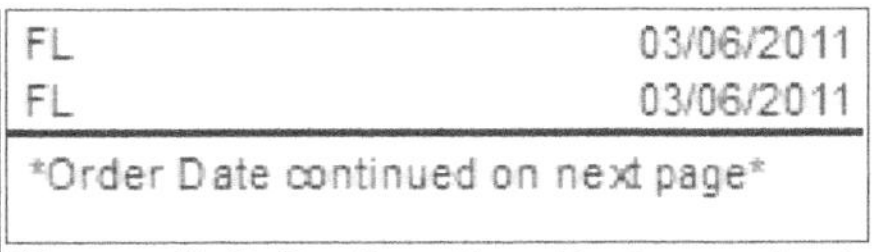

Figure 7-2 Continuation Footer content displayed

The reason that there are records at the top of the first page that do not have an Order ID is because the customers do not have a record in the Orders table. There are records for these customers in the Order Detail table. If this database were live, this would be a problem because there should not be records in an Order Detail table without a matching record in the Orders table.

Copy Layout To Option

The feature is available for all layouts. It is used to select a different table or set that the layout will be based on. To use this feature, the new table or set must have the same field names as the ones used on the layout that is being copied.

Exercise 7.2: Use The Copy To Option To Modify A Report

In this exercise you will change the set that a report is based on so that the report can be displayed on a form in a slightly different way. Because of the set that the Grouped by order date report is based on, the report cannot be used to display data based on the order selected on the embedded browse. In this exercise, you will select a different set for the report, then display the report on a copy of a form.

1. Right-click on the aGroupedByOrderDate report and select **COPY TO**.

2. Type an `a` at the beginning of the Object Name field.

3. Select the Customers-orders set in the list. You should have the options shown in Figure 7-3.

   Click OK.

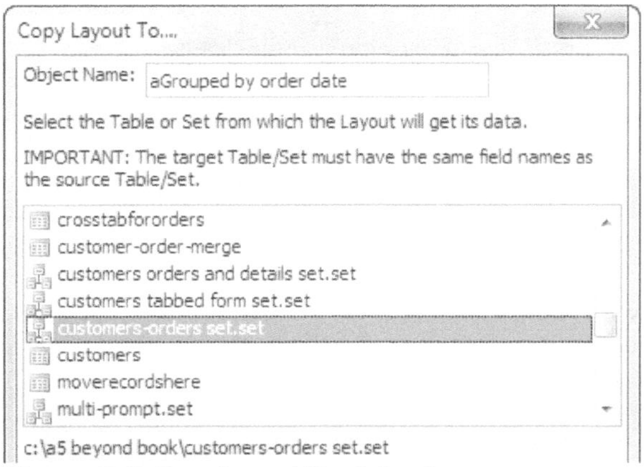

Figure 7-3 Copy Layout To dialog box

Modify The Form To Display A Different Report

1. Save the aReportPreview2 form as `aReportPreview3`.

2. On the form, click the button in the upper right corner of the Report Preview control, as illustrated in Figure 7-4.

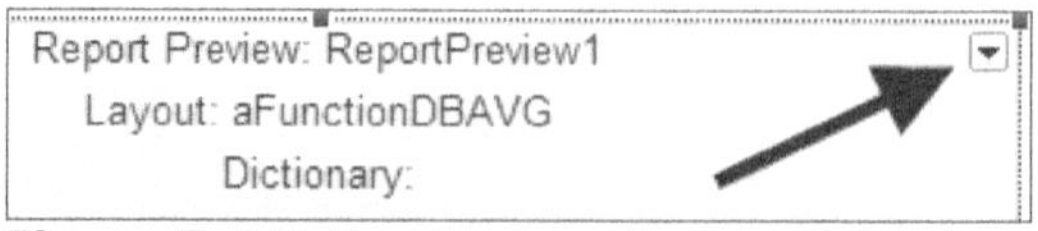

Figure 7-4 Button to open the Report Preview dialog box illustrated

3. Select the aGroupedByOrderDate report. When you view the report, select an order in the browse on the left. The corresponding detail records will be displayed on the report.

Exercise 7.3: Use A Hyperlink To Open A Form From A Report

In this exercise you will add a hyperlink to fields on a report that will open a form that displays the detail information for the selected order or customer. Keep in mind that hyperlinks on a report are only useful when the report is viewed. If the report is printed, the hyperlinks have no value.

Create The Order ID Hyperlink

By default, Alpha Five will display a field as a hyperlink when the mouse pointer hovers over the field. I prefer to have fields look like a hyperlink whether or not the mouse pointer is hovered over a field. That way the user knows that the link is there. In this part of the exercise you will create a link for the Order ID field that opens a form.

1. Save the Orders report as `aViewOrders`.

2. On the properties dialog box Font tab for the Order ID field, select the Underline option and change the font color to blue.

3. Double-click on the Order ID field on the Events for dialog box. Click the Add New Action button.

4. Select the Form/Browse category, then select the Open Form or Browse Layout action. Click OK.

5. Select the View Orders form, then click Next.

6. Select the **RECORDS THAT MATCH THE VALUE IN A CONTROL** option. Select the Order ID field in both drop-down lists on the Filter tab, as shown at the bottom of Figure 7-5, then click Finish.

7. Add this comment to the action. `Opens the View Orders form when the Order ID field in the report is clicked on`, then click the Save button.

8. When you click on an Order ID number in the aViewOrders report, the View Orders form opens and displays detail data for the order, as shown in 7-6.

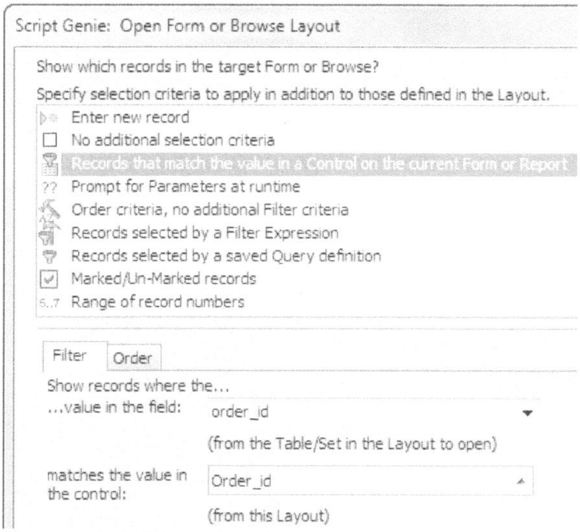

Figure 7-5 Filter tab options

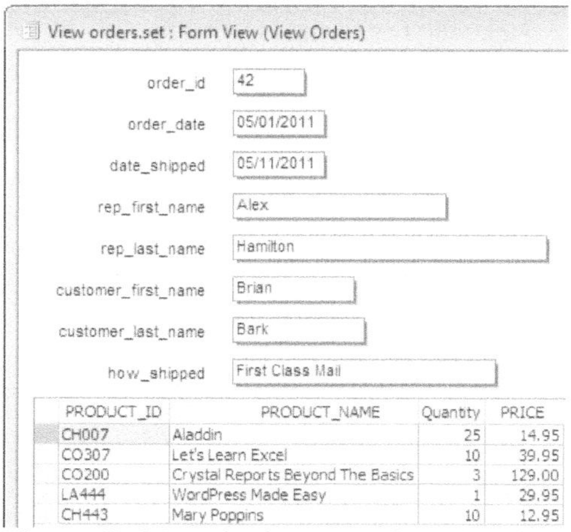

Figure 7-6 Detail information for order the selected on the report

Create The Customer ID Hyperlink

The process of creating this hyperlink is almost the same as the one that you created for the Order ID field.

1. Follow the steps starting with step 2 in the previous section, with the changes listed in Table 7-2.

Step	Change
2	Order ID to Customer ID.
3	Order ID to Customer ID.
5	View Orders form to aReportPreview2 form.
6	Order ID to Customer ID.
7	View Orders form to aReportPreview2 form.
7	Order ID to Customer ID.
8	Order ID to Customer ID.
8	View Orders form to aReportPreview2 form.

Table 7-2 Changes needed to create the Customer ID hyperlink

2. Click on the Customer ID link. You will see the aReportPreview2 form, which displays the Customer information and their orders.

Exercise 7.4: Suppress Fields And Bands

There may be times when the report does not need to display the same data for every detail row. Some sections on a report may only have one field and sometimes that field does not have data for every record. An example would be the second address field in a table. By default, the space where this field would print on the report would be blank. That is probably not what you want to have happen. In this exercise you will learn how to suppress a field that does not have data and how to suppress a section that has fields that do not have data.

How To Suppress A Field

1. Save the aContactList report as `aSuppressField`.

2. Make the Detail section longer, then add the Note field to it, not the title, below the fields, as shown in Figure 7-7.

   View the report. It should look like the one shown in Figure 7-8. As you can see, not every record has data in the Note field.

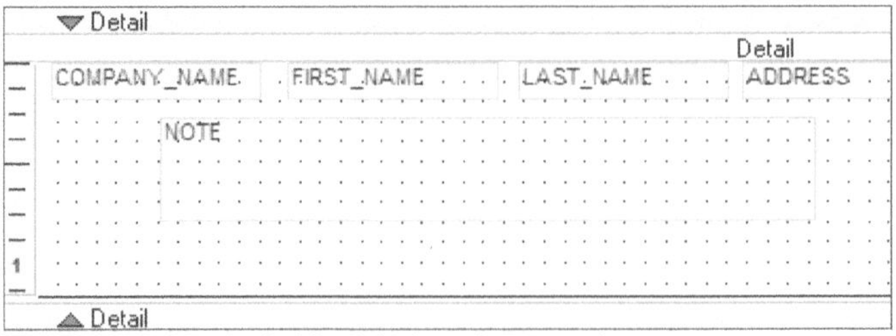

Figure 7-7 Note field added to the Detail section

3. On the properties dialog box for the Note field, check the **ALLOW SHRINKING** option. Save the changes. If you preview the report, you will see that there is less white space between the records, as shown in Figure 7-9.

Figure 7-8 Preview of report with the Note field

Figure 7-9 Report with the Note field allowed to shrink

How To Suppress Data In A Rich Text Control

In this part of the exercise you will add the Note field to a Rich Text control and enable suppression on the control. The benefit of adding a field like a Note field that will not always have data to a Rich Text field and each record can have a different amount of data in the Note field is that you can make the field any length you want and enable scrollbars, which allows the user to scroll to see all of the data in the field.

The Rich Text control can contain more than one field, as shown in Figure 7-10. It is often used to print address information on a form, letter or label because any field in the rich text control that does not have data will be suppressed.

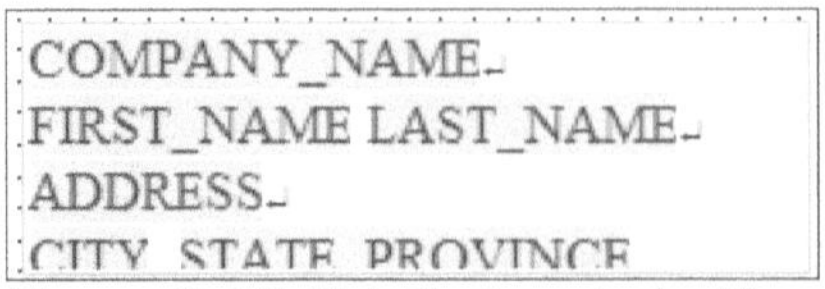

Figure 7-10 Rich Text control with multiple fields

1. Save the aSuppressField report as `aSuppressRichTextControl`.

2. Delete the Note field, then add the Rich Text control to the bottom of the Detail section.

3. Drag the Note field into the Rich Text control.

   On the shortcut menu for the control, select the **CAN SHRINK** option.

   This option enables the **ALLOW SHRINK WHEN PRINTING** option, shown in Figure 7-11.

   Save the changes.

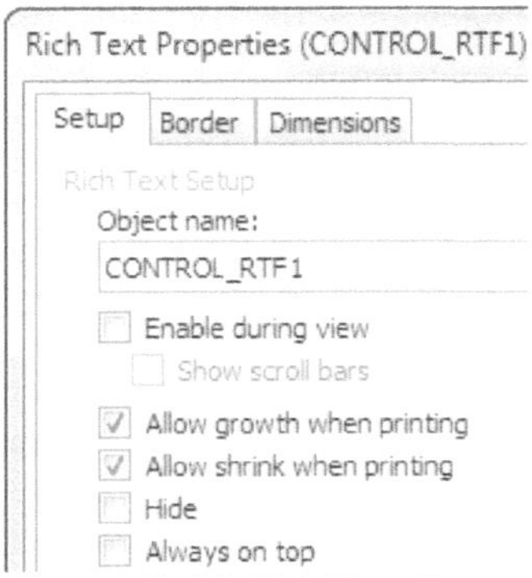

Figure 7-11 Rich Text Properties dialog box

Suppress A Section (Report Band)

As shown earlier in Figure 7-7, there is extra space below the Note field. As you saw, this space is displayed on the report. The steps below show you how to suppress the extra space in a section of the report.

1. Save the aSuppressField report as `aSuppressReportSection`.

2. Right-click on the Detail bar without an arrow (the second one at the top of Figure 7-7) and select Properties.

3. On the Region tab, select the **SHRINK CONTENTS OF BAND** option shown in Figure 7-12.

   When you view the report, you will see that there is less space between the rows of data, as shown in Figure 7-13, then there is shown earlier in Figure 7-8.

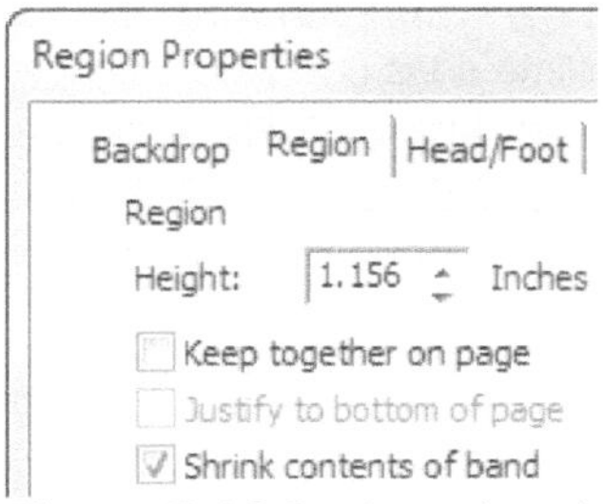

Figure 7-12 Region tab options

Figure 7-13 Report with Shrink contents of band option enabled

Changing The Background Color

One of the more popular uses of the Color tab on the properties dialog box is to add a background color to every other detail record on the report. If you have ever seen what is known as "green bar" computer paper, you already know the color effect that you will create in this exercise.

The **FRAME CONTROL** is placed around the fields in the Detail section to control the background color that is displayed.

The **DYNAMIC** option is used when you need to create a condition that will determine if something happens. In order to change the background color of every other row, the functions discussed below are needed.

① **MOD** Divides one number by another number and returns the remainder, instead of the result of the division.
② **MRECNO()** This function returns the row number in the Detail section of the report.

Exercise 7.5: Alternate The Background Color Of Rows

In this exercise you will learn how to create a report that has alternating row background colors.

Add The Frame To The Detail Section

1. Save the aContactList report as `aBackgroundColor`.

2. Move the bottom Detail bar separator down a little, so that you will be able to select all of the fields in the section. Make sure that all of the fields are covered. Move the bottom Detail bar separator back up.

3. Select the Frame control in the Toolbox, then draw a box around the fields in the Detail section. The frame does not need a heading, so leave the Frame Heading field on the Frame Genie dialog box blank. Click OK.

4. On the Properties panel for the frame, change the following options, as illustrated in Figure 7-14. I find it easier to use the Properties panel instead of the Properties dialog box to make these changes, but either can be used. In the Border section, clear the check mark for the bottom, left, right and top edge options. In the Fill section, change the Color to white, then change the Style option to solid.

Create The Expression To Apply The Background Color

1. Click the Fill Color Dynamic button shown in Figure 7-14. Select the color and type the expression shown in Figure 7-15. Change the color at the bottom of the dialog box to white. The report should look like the one shown in Figure 7-16.

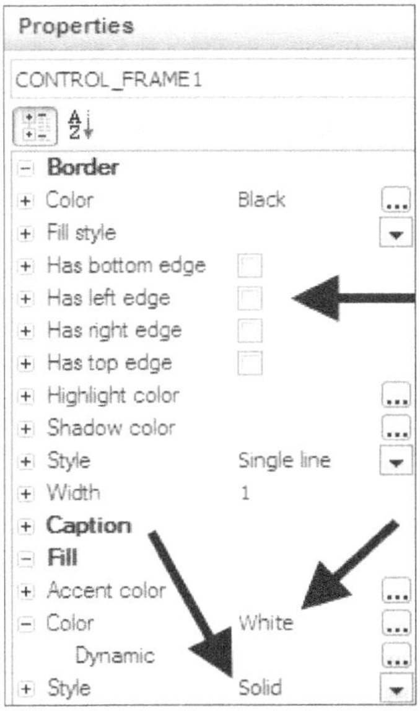

Figure 7-14 Properties panel for the frame

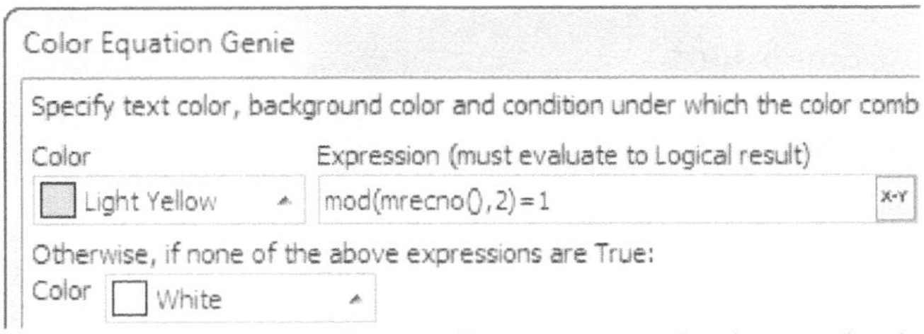

Figure 7-15 Options for an alternating row background color

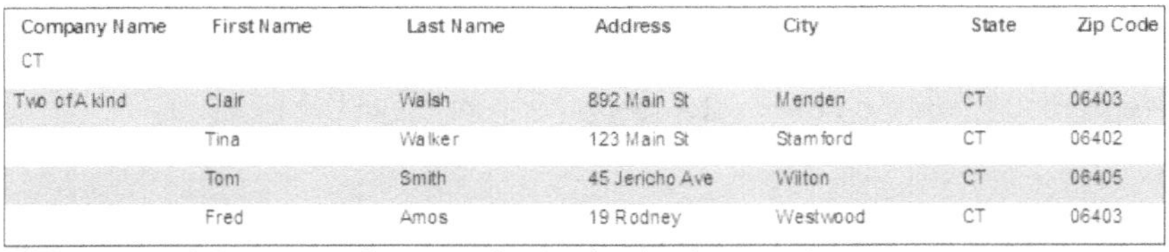

Company Name	First Name	Last Name	Address	City	State	Zip Code
CT						
Two of A kind	Clair	Walsh	892 Main St	Menden	CT	06403
	Tina	Walker	123 Main St	Stamford	CT	06402
	Tom	Smith	45 Jericho Ave	Wilton	CT	06405
	Fred	Amos	19 Rodney	Westwood	CT	06403

Figure 7-16 Report with one color in the background

The expressions and options shown in Figure 7-17, create the report shown in Figure 7-18.

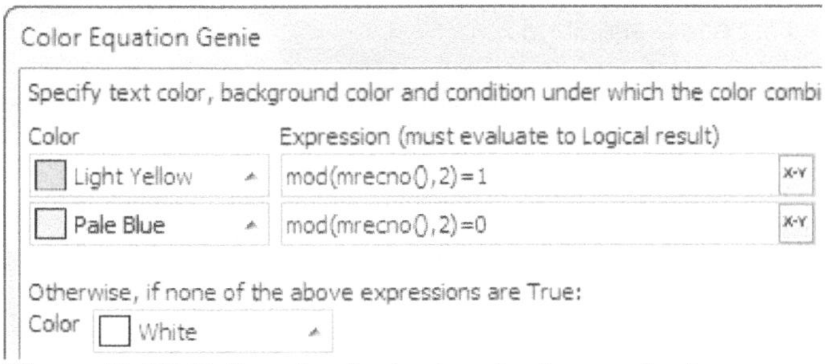

Figure 7-17 Options to display two background colors

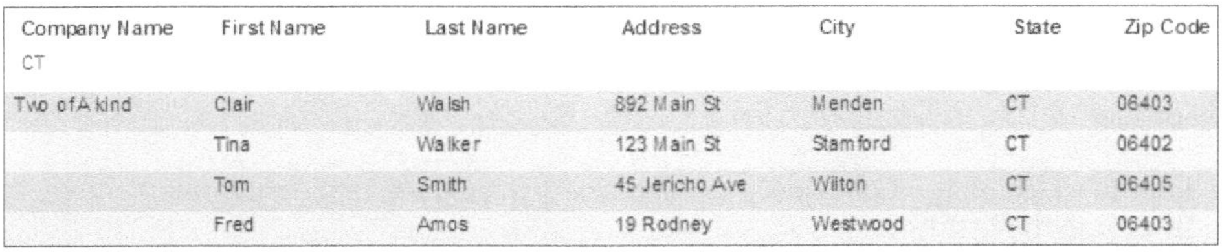

Company Name	First Name	Last Name	Address	City	State	Zip Code
CT						
Two of A kind	Clair	Walsh	892 Main St	Menden	CT	06403
	Tina	Walker	123 Main St	Stamford	CT	06402
	Tom	Smith	45 Jericho Ave	Wilton	CT	06405
	Fred	Amos	19 Rodney	Westwood	CT	06403

Figure 7-18 Report with two colors in the background

Using Conditions

Conditions are used to create the filter expressions. Some filter expressions only require one condition, like display all records where the sales rep equals 4.

Using Multiple Conditions

When you need to create multiple conditions like display customers in CA that placed an order after 9/19/11, there are two types of conditions that you can create, as explained below.

① Use the **OR CONDITION** when any of the conditions can evaluate to True to satisfy the requirement. For example, Customers in CA **OR** order was placed after 9/19/11.
② Use the **AND CONDITION** when all conditions have to evaluate to True to satisfy the requirement. For example, Customers in CA that placed an order after 9/19/11. The multiple conditions that you have created in this book up to this point have been And conditions.

Exercise 7.6: Use The AND Condition To Create A Filter Expression

In this exercise you will learn how to create two conditions that both must evaluate to True for the record to appear on the report.

Create The Report

1. Create a blank free-form report based on the Customers-orders set. Save the report as `aANDFilter`.

2. Add a Page Header section. This is where the field headings will be placed.

3. From the Customers table, add the following fields to the Detail section: Customer ID, First name, Last name and State.

4. From the Orders table, add the following fields to the Detail section: Order ID, Sales Rep ID and Order Date.

Create The Filter Expression

In this part of the exercise you will create two conditions:

① The Sales Rep ID must be equal to four.
② The Order Date must be greater than or equal to 6/1/2011.

1. Click the **SELECT RECORDS** button on the toolbar. Click the Filter field button on the **SELECT RECORDS TO PRINT DIALOG BOX**, then click the Create Filter Using Genie button on the Expression Builder.

2. Open the drop-down list on the Condition 1 tab and select the Orders table, then select the Sales Rep ID field in the first list.

3. The **IS EQUAL TO** operator should be selected in the second list.

   Type `4` in the field to the right.

   These options will select orders whose Sales Rep ID equals 4.

   You should have the options shown in Figure 7-19.

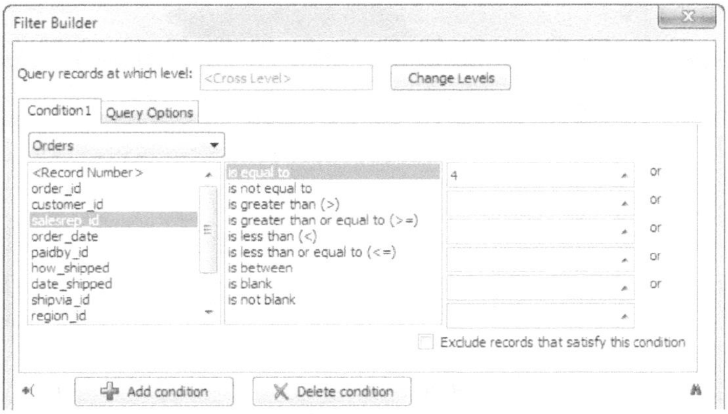

Figure 7-19 Condition 1 tab options

4. Click the **ADD CONDITION** button, then select the Orders table.

5. Select the Order Date field, then select the **IS ON OR AFTER THE DATE** operator. This operator is the same as the **IS GREATER THAN OR EQUAL TO** operator.

6. In the field type `6/1/11`.

   Select the **AND THIS CONDITION** option shown in Figure 7-20, if it is not already selected.

Figure 7-20 Condition 2 tab options

7. Click the binoculars icon in the lower right corner of the dialog box, as show earlier in Figure 7-19. Figure 7-21 shows the expression that was created from the options that you selected on the Condition tabs. Close the Filter Expression dialog box. Click OK to close all of the dialog boxes.

Figure 7-21 Filter expression

8. Add the **CURRENT FILTER** System field to the top of the Page Header section.

9. Save the changes. When you view the report, you will see that the Sales Rep ID for all records displayed is 4 and that the order date for each row is greater than or equal to 6/1/11, as shown in Figure 7-22.

Current filter (Orders->salesrep_id = 4) .and. (Orders->order_date >= ctod("6/1/11"))

Customer id	First name	Last name	State	Order id	Salesrep id	Order date
11	Tom	Smith	CT	23	4	06/03/2011
28	William	Olin	NJ	91	4	06/03/2011
202	Thomas	Axen	CA	357	4	04/30/2012
209	Roland	Wacker	IL	375	4	05/11/2012

Figure 7-22 Report with the .AND. condition

Exercise 7.7: Use The OR Condition To Create A Filter Expression

In this exercise you will learn how to create a filter where either of two conditions have to evaluate to True for the record to be displayed on the report.

1. Save the aANDFilter report as `aORFilter`.
2. Click the Select Records button on the toolbar. Delete the expression in the Filter field. The Filter Genie is not available if an expression already exists. Open the Filter Builder.
3. Create a condition to select orders that have the sales rep 4.
4. Create a condition to select orders that have the sales rep 10, then select the **OR THIS CONDITION** option. Yes, you could have put both sales rep numbers on the Condition 1 tab, but I wanted to illustrate the **OR** condition option.
5. Create a condition to select orders with an order date greater than 6/1/11, then select the **AND THIS CONDITION** option.

If you look at the tabs shown in Figure 7-23, you will see which condition type the tab contains. The tabs read Condition 1 or Condition 2 and Condition 3.

Figure 7-23 Two OR conditions and one AND condition

This means that if either of the filter expressions on the first two tabs evaluate to True and the filter expression on the third tab evaluates to True, the record will be displayed on the report. Figure 7-24 shows the expression.

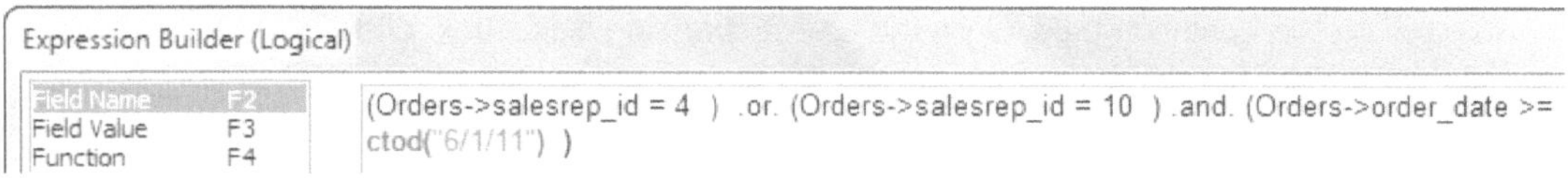

Figure 7-24 Filter expression

The last page of the report should look like the one shown in Figure 7-25.

Current filter (Orders->salesrep_id = 4) .or. (Orders->salesrep_id = 10) .and. (Orders->order_date >= ctod("6/1/11"))

Customer id	First name	Last name	State	Order id	Salesrep id	Order date
302	Fasan	Jane	RI	295	10	03/07/2012
302	Fasan	Jane	RI	468	10	07/21/2012
303	Edwards	Donald	CA	469	10	07/23/2012
304	Bodnar	Stacy	IA	470	10	07/23/2012
307	Esler	Jerry	OR	300	4	03/09/2012
309	Walter	Robert	IL	475	4	07/25/2012

Figure 7-25 Report with the .OR. condition

The orders have sales rep 4 or 10 and the order date is greater than or equal to 6/1/2011.

Top N Reports

Top and Bottom N reports, commonly known as Top N reports (and how I refer to them), are used to show the first N or last N records in a group. The default value for N is usually 10, which is where "Top 10" comes from. You can use a different number for N. Instead of displaying all orders in a certain date range, you could only show the largest 10 orders in the date range. This type of report is popular because it allows the reader to quickly see the highest (often thought of as the best) or lowest (often thought of as the worse) data.

Top N Options

The bottom of Figure 7-26 illustrates the Top N options that you can use.

Use these options if you do not want to use the functions or write code.

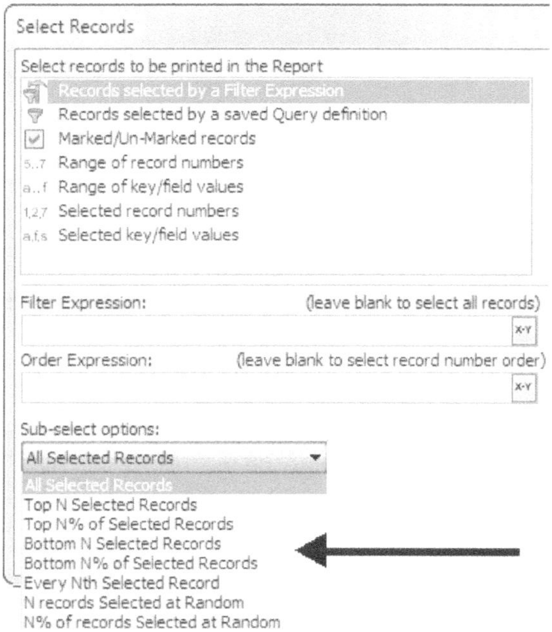

Figure 7-26 Top N options illustrated

Exercise 7.8: Create A Top 10 Sales Report

In this exercise you will modify an existing list report that displays last years sales total amount for each customer, as shown in Figure 7-27.

The modified report will only display the 10 records with the highest sales total amounts.

Last Years Sales

Customer #	Name	State	Last years sales
1	Tina Jones	FL	55664.35
2	Jamie Walker	NV	3239.85
3	Stuart Thomas	FL	1621.20
4	Todd Green	FL	10662.75

Figure 7-27 Last Years Sales report

1. Save the Last Years Sales report as `aTop10LastYearsSales`.

2. Click the Select Records button, then click the Create Filter/Order Using Genie button.

3. In the Order Expression field, select the Last Years Sales field.

4. Open the **SUB-SELECT OPTIONS** drop-down list and select Top N Selected Records.

   Accept the default **N** value shown to the right of the field.

   You should have the options selected, shown at the bottom of Figure 7-28.

   Click OK.

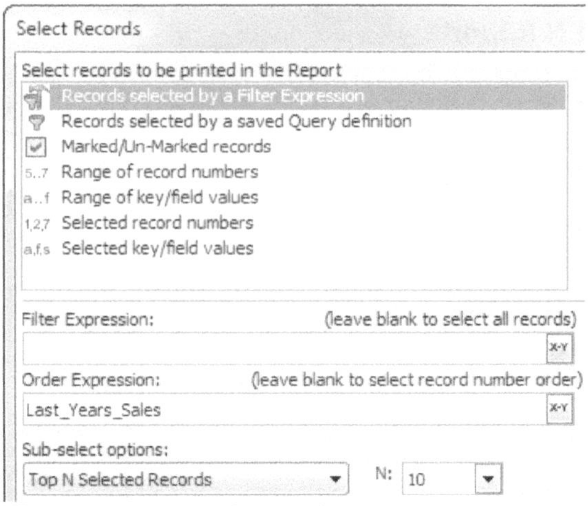

Figure 7-28 Top 10 records options

5. Select the Descending order option.

   When you view the report, you should see the 10 records shown in Figure 7-29.

   If you viewed the Chart Customers table in the Default Browse and sorted the Last Years Sales field in descending order, the first 10 records displayed would be the same as the ones on the report.

Last Years Sales

Customer #	Name	State	Last years sales
200	Anna Bedecs	WA	500000.00
239	Tim Smith	MI	500000.00
311	Lee-Johnson Laurie	CA	401000.00
236	Laura Callahan	VA	300000.00
341	Zalapski Aaron	NC	298356.22
10	Tina Walker	CT	201000.00
255	Daryl Patterson	NM	201000.00
257	Lori Martin	NY	201000.00
284	Aaron Baker	CT	201000.00
293	Manon Patricia	WI	201000.00

Figure 7-29 Top 10 sales report

Top/Bottom Percent Reports

Bottom N Percent reports display the lowest values from the data. Before running a percent report, (Top or Bottom) you do not know how many records will be displayed on the report.

This is because you do not know how many records it will take to reach the percent selected.

The number of records displayed also depends on any other filter criteria that the report has.

309	Walter Robert	IL	201000.00
310	Christianso Chris	MI	201000.00
14	Louis Riker	CT	200000.00
254	Dan Smith	PA	181444.66
20	Karen John	PA	133551.30
340	Rubens Danielle	MT	123658.46
275	Anthony Shoemaker	MA	100000.00
289	Andrea Trueman	AL	100000.00
48	Stella Muldoon	NV	97459.70
315	Mast Alexander	AL	95900.85
252	Ian Dodsworth	ND	90000.00
250	Kim King	MT	87906.45
354	Zarcalister Bob	VT	85642.56

Figure 7-30 Top N Percent report

For example, if the Top N report created in Exercise 7.8 was changed to a Top N Percent report, the report would display the records shown in Figure 7-30.

In addition to the 10 records displayed in the Top N report, the report displays more than 10 records because a percent is not a specific number. In this example, it displays 23 records. That may not always be the case. As data is added to the table(s) that the report is based on, the number of records displayed on the report can change.

Exercise 7.9: Create A Bottom N Percent Report

In this exercise you will modify the report shown earlier in Figure 7-27 to display the bottom 25% of last years sales.

1. Save the Last Years Sales report as `aBottomPercentSales`.

2. Add `Bottom 25% of` to the beginning of the report title.

3. Click the Select Records button, then click the Create Filter/Order Using Genie button.

4. In the Order Expression field, type `invert(Last_Years_Sales)`. This is the same as selecting the Descending option on the Select Records to Print dialog box.

5. Open the Sub-select options drop-down list and select **BOTTOM N% OF SELECTED RECORDS**.

6. Open the N drop-down list and select 25%, as shown in Figure 7-31.

   When you view the report, you will see the records shown in Figure 7-32. There are more records on the report, then displayed in the figure.

Figure 7-31 Bottom N percent options

Bottom 25% of Last Years Sales

Customer #	Name	State	Last years sales
279	Xena Pratt	KY	2944.00
241	Justin Brid	FL	2939.29
286	Samuel Davidson	DE	2934.94
25	Sidney Queen	NV	2850.85
373	Danforth Fred	CO	2826.90
372	Smithers Seth	AZ	2781.60

Figure 7-32 Bottom N percent records report

Make Certain Data Stand Out On The Report

There may be times when you want data that meets a condition to be displayed differently on the report from the other data in the column. For example, you may want to change the fill or border color of data when a condition is met. Earlier in this chapter you learned how to use the Fill properties to change the background color of detail rows on a report. The same technique can be applied to individual pieces of data.

Exercise 7.10: Conditionally Customize How Data Is Displayed

In this exercise you will learn how to conditionally change how data is displayed.

Customize The Fill Color

In this part of the exercise you will learn how to create an expression that changes the fill color of the Qty field to light yellow if the value is between 10 and 20.

1. Save the Quantity Ordered report as `aCustomizeData`.

2. Delete the Average quantity field and title. Delete the Report Header section.

3. Click on the Qty field. In the Fill section of the Properties panel, click the **COLOR DYNAMIC** button.

4. Select the color Light yellow, then type this expression. `Between(Qty, 10, 20)`

5. Change the Otherwise color option at the bottom of the dialog box to Winback, as shown in Figure 7-33.

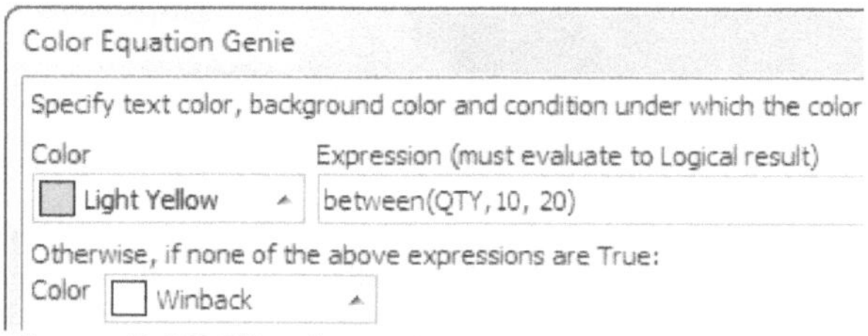

Figure 7-33 Fill color options

6. Change the Fill Style option to Solid.

   The report should look like the one shown in Figure 7-34.

Order id	Product id	Quantity	Price	line total
1	CO295	10	79.95	799.50
1	CH007	10	14.95	149.50
2	LA044	1	29.95	29.95
3	CH100	25	12.95	323.75
3	CH101	10	12.95	129.50

Figure 7-34 Fill color customization

Customize The Border Color And Style Options

In this part of the exercise you will learn how to create an expression that changes the border color to orange and the border style of the Line total field to long dashes if the Line total value is greater than or equal to $500.

Customize The Border Color

1. Click on the Line total field. In the Border section of the Properties panel, click the Color Dynamic button.

2. Select the color Orange, then type this expression, as shown in Figure 7-35.

   `calc->line_total >= 500.`

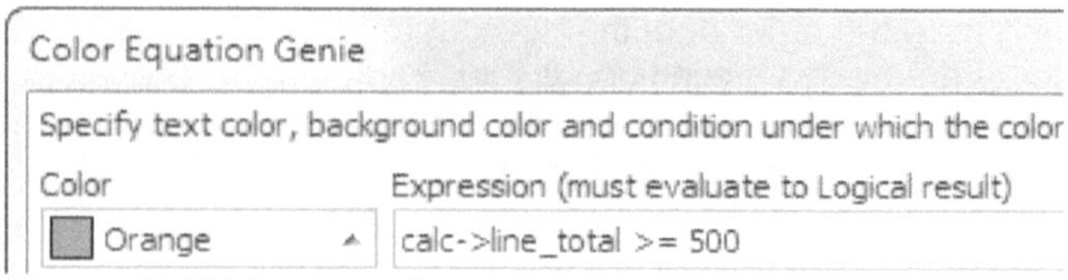

Figure 7-35 Border color options

Customize The Border Style

1. Click on the Line total field. In the Border section of the Properties panel, click the **STYLE DYNAMIC** button.

2. Type this expression. You will see the **<INVALID OR INCOMPLETE EXPRESSION>** message, even though the expression works.

```
If(Calc->Line_total >= 500, "Long dashes", "No border")
```

3. Change the Border width to 2.

   The report should look like the one shown in Figure 7-36.

Order id	Product id	Quantity	Price	line total
1	CO295	10	79.95	799.50
1	CH007	10	14.95	149.50
2	LA044	1	29.95	29.95

Figure 7-36 Border color customizations

Using Groups

You have seen a few reports in this book that have at least one group. Groups help organize records in the Detail section. Reports can have more than one group. There is no manual way to change the order of the groups on the report. When adding additional groups to a report, the section or region band that you click on determines where the next group will be placed. If you click on the region band to add a group, the group is created as the last group. If you click on the section band to create the group, the group is created directly above the section band that you right-clicked on.

Exercise 7.11: Create Groups

In this exercise you will create a report that demonstrates where groups appear, based on the section or band that was selected.

1. Save the aORFilter report as `aCreateGroups`.

2. Add the City field to the report before the State field.

3. Delete the Current filter field from the report. Delete the Report Header section.

Create The Groups

1. Right-click on the Detail region band and select Insert Group, then select the following options.
   Break on change in - Order Date
   Label - `Group 1`

2. Add a Text control to the Group Header section and type `Group 1 detail band order date`.

3. Right-click on the Detail region band and select Insert Group, then select the following options.
   Break on change in - Sales Rep ID
   Label - `Group 2`

4. Add a Text control to the Group 2 Header section and type `Group 2 detail band sales rep id`. The layout should look like the one shown in Figure 7-37. The report should look like the one shown in Figure 7-38.

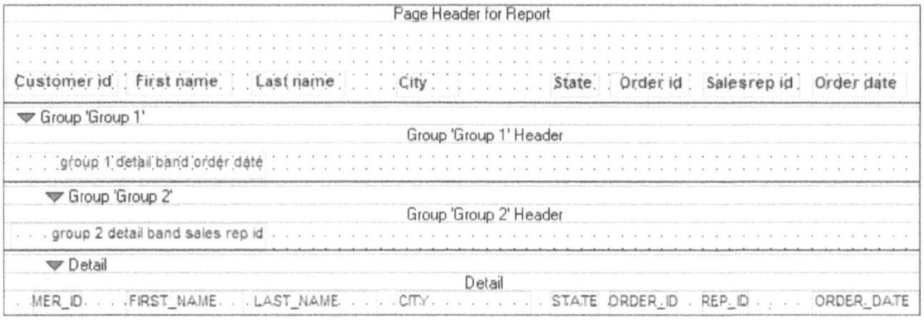

Figure 7-37 Group report layout

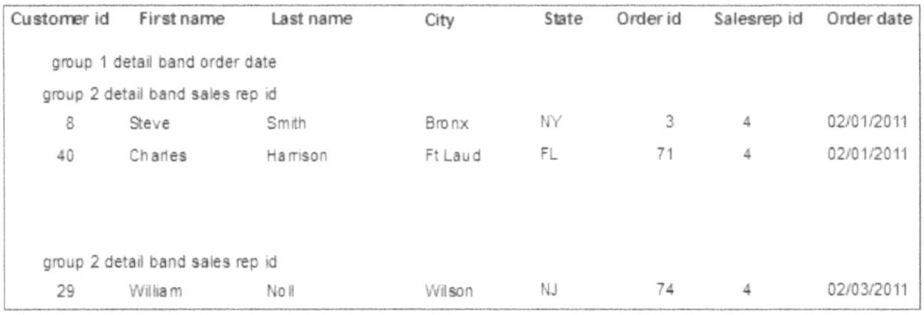

Figure 7-38 Report with two groups

5. Right-click on the Detail section band and select Insert Group, then select the following options.
   Break on change in - State
   Label - `Group 3`

6. Add a Text control to the Group 3 Header section and type `Group 3 detail band state`.

7. Right-click on the Group 3 State section and select Insert Group, then select the following options.

   Break on change in - City
   Label - `Group 4`

   The layout should look like the one shown in Figure 7-39.

   Notice that the Group 3 (State) name changed to Group 4 and that the new Group 4 was placed below Group 2.

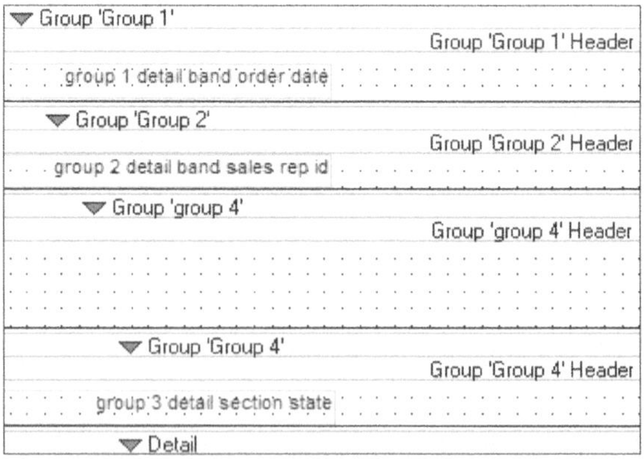

Figure 7-39 Group 4 added from the Group 3 section

8. Save the report as `aCreateGroups2`.

9. Delete the Group 4 section that does not have a text control.

10. Right-click on the Detail region band and select Insert Group, then select the following options.
    Break on change in - City
    Label - `Group 5`

11. Add a Text control to the Group Header section and type `Group 5 detail band city`.

    The layout should look like the one shown in Figure 7-40.

    I am sure that the location of groups is not what you were expecting.

    Save the changes.

Figure 7-40 Group 5 added via the Detail band

Most reports do not require this many groups. It was done here to illustrate where new groups will be placed. If the new group is not in the location that you need, click the Undo button to remove it, then select the appropriate band or section to create the group from.

Reports Grouped By Date

More than likely you will have the need to create reports that are grouped by month, like reports that display a monthly total amount of orders and a count of orders for the month or the famous "quarterly reports". If you have looked through the functions, there aren't any specifically for grouping records by a date field. You can use the Month function to create a group.

Exercise 7.12: Create A Report Grouped By Month

In this exercise you will modify a report that displays order information for every record in the table in list format.

When finished, the list report shown in Figure 7-41 will look like the one shown later in Figure 7-43. For this report, only orders in 2011 will be displayed.

Customer #	Name	Order date	Order #	Date shipped	Order Total
1	Tina Jones	02/02/2011	5	03/02/2011	$29.00
1	Tina Jones	02/15/2011	13	03/05/2011	$1,142.13
2	Jamie Walker	02/01/2011	2	02/13/2011	$5,060.28
2	Jamie Walker	03/02/2011	9	03/20/2011	$29.00
3	Stuart Thomas	02/15/2011	10	03/01/2011	$14,872.30
3	Stuart Thomas	02/14/2011	12	03/05/2011	$10,259.10
4	Todd Green	02/03/2011	7	03/05/2011	$49.50

Figure 7-41 Order List report

1. Save the Order List report as `aOrdersGroupedByMonth`.

2. Add a group to the report, then select the following option.
   Break on change in - `month(chartorders->order_date)`
   This code will only use the month portion of the date field to create the group.

3. In the Label field type `ByMonth`, as shown in Figure 7-42.

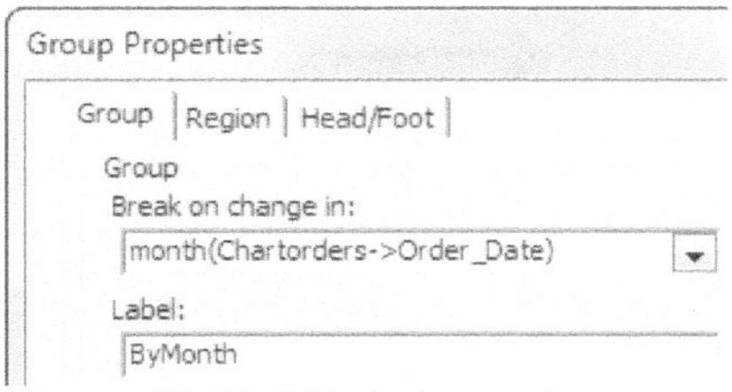

Figure 7-42 Criteria to create a group by month

4. Create a filter that selects records with an order date in 2011. Sort the records by the Order Date field.

5. Move the field titles in the Report Header section to the Group Header section.

6. Add a Text control to the Report Header section, then type `Monthly Order Report For 2011`. Make the text bold and size 12.

7. View the end of the orders for February. You will see a blank space and then the orders for March, as shown in Figure 7-43.

If you view the bottom of the last page of the report, you will see that the only orders in the report have an order date in 2011. If you want, you can create calculated fields for the Group Footer section.

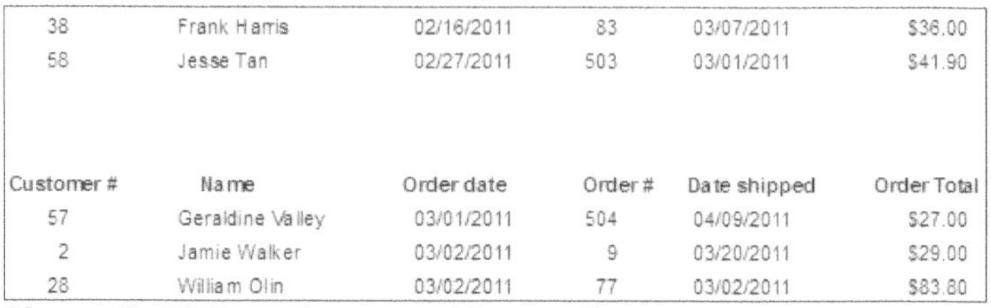

38	Frank Harris	02/16/2011	83	03/07/2011	$36.00
58	Jesse Tan	02/27/2011	503	03/01/2011	$41.90
Customer #	Name	Order date	Order #	Date shipped	Order Total
57	Geraldine Valley	03/01/2011	504	04/09/2011	$27.00
2	Jamie Walker	03/02/2011	9	03/20/2011	$29.00
28	William Olin	03/02/2011	77	03/02/2011	$83.80

Figure 7-43 Records grouped by month

Use Date Functions To Display Parts Of A Date Field

The report that you created in the previous exercise displays the orders in 2011 by month. It would be helpful if the report at least displayed the order month in the Group Header section.

Exercise 7.13: Display The Group Month And Year

In this exercise you will create an expression that uses the **CMONTH** and **CYEAR FUNCTIONS** to display the month and year of the group in the Group Header section. This report is currently filtered to only display orders in 2011. Displaying the year in the Group Header section is not really necessary. I am showing you how though because on your own you may have the need to create a similar report that spans multiple years. You can thank me later.

1. Save the aOrdersGroupedByMonth report, as `aGroupedByMonth&Year`.

2. Open the Calculated Values dialog box, then type this expression.

```
Group_Month = "Orders for " + cmonth(chartorders->order_date)
+ " " + cyear(chartorders->order_date)
```

3. Add the calculated field, not the title, to the top of the Group Header section. Make the field bold and size 10. The first page of the report should look like the one shown in Figure 7-44.

Monthly Order Report For 2011

Orders for February 2011

Customer #	Name	Order date	Order #	Date shipped	Order Total
2	Jamie Walker	02/01/2011	2	02/13/2011	$5,060.28
7	Brenda Taylor	02/01/2011	1	02/13/2011	$41.90
8	Steve Smith	02/01/2011	3	02/14/2011	$186.87

Figure 7-44 Report with custom Group Header field

Exercise 7.14: Create A Quarterly Order Report

Like the monthly report that you created in the previous two exercises, quarterly reports are also popular. In this exercise you will learn how to create groups that have three months of data.

The **CEILING FUNCTION** calculates the smallest integer that is greater than or equal to the number that you select. This function can be used to create a group, if you will, that puts records in the range that you supply. For example, each quarter of the year has three months, so you would want three months in a quarter displayed together on the report to look like a group.

1. Save the Order List report as `aOrdersByQuarter`.
2. Add a group to the report, then select the following options.
   Break on change in - `ceiling(month(chartorders->order_date)/3)`
   Label - `ByQuarter`
3. Create a filter that selects records with an order date in 2011. Sort the records by the Order Date field.
4. Move the field titles in the Report Header section to the Group Header section.
5. Add a Text control to the Report Header section, then type `Quarterly Order Report For 2011`. Make the text bold and size 12.
6. Create a calculated field that totals the order amount field for the group. Format the field with a dollar sign, then add the calculated field to the Group Footer section. Line it up with the Order Total field in the Detail section.
7. View the last page of the report. You should see the end of the third quarter and all of the 4th quarter, as shown in Figure 7-45.

56	Annie Nyland	09/01/2011	524	09/05/2011	$33.00
57	Geraldine Valley	09/01/2011	523	09/01/2011	$548.70
47	Ronald Lugo	09/05/2011	527	12/05/2011	$33.90
			Total order amount for the quarter		$18,927.56
Customer #	Name	Order date	Order #	Date shipped	Order Total
46	Max Murray	12/04/2011	528	01/03/2012	$989.55
41	Sharon King	12/05/2011	530	02/14/2012	$959.70
60	Gloria Vallis	12/05/2011	529	01/04/2012	$59.70
			Total order amount for the quarter		$2,008.95

Figure 7-45 Orders grouped by quarter

Control Library

Because forms and reports are both layouts, they use the same Control Library dialog boxes.

Exercise 7.15: Add An Object From A Report To The Control Library

1. Open the aContinuationFooter report.
2. Right-click on the text object in the Continuation Footer section (to the far right) and select Add selected controls to Control Library.
3. In the Name field, type `continuation_footer_rpt`, then click OK. If you look in the Control Library in the Toolbox, you will see the control.

Using Controls On A Report

Just like you can add controls to a form, they can also be added to a report. Usually, controls on a report are for display purposes.

Exercise 7.16: Add The Check Box Control To A Report

In this exercise you will add the Check Box control to a report.

1. Save the Paid By Check report as `aCheckBoxControl`.

2. Delete the calculated field in the Page Header section.

3. Add the Check Box control to the Detail section.

   The options shown in Figure 7-46 are exactly what you need.

   Click OK.

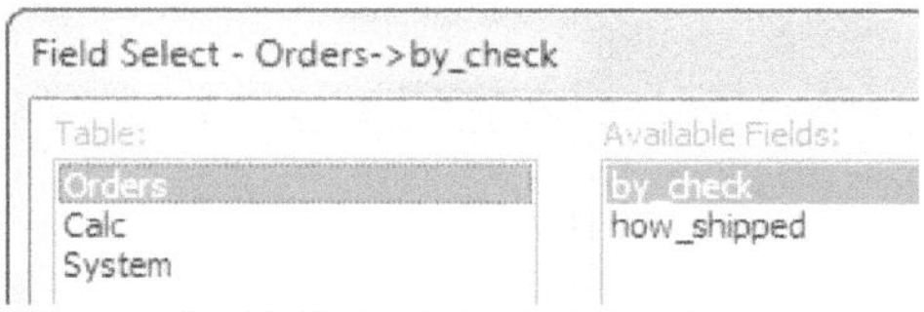

Figure 7-46 Field Select dialog box

4. On the Properties panel, clear the check mark for the four Border Edge options.

5. Add a Text control to the Page Header section.

   Type `Paid By Check`.

   The report should look like the one shown in Figure 7-47.

Order id	Customer id	Order date	Paid By Check
1	7	02/01/2011	☒
2	2	02/01/2011	☐
3	8	02/01/2011	☒
4	15	02/01/2011	☒
5	1	02/02/2011	☐

Figure 7-47 Report with Check Box control

Exercise 7.17: Use A Saved Query To Filter A Report

In this exercise you will create a basic list report that is filtered by that query.

1. Create a new blank free-form report based on the Chart Orders table.

2. Add the following fields to the report: Order ID, Customer ID, Order Date, Order Amount and Customer State.

3. Save the report as `aFilterOnSavedQuery`, then close the report.

How To Attach A Query To A Report

In this part of the exercise you will attach the query to the report. You would use these steps to attach the query to the other layout types also. This process does not allow you to save the query with the report. This option is best suited for situations where you want to run the report using several different queries. In the next exercise you will learn how to save the query with the report.

1. On the Operations tab, right-click on the Query Chart Orders query and select **RUN SPECIAL**.

2. On the dialog box shown in Figure 7-48, select the Report **LAYOUT TYPE** and the aFilterOnSavedQuery report.

   Click OK.

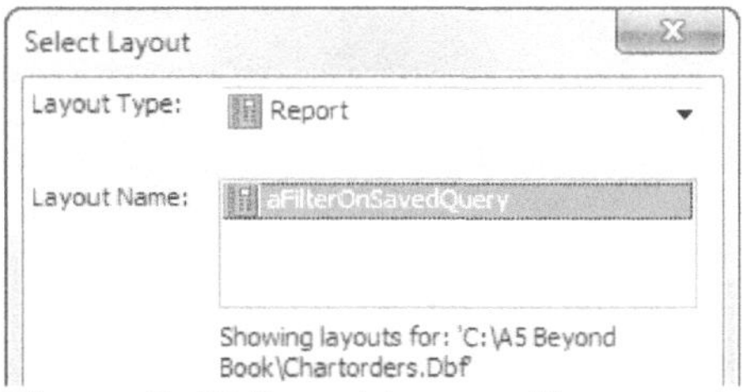

Figure 7-48 Report to run with a saved query

3. The report will automatically open and be displayed, as shown in Figure 7-49.

   There are 71 records on the report, which is the same number of records the Query By Form retrieved.

Order id	Customer id	Order date	Orderamount	Customerstate
177	202	01/03/2012	2654.56	CA
179	368	01/05/2012	21.60	CA
201	215	01/18/2012	31.00	CA
204	218	01/19/2012	67.80	CA
260	278	02/21/2012	6116.82	CA
271	231	02/27/2012	139.48	CA
5	1	02/02/2011	29.00	FL

Figure 7-49 Report based on a saved query

Exercise 7.18: How To Save The Query With The Report

In this exercise you will learn how to save a query with the report.

1. Save the aFilterOnSavedQuery report as `aBasedOnSavedQuery`. Click the Select Records button, then click the Create Filter/Order Using Genie button.

2. At the top of the dialog box, select the **RECORDS SELECTED BY A SAVED QUERY DEFINITION** option.

3. Open the Query Name drop-down list and select the Query Chart Orders query, then click OK.

   You should have the options shown in Figure 7-50.

   If checked, the **SAVE FILTER/ORDER EXPRESSION** option will add the expression in the query to the Filter and Order fields on the dialog box shown in Figure 7-51.

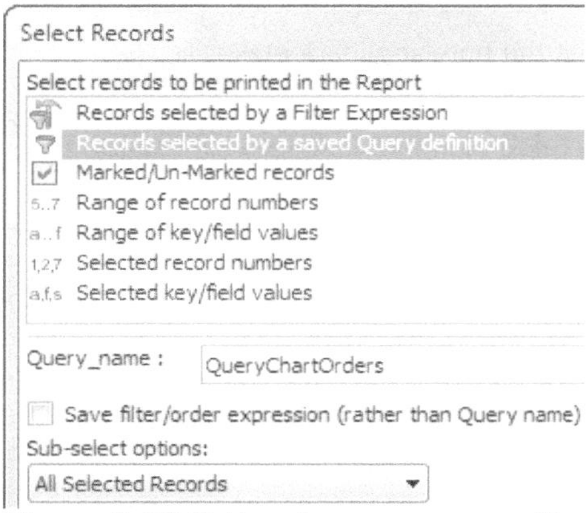

Figure 7-50 Options to save a query with a report

   This means that you can modify either or both expressions because the query is detached from the report. The downside to this is any changes that are made to the saved query will not be reflected in this report.

   The **SUB-SELECT OPTIONS** are the same Top N options that you learned about earlier in this chapter. Selecting one of these options applies it to the Filter Expression and also detaches the query from the report.

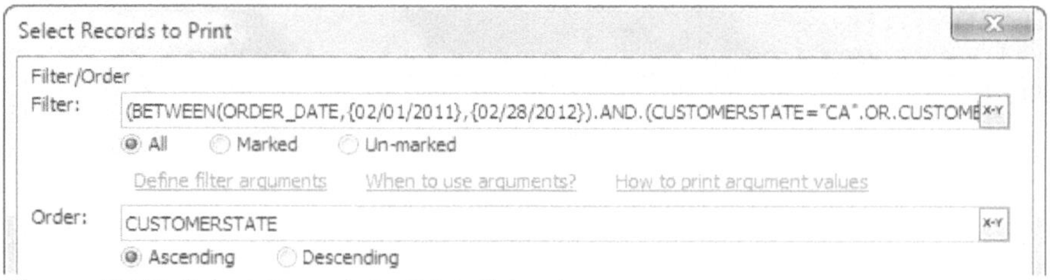

Figure 7-51 Select Records to Print dialog box

> The Select Records to Print dialog box has many of the options that the Select Filter dialog box has.

4. Save the changes. When you preview the report, it should look like the one shown earlier in Figure 7-49.

What Is A Subreport?

All of the reports that you have created or modified so far in this book are individual reports that used a single data source. Subreports are a very powerful and flexible tool in Alpha Five. A subreport is a report within a report. Subreports are their own reports that can use the same data source as the main report, a completely different, but related data source or an unrelated data source. This means that the main report could be created from data in an Excel spreadsheet and the subreport could be created from data in a database.

Subreports can be placed in any section of the report except the Report Header or Page Footer. They are created the same way any other report is created - either from scratch or by using a genie. Existing reports can also be used as a subreport. The main report can display several subreport. Subreports also allow what appears to be unrelated data to be presented on one report, in a way that the unrelated data makes sense.

Believe it or not, there are limitations to standard reports. The biggest limitation of standard reports is that they can only display a single view of the data. Yes, I know what you are thinking, is that not the main purpose of relational data? My answer to that question is "Yes that is the purpose of relational data, but only to a point." For example, relational data will let you create a report that displays last year's total sales by sales rep by region. By adding a subreport to the report, you could also display the orders for the top three sales reps in the same report.

Subreports are especially helpful when the data sources needed to create the report do not have a common field with the same data type. For example, the Orders table could store the Customer ID field as a numeric field and the Invoice table could store the Customer ID field as a string field. This is when using a subreport will allow you to create a report that shows customers and their invoices.

Differences Between A Main Report And A Subreport

① A subreport does not have Page Header or Page Footer sections.
② The entire subreport prints in the section of the main report that it is placed in.
③ A subreport cannot contain another subreport.
④ A main report can contain several subreports.
⑤ A subreport is not a stand-alone report once it is embedded in the main report.

Subreport Size

Selecting the correct **HORIZONTAL WIDTH** is important because all of the fields on the subreport need to be displayed in the main report. If the subreport box is not wide enough, when you preview the report, just make it wider. The **VERTICAL LENGTH** of the subreport box does not matter because the subreport will expand as needed.

> **Editing A Subreport**
> Double-click on the Subreport control to open it.

Exercise 7.19: Use The Sub-Report Control

In this exercise you will learn how to use the Subreport control by creating a subreport to display counts of how each order was shipped. You will also create a filter for the data displayed in the subreport.

1. Save the Sub Report Counts report as `aSubreport`.

2. Add the Sub-Report control to the Report Footer section.

3. In the Name field type `ShipViaSubreport`.

   Select the **SPECIFY FILTER** option, then type the expression shown in Figure 7-52.

   Click OK.

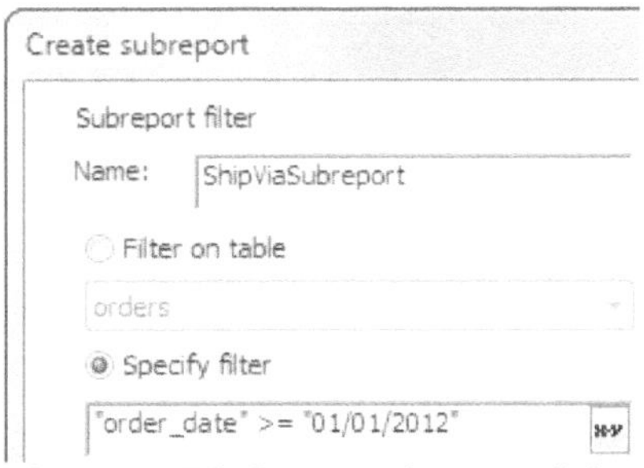

Figure 7-52 Create subreport dialog box

Create The Subreport

As you will see, the Subreport Editor has the same features that the Report Editor has.

1. Make the Subreport Header section a little longer.

2. Add the three calculated fields to the bottom of the section.

3. On the Properties panel, change the Field width of the three calculated fields to 4, then clear the four Border edge options.

4. In the Subreport Header section, create the titles shown in Figure 7-53.

5. Open the Region Properties dialog box, Region tab for the Detail section, select the **SHRINK CONTENTS OF BAND** option.

6. Click on the X in the upper right corner to close the Subreport Editor. Save the changes. The layout should look like the one shown in Figure 7-54. When you preview the last page of the report, you will see the subreport data, as shown in Figure 7-55.

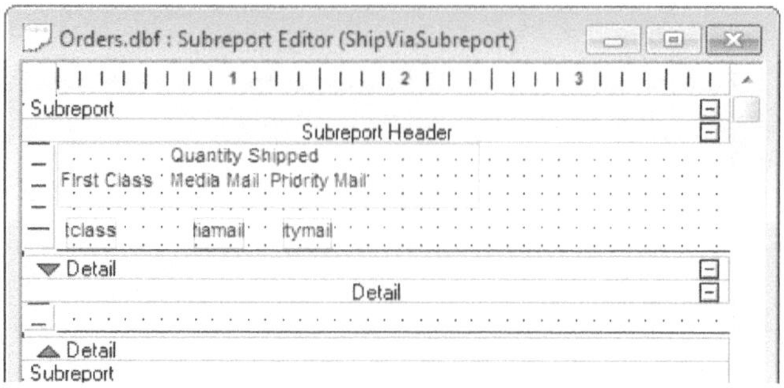

Figure 7-53 Subreport Editor

Figure 7-54 Report layout

Figure 7-55 Subreport data

> **Section Bar Shortcut Menu**
> The section bar of the section that has the Subreport control has the shortcut menu shown in Figure 7-56. In the exercise above, that would be the Report Footer section. The **ACTIONS** option does not seem to work.

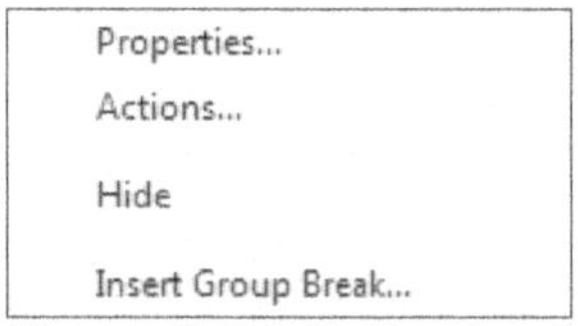

Figure 7-56 Section bar (with a subreport) shortcut menu

Linked Reports

This type of report is similar to a subreport because it is viewed from another report. Like subreports, there is a control for Linked Reports. This biggest difference is that Linked Reports have to be created from the Layout Table Report Editor. Linked reports are actually Layout Table reports that are embedded in another report. The same linked report can be used in a Free Form and Layout Table report.

While the Linked Report requires a common field with the report that it will be linked to, the reports can be created from different tables or sets. Linked Reports are usually placed in the Detail section of the report because the goal is to provide more information about the corresponding record in the main report, but they can be placed in any section. Most of the time a linked report will not have groups, but it can.

More than one linked report can be added to a report. One benefit that linked reports have that subreports do not, is that calculated total fields in a linked report can be used in the main report.

Parent-Child Report Relationship

When you create a set, each table in the set is either a parent or child table in the relationship. The same is true for linked reports. The main report is the **PARENT REPORT** and the linked report is the **CHILD REPORT**.

Exercise 7.20: Use The Linked Report Control

In this exercise you will learn how to:

① Create a Layout Table report.
② Add a Linked Report to a Free Form report.
③ Add a Linked Report to a Layout Table report.

Create The Layout Table Report

The linked report will display the following fields from the Orders table: Order ID, Order Date and Date Shipped.

1. Start a new Quick Report using the Orders table.

2. Add the fields in Table 7-3 to the report and change the Label name.

   Make the **JUSTIFICATION** Center for the first two fields in the table.

   Make the Justification Left for both date fields in the table.

Field	Label Name
Order ID	Order #
Customer ID	Customer #
Order Date	Order Date
Date Shipped	Shipped On

Table 7-3 Fields for the Linked Table report

3. On the Report Settings tab, in the Title field type `Orders`, then change the report font size to 10.

4. On the Filter/Order tab, sort the records by Customer ID, then by Order ID, as shown in Figure 7-57.

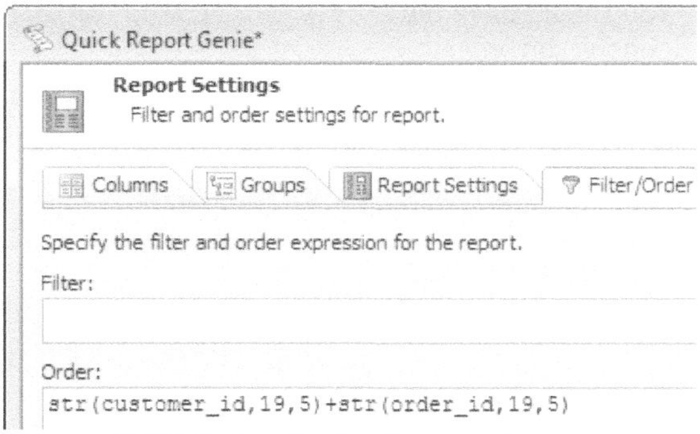

Figure 7-57 Sort order for the report

5. Click the Open in Report Editor button on the toolbar. Select the Layout Table report option, then click the Save Report and Open in Report Editor button.

6. Save the report as `aCustomerListLinkRpt`.

7. Select the four field titles in the Report Header section, change the Fill Color to a light color, then change the Fill Style to Solid. Save the changes.

Link A Report To A Free Form Report

1. Save the Customer List Free Form report as `aCustomerListLinkFree`.

2. Make the Detail section longer, then add the Linked Report control below the fields in the Detail section.

3. On the Edit Linked Report dialog box, click the **SELECT REPORT** button, then select the aCustomerListLinkRpt report on the dialog box shown in Figure 7-58.

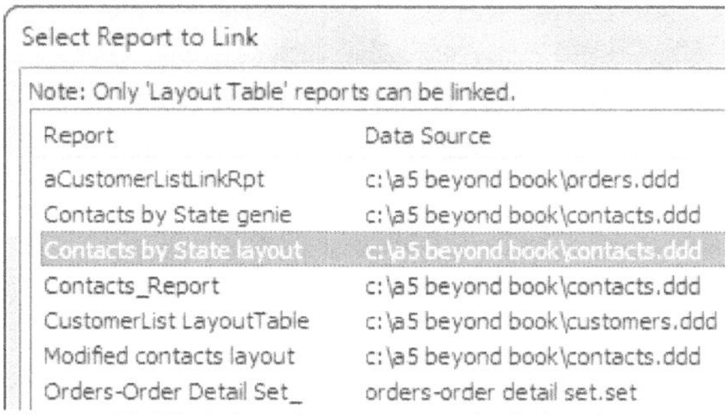

Figure 7-58 Select Report to Link dialog box

4. Click the Define Link button, then click the Add Field button. Open the Field drop-down list and select the Customer ID field. The same field should have automatically been filled in the other drop-down list, as shown in Figure 7-59. Click OK.

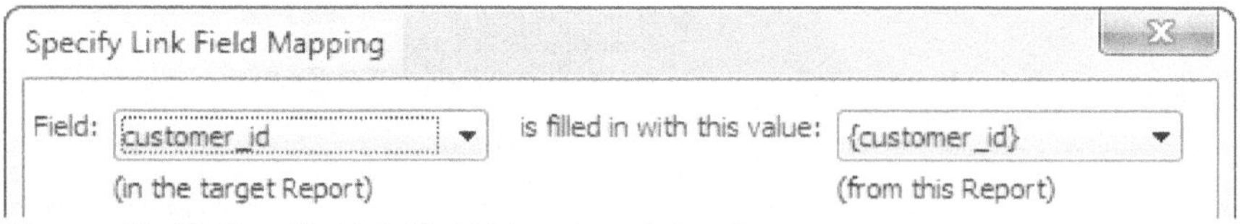

Figure 7-59 Specify Link Field Mapping dialog box

5. You should have the options shown in Figure 7-60.

   Click OK.

   You should have the linked report options shown in Figure 7-61.

   Click OK.

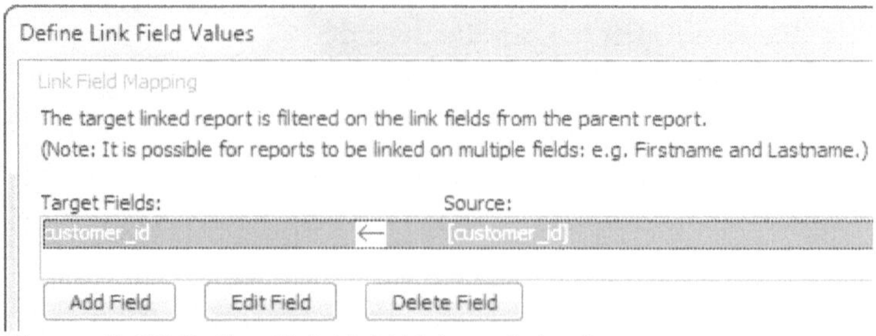

Figure 7-60 Define Link Field Values dialog box

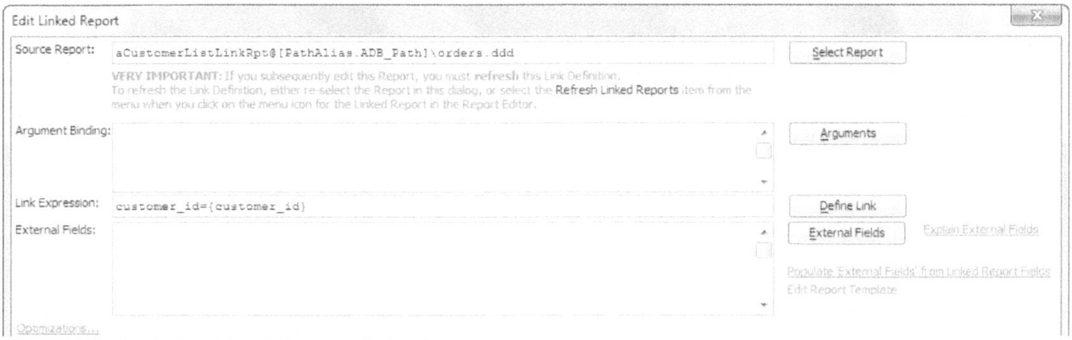

Figure 7-61 Edit Linked Report dialog box

6. Add a border style of your choice to the Linked Report control. Change the Border Width to 1.

7. Open the Region Properties dialog box for the Detail section. On the Region tab, check the **KEEP TOGETHER ON PAGE** option. This will force the fields in the Linked Report control to be displayed on the same page.

8. The Free Form linked report layout should look like the one shown in Figure 7-62.

   Make sure that all four fields in the Linked Report control in the Detail section are visible.

   Save the changes.

   When you view the report, it should look like the one shown in Figure 7-63.

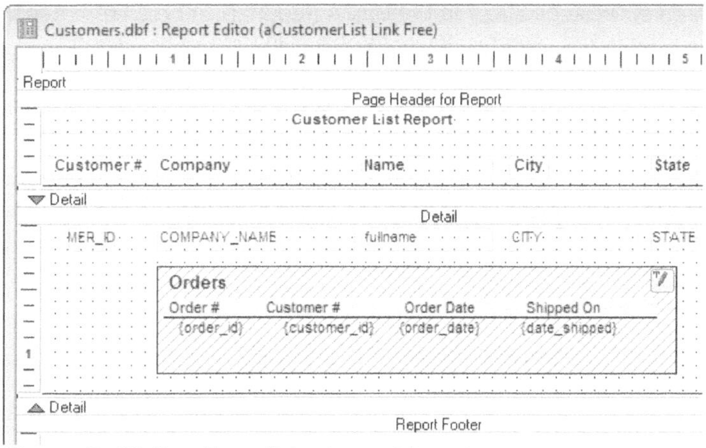

Figure 7-62 Free Form linked report layout

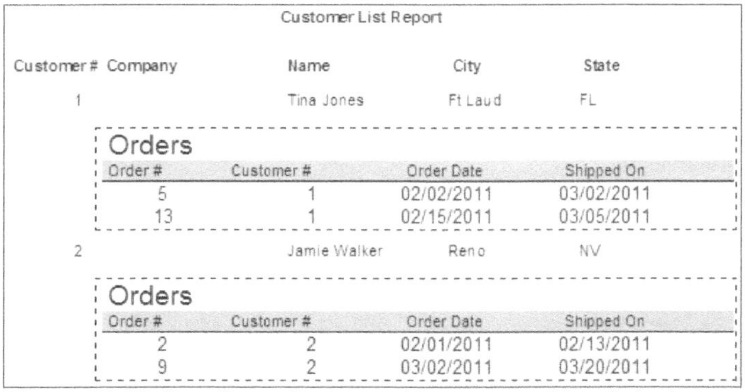

Figure 7-63 Free Form Customer List report with a linked report

Link A Report To A Layout Table Report

For the most part, linking to a Layout Table report is the same as linking to a Free Form report.

1. Save the Customer List Layout Table report as `aCustomerListLayout`.

2. Click on a cell in the Detail section, then click the **NEW LINKED REPORT** link in the Toolbox, as shown in Figure 7-64.

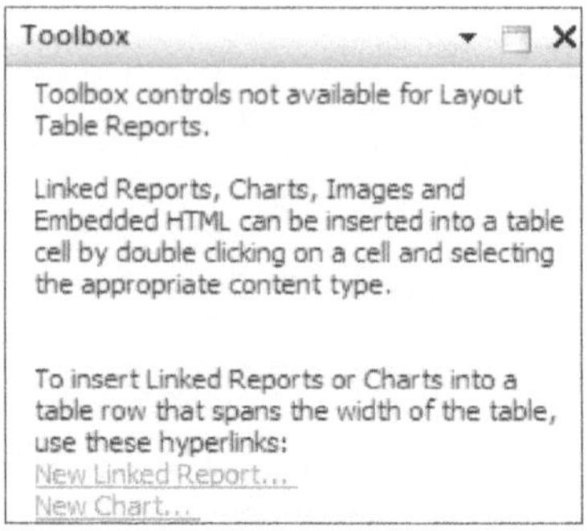

Figure 7-64 Layout Table Toolbox

3. Follow steps 3 to 7 in the Link A Report To A Free Form Report section above. As you can see, the linked report is above the fields in the Detail section.

4. Click on the linked report. Hold the mouse pointer over the square on the left side of the report, as illustrated in Figure 7-65.

   The background color should change to pink.

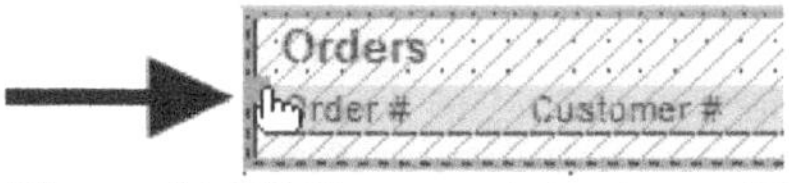

Figure 7-65 Mouse pointer in position to move report

5. Drag the linked report down.

   It should be below the fields, as shown in Figure 7-66.

   Save the changes.

   The report should look like the one shown in Figure 7-67.

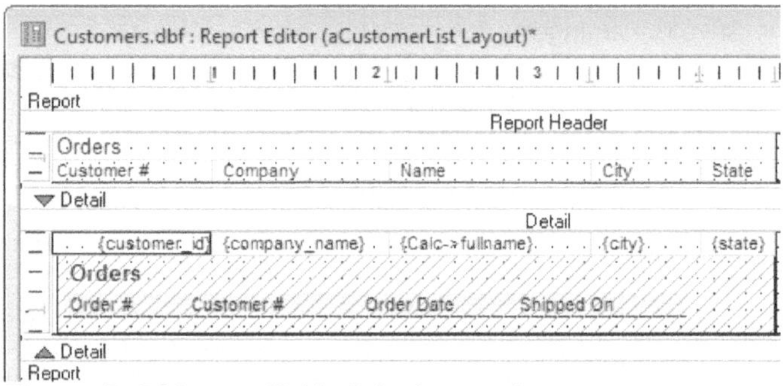

Figure 7-66 Layout Table linked report layout

Figure 7-67 Layout Table Customer List report with a linked report

Refreshing Linked Reports

If you modify a linked report, the report(s) that it is linked to will not have the changes until you refresh the linked report in the main report. To refresh the link, follow the steps below.

1. Open the report that has a linked report.

2. Right-click on the linked report and select **REFRESH LINKED REPORT**. You will not see any message that informs you that the refresh is complete.

Exercise 7.21: Create A Report Based On Crosstab Data

1. Use the Quick Report Genie to create a report based on the aCrosstabBySalesRep table.

2. Add all of the fields to the report.

3. For all of the State fields, complete the following:
   ☑ Select a format expression with a dollar sign. (**TIP:** Select the expression, right-click and select Copy, then paste it in the field for the other State fields instead of opening the Display Format dialog box over and over.)
   ☑ Check the **TOTAL** Summary option.

4. On the Report Settings tab, clear the check mark for the **USE LAYOUT TABLES** option.

5. On the Style tab, select the **SECTION BORDERS** and **COLOR ALTERNATING ROWS** options.

6. Click the Open in Report Editor button. Select the Free form report option, then click the Save Report and Open in Report Editor button.

7. Select the State headings in the Report Header section, then change the Layout Align option to Center.

8. In the Report Footer section, add a text object to the beginning of the section, with the text `Sales rep totals by state`.

9. Save the report as `aCrosstabForSalesRep`. It should look like the one shown in Figure 7-68.

REPNAME	CT	FL	NJ	NV	NY	PA
Alex Hamilton	$0.00	$2,939.85	$0.00	$2,322.74	$2,939.85	$1,749.20
April Smith	$890.61	$3,685.44	$605.55	$0.00	$186.87	$203.60
Bill David	$1,099.25	$0.00	$0.00	$832.35	$823.05	$43.50
Bob Thomas	$988.51	$0.00	$0.00	$1,396.05	$0.00	$168.00
June Cable	$0.00	$49.50	$0.00	$1,498.24	$17.50	$194.70
Karen Williams	$0.00	$49.50	$2,792.86	$623.65	$27.00	$0.00
Mark Hill	$3,349.20	$20,246.65	$29.00	$3,493.20	$0.00	$0.00
Stanley Banks	$0.00	$0.00	$41.90	$9,323.42	$0.00	$1,823.65
Tom Carter	$0.00	$0.00	$0.00	$5,923.20	$0.00	$65.00
Veronica Smith	$10,001.17	$41.90	$2,714.08	$5,060.28	$1,799.70	$0.00
Sales rep totals by state	$16,328.74	$27,012.84	$6,183.39	$30,473.13	$5,793.97	$4,247.65

Figure 7-68 Crosstab report

ADDING BOOKMARKS, AN INDEX AND TABLE OF CONTENTS TO A REPORT

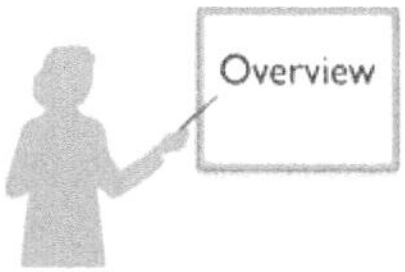

In this chapter you will learn how to add features commonly found in books to a report.

CHAPTER 8

Using Bookmarks

This feature is very useful in reports that are viewed on a computer screen or in a PDF file and have a lot of data or reports that have a lot of groups. Bookmarks allow you to drill down to the specific data that you are looking for in the report. For example, if a report is grouped by state, then by city, it would be much easier to find records in a specific city using bookmarks. The user would select the state bookmark, then select the city bookmark to view the detail records for a specific city. Later in this book, you will learn how to save these bookmarks in a report that is saved in PDF format. In addition to bookmarks, a table of contents and index, like the ones in books, can also be created for reports.

Edit Bookmark For Report Dialog Box

The structure of bookmarks will remind you of the Tree control that is available for forms. The dialog box shown in Figure 8-1 is used to set up the bookmarks. The dialog boxes to set up a table of contents and index are similar to the one for bookmarks.

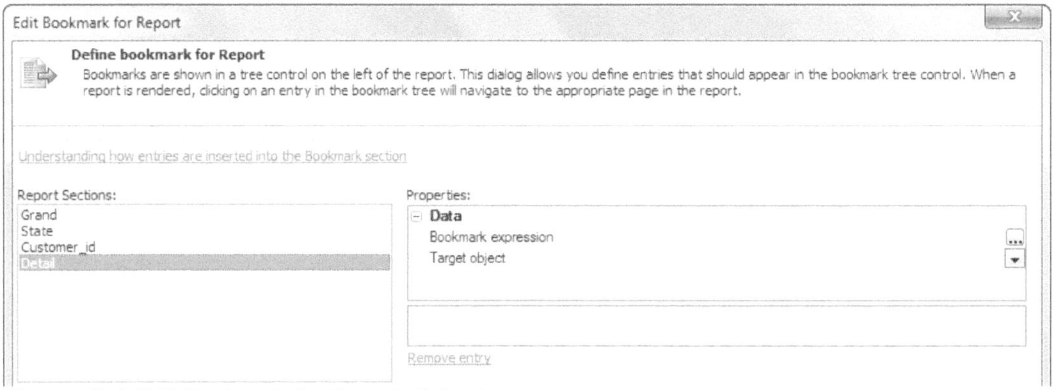

Figure 8-1 Edit Bookmark for Report dialog box

The **REMOVE ENTRY** option will delete the properties for the report section that is selected. This option is also available for Table of Contents and Index entries.

Report Sections

The options in this list correspond to a section of the report. Objects (also known as **TARGETS** for bookmarks, Table of Contents and an Index) in each section of the report can be used as a link for a bookmark. The order that they are listed in is the order that they will appear in the **BOOKMARK PANEL** when the report is previewed. If a report does not have any groups, only the Grand and Detail options will appear in this list. They are referenced by their **OBJECT NAME**. This is one of the times when giving certain objects a descriptive name would be useful. The options are explained below.

① The **GRAND** option is used to select an object in the Report Header or Footer section to use as a bookmark. Unlike the other report sections, multiple objects in the Report Header and Footer sections can be used to create bookmarks. The dialog box shown in Figure 8-2 is used to set up bookmarks for objects in the Report Header and Footer section. As shown, there are three objects in the report that can be set up as bookmarks.

② In Figure 8-1 above, the State and Customer ID options are objects in a **GROUP HEADER** or **FOOTER** section of the report that can be used as a bookmark.

③ The **DETAIL** option is used to select an object in the Detail section to use as a bookmark.

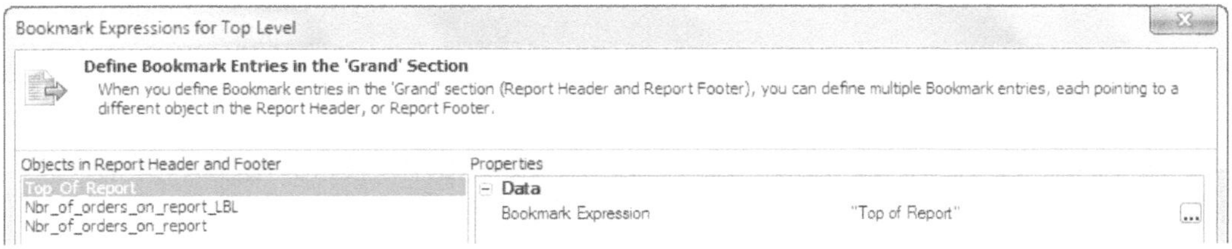

Figure 8-2 Bookmark Expressions for Top Level dialog box

Properties

The options in this section are used to select the data that will be linked to and what will be displayed as the bookmark name.

① **BOOKMARK EXPRESSION** Is used to select a field or create an expression that will be used as the content displayed in the list of bookmarks.

② **TARGET OBJECT** Is used to select a field or object that will be displayed (jumped to) on the report when the item in the bookmark panel is clicked on. This property is not available for the Grand report section. The options in the drop-down list are the fields, objects and calculated fields in the section(s) of the report that the bookmark link is in. This selection will automatically be highlighted on the report.

The Bookmark Expression and Target object options can use the same field.

Exercise 8.1: Adding Bookmarks To A Report

In this exercise you will create calculated fields and bookmarks for a report that has two groups.

1. Save the aGroupTotals report as `aBookmarks`.

2. Add the Customer ID field and title to the Group Customer ID Header section. Change the Customer ID title to `Customer #`.

3. Move the First and Last name fields to the Group Customer ID Header section. Move the City and State fields in the Detail section to the left.

4. Add the Report Header section to the report. Add a Text control to the section.
   Type `Orders By State And Customer Number` in the object.
   Change the Object name property of the control to Top_Of_Report.
   Change the font size to 12 and bold.

5. Add the Detail Header section. Drag the Order ID and Order Date field titles in the Page Header section to the Repeating Detail Header section, then delete the Page Header section.
   Change the Order ID title to `Order #`.

6. Delete the calculated field and title in the Group State Footer section.

7. Create a calculated field named `Nbr of orders for state` that provides a count of orders per state. Place the field in the Group State Footer section.

8. Create a calculated field named `Nbr of orders on report` that provides a count of orders for the entire report. Place the field in the Report Footer section.

9. Add the Sales Rep ID and Date Shipped fields to the Detail section. Change the Sales Rep ID title to `Sales Rep #`.

If you viewed the report now, you would see duplicate rows of data, as shown in Figure 8-3.

That is because many orders have more than one item and because of the set that the report is based on.

If the report does not need fields from a table (in this exercise, the Order detail table), you should remove the table from the set, if this is the only layout that uses the set. Otherwise, copy the report to a set that does not have the table that you are not using.

Orders By State And Customer Number

AL

Customer # 289 Andrea Trueman

Order Nbr	Order date	Salesrep #	Date shipped
282	03/03/2012	4	03/06/2012
282	03/03/2012	4	03/06/2012
282	03/03/2012	4	03/06/2012
455	07/09/2012	6	07/10/2012

Customer # 292 Witt Jon

Order Nbr	Order date	Salesrep #	Date shipped
285	03/05/2012	2	03/06/2012
285	03/05/2012	2	03/06/2012
458	07/10/2012	4	07/11/2012

Figure 8-3 Report with duplicate records displayed

10. Copy the aBookmarks report to the Customers-Orders set.

11. On the Control panel, delete the aBookmarks report that is attached to the Customers orders and details set.

12. If you preview the report that you just copied to another set, you will not see duplicate records.

When you copy a report to a different table or set, bookmarks are not copied.

Create The Bookmarks

In this part of the exercise you will create the following bookmarks: Top of Report, State, Customer Name and count of orders on report.

Create The Grand Report Section Bookmarks

1. Report ⇒ Define Bookmarks.

2. Select the Grand report section. Click the Bookmark expressions field button.

3. The Top of Report object should be selected. Click the Bookmark Expression field button.
   Type `"Top of Report"` in the Expression Builder. The Bookmark Expressions for Top Level dialog box should look like the one shown earlier in Figure 8-2. This bookmark will jump to the top of the first page of the report.

4. Select the Nbr of orders on report field, then click the Bookmark Expression field button.
   Type `"Count of orders on report"`.
   Click OK to close the Bookmark Expressions for Top Level dialog box.

Create The Bookmarks For The Other Sections

1. Select the State report section, then select the following options.
   Bookmark expression - State
   Target object - State

2. Select the Customer ID report section, then select the following options, as shown in Figure 8-4.
   Bookmark expression - `trim(first_name) + " " + last_name`
   Target object - Customer ID

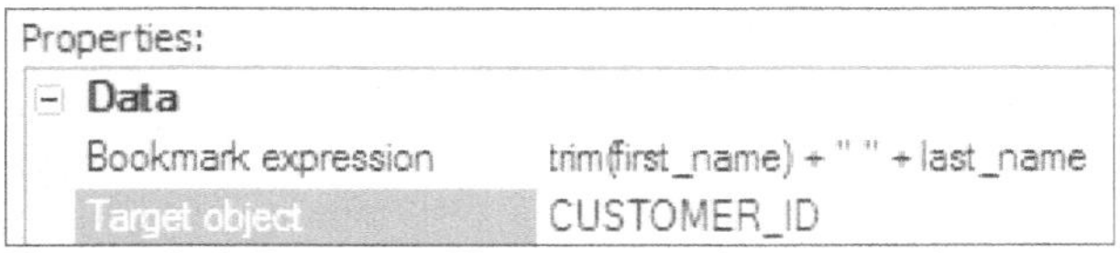

Figure 8-4 Customer ID report section properties

> If you want the first and last name fields to look like one field and do not want to create an expression to combine them, follow the steps below.
>
> 1. Set the horizontal alignment of the first name field to right.
> 2. Set the horizontal alignment of the last name field to left.
> 3. Move the last name field to the left so that the border touches the first name field.

3. Select the Detail report section, then select the following options.
   Bookmark expression - `"Order #" + alltrim(str(Orders ->Order_id))`
   Target object - Order ID

4. Save the changes.

   Preview the report.

   The top of the Bookmark panel should look like the one shown in Figure 8-5.

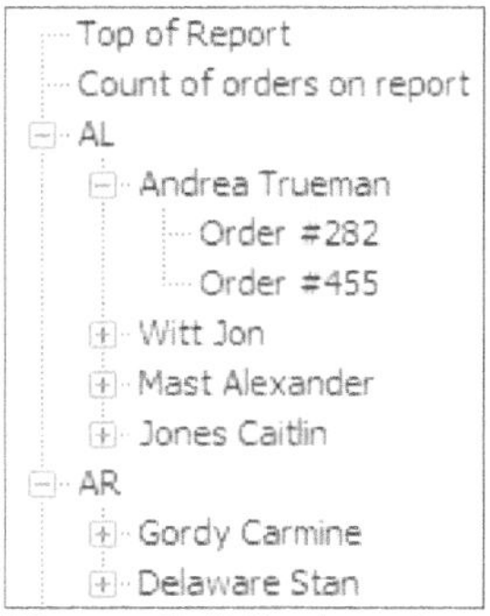

Figure 8-5 Bookmark panel

Test The Bookmarks

1. Clicking on the Count of orders on report bookmark jumps to the end of the report and displays the total number of orders on the report.

2. Click on the Top Of Report bookmark to jump to the beginning of the report.

3. Click on the GA (state) bookmark. You will see the orders for the state of Georgia.

4. In the state of FL, display the orders for Robert Emerson, then click on Order #34.
   The detail header record for this order is displayed on the report.

Bookmark Observation
I noticed that the bookmark created in the Grand report section of the Edit Bookmark for Report dialog box appears at the top and bottom of the bookmark list on the left side of the report. I expected to see them at the top of the report, but not at the bottom.

Adding A Table Of Contents To A Report

The dialog box shown in Figure 8-6 is used to create a Table of Contents. As you can see, it has similar options to the dialog box that is used to create bookmarks. The major difference is that a Table of Contents can be customized. Alpha Five will create a default layout for the Table of Contents. You can customize the layout of a Table of Contents by creating a report called **TABLE OF CONTENTS REPORT**.

The **ADD NEW CUSTOM TABLE OF CONTENTS REPORT LINK** is used to create a custom Table of Contents. (1)

The **EDIT CUSTOM TABLE OF CONTENTS REPORT LINK** opens the Custom Table of Contents report, discussed earlier. The report can also be opened from the Control panel. (1)

(1) This option is also available for a custom Table of Contents.

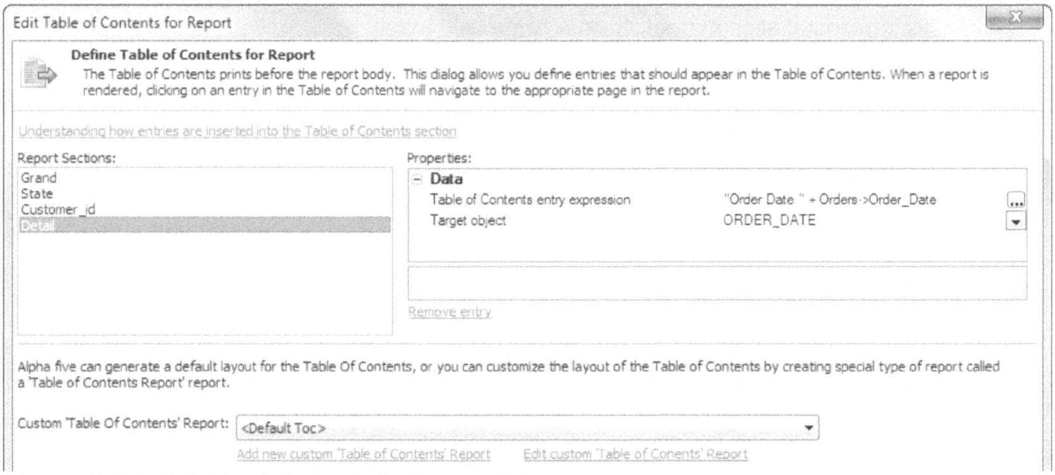

Figure 8-6 Edit Table of Contents for Report dialog box

Exercise 8.2: Create A Table Of Contents Using The Default Layout

In this exercise you will create a Table of Contents that uses the default layout. The Table of Contents will display states, customer names and order dates.

1. Save the aBookmarks report as `aTableOfContentsDefault`.

2. Report ⇒ Define Table of Contents. No fields or objects in the Grand report section will be added to the Table of Contents.

3. Select the State report section, then select the following options.
   Table of Contents entry expression - State
   Target object - State

4. Select the Customer ID report section, then select the following options.
   Table of Contents entry expression - `trim(first_name) + " " + last_name`
   Target object - First name

5. Select the Detail report section, then select the following options, as shown earlier in Figure 8-6.
   Table of Contents entry expression - `"Order Date " + Orders->Order_Date`
   Target object - Order Date

6. Add the Page Footer section to the report. Add the Page X of Y System field to the Page Footer section without the title.

7. Save the changes. Preview the report. The Table of Contents should look like the one shown in Figure 8-7. I know that you may be thinking that displaying the order date in the Table of Contents is strange, but if you view a customer that starts at the bottom of the page, you may see that at least one of their orders is on a different page.

   If you click on an entry in the Table of Contents, the corresponding section of the report will be displayed.

   On the left of the figure you will see the bookmarks.

   Notice that there is an entry at the top of the Bookmark panel for the Table of Contents.

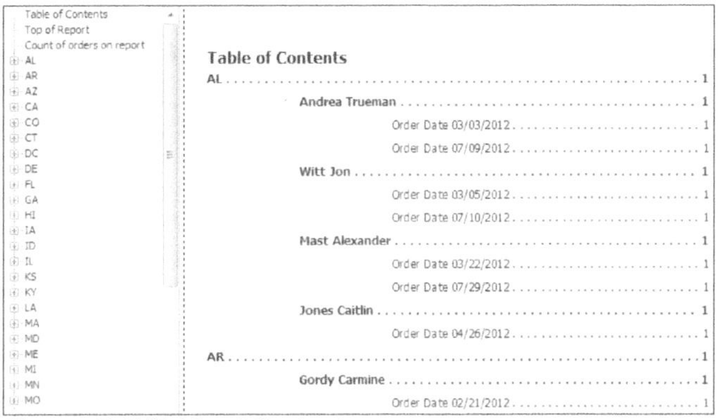

Figure 8-7 Table of Contents

Table Of Contents Page Numbers
The page numbers for this section of the report are automatically created. If you scroll to the bottom of any page of the Table of Contents, you will see the roman numeral page number.

Table Of Contents Observation
On a report that has a Table of Contents, the **PAGE X OF Y SYSTEM FIELD** in the Page Footer section of the report does not display the correct page count. For example, Page 31 of 20 will be displayed on the last physical page of the report, as shown in Figure 8-8. The report actually has a total of 51 pages including the Table of Contents, which is the first 20 pages. The main portion of the report has the remaining 31 pages. I also tested the **PAGE COUNT SYSTEM FIELD**. After a certain point, the page number field stops incrementing. The field seems to only count the pages in the main portion of the report, not the actual report pages. The page numbers for entries in the Table of Contents are not correct after a certain point, but when clicked on, the correct section of the report is displayed.

Figure 8-8 Incorrect page number

Custom Table Of Contents

There may be times when the default Table of Contents layout that you used in the previous exercise is not enough. When that is the case, you can create a custom Table of Contents. When selected, Alpha Five will create a report named Table of Contents that is used to create a custom Table of Contents.

Dictionary Options For Storing A Custom Table Of Contents Layout

As explained below, there are two dictionaries that the custom Table of Contents layout report can be stored in.

① **LOCAL DICTIONARY** Selecting this option will store the custom layout in the dictionary for the table or set that the report is based on. This option must be selected if the custom Table of Contents will be used in a Web application.
② **GLOBAL DICTIONARY** Select this option if you want the custom Table of Contents to be available for other reports, even if the reports are based on a different table or set.

Exercise 8.3: Create A Custom Table Of Contents

In this exercise you will use the report from the previous exercise as the starting point to create a custom Table of Contents because the beginning steps are the same.

1. Save the aTableOfContentsDefault report as `aTableOfContentsCustom`.

2. Report ⇒ Define Table of Contents. Click the **ADD NEW CUSTOM TABLE OF CONTENTS REPORT** link at the bottom of the dialog box.

3. In the Enter report name field on the dialog box shown in Figure 8-9, type `aTOCCustom`. The Store custom Table of Contents report in a local dictionary option should be selected. After you click OK, you will see the custom Table of Contents layout.

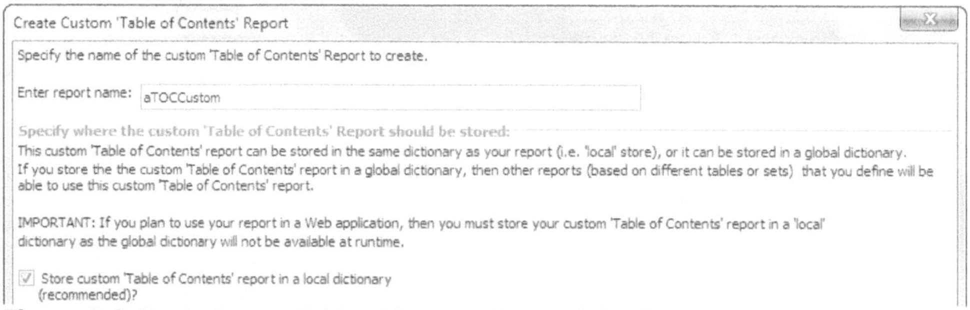

Figure 8-9 Create Custom Table of Contents Report dialog box

Modify The Table Of Contents Custom Layout Report

Figure 8-10 shows the custom layout report. It was created based on the options that you selected on the Edit Table of Contents for Report dialog box.

Figure 8-11 shows the calculated fields that were automatically create for the custom layout. This report can be modified like any other report. The steps below demonstrate some of the changes that can be made to customize the Table of Contents.

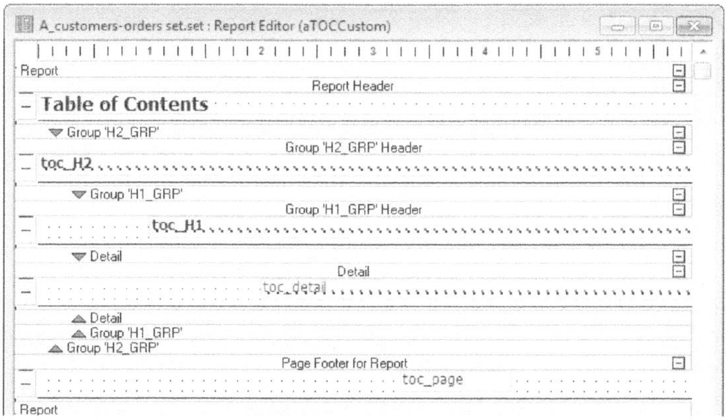

Figure 8-10 Custom Table of Contents layout report

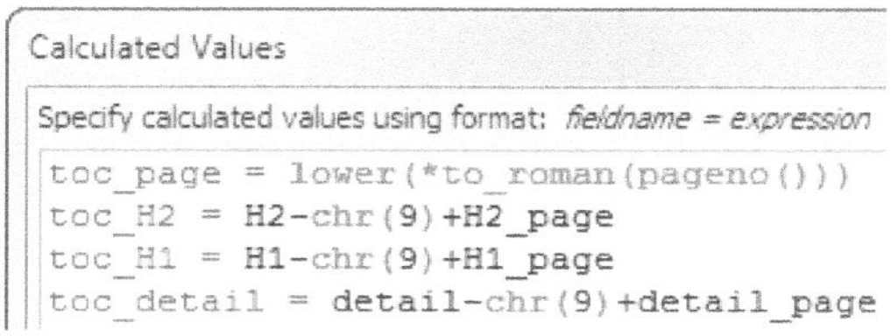

Figure 8-11 Calculated fields for the custom layout

1. Add a Text object to the bottom of the Report Header section. Start it at the 1 inch mark. Type `For the Orders By State and Customer Number Report.`

2. Add another Text object to the Report Header section. Type `Print -`.

3. Add the Date system field to the report, next to the last text object. Delete the field title. On the properties dialog box, change the Format Style to December 31st, 1998.

4. Select the toc_H2 field, then change the Fill Color to Light yellow.

5. Select the toc_detail field, then change the Fill Style to Transparent.

6. Follow the steps in Chapter 7, Exercise 7.5 Alternate Row Background Color, to change the background color of the Detail section of this report. Use the background color of your choice.

> **Previewing A Custom Table Of Contents Report**
> If you try to preview the aTOCCUstom report, you will see that nothing happens. That is because it is not a standalone report and requires data from the main report.

7. Save the changes.

   Preview the aTableOfContentsCustom report.

   The first page of the Table of Contents should look like the one shown in Figure 8-12.

   What you will notice is that every other row, regardless of whether or not it is the first detail record for the customer has a colored background, as shown at the bottom of the figure.

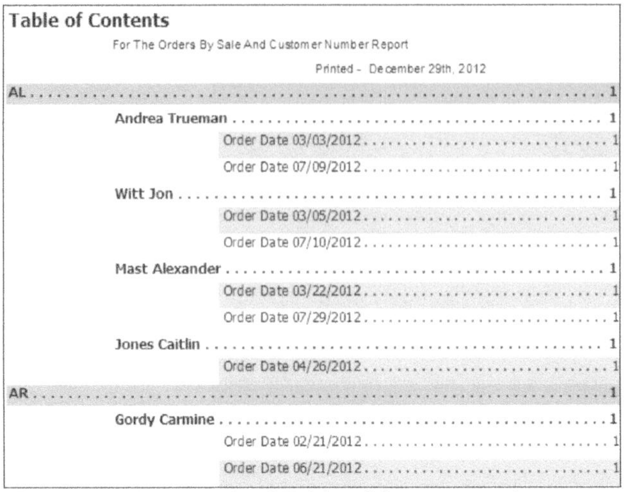

Figure 8-12 Customized Table of Contents and unexpected output of alternate row background color

Adding An Index To A Report

Like the Table of Contents, you can use the default index layout or you can create a custom index. The dialog box shown in Figure 8-13 is used to create an index. It is not a requirement to use the same fields in an index that are used in a Table of Contents. The purpose of an index is to include specific items that someone may need to look for in the report.

The index uses its own page numbers, meaning that they do not continue from the report. The biggest difference between the Table of Contents and index is that the index is located after the report.

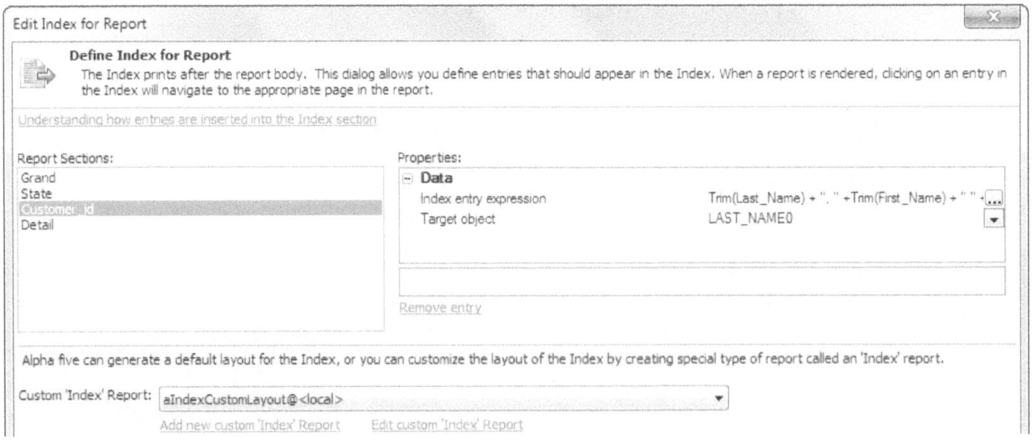

Figure 8-13 Edit Index for Report dialog box

Exercise 8.4: Create A Default Index

In this exercise you will create an index that displays the customer last name and page number.

1. Save the aTableOfContentsDefault report as `aIndexDefault`.

2. Report ⇒ Define Index.

3. Select the State report section, then select the following options.
   Index entry expression - State
   Target object - State

4. Select the Customer ID report section, then select the following options.
   Index entry expression - Last name
   Target object - Last name

5. Save the changes. Preview the report. Scroll to the bottom of the Bookmark panel, then click on the Index option.

   The index should look like the one shown in Figure 8-14. The index is not very informative or appealing.

   In the next exercise you will learn how to customize the index.

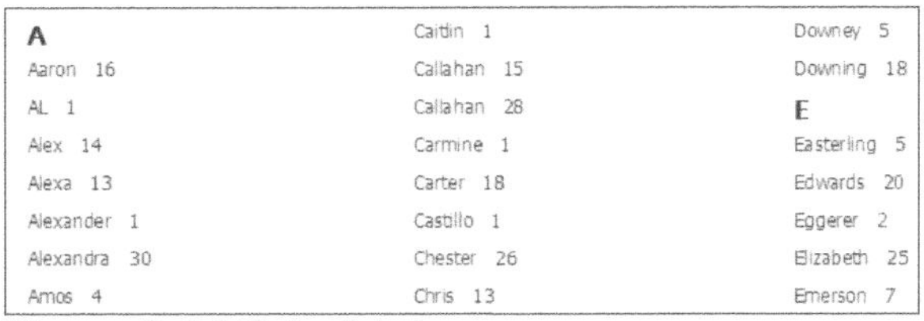

A	Caitlin 1	Downey 5
Aaron 16	Callahan 15	Downing 18
AL 1	Callahan 28	**E**
Alex 14	Carmine 1	Easterling 5
Alexa 13	Carter 18	Edwards 20
Alexander 1	Castillo 1	Eggerer 2
Alexandra 30	Chester 26	Elizabeth 25
Amos 4	Chris 13	Emerson 7

Figure 8-14 Default index

> **Index Observation**
> When I click on the index option in the Bookmark panel, the index is not displayed if the report has a Table of Contents. A part of the report above the index is displayed.

Exercise 8.5: Create A Custom Index

As you saw in Figure 8-14 above, the default index is not very appealing. In this exercise you will make the following changes:

① Display the customers first name.
② Display the order date.
③ Change the number of columns to 2.

1. Save the aIndexDefault report as `aIndexCustom`.

2. Report ⇒ Define Index. Click the **ADD NEW CUSTOM INDEX REPORT** link.

3. Type `aIndexCustomLayout` as the report name, then click OK.

   You should see the layout report shown in Figure 8-15.

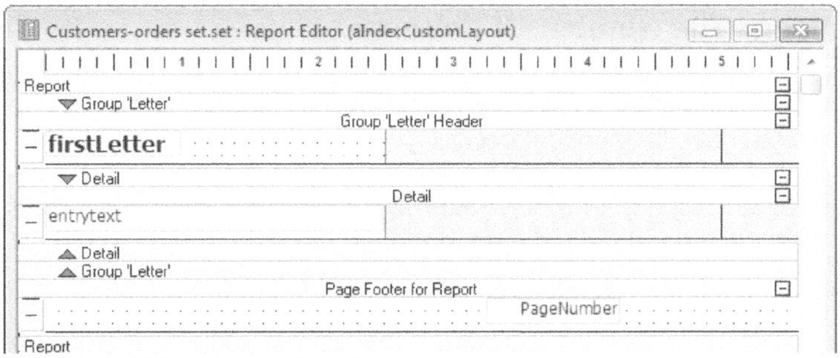

Figure 8-15 Index custom layout report

This report has the expressions shown in Figure 8-16.

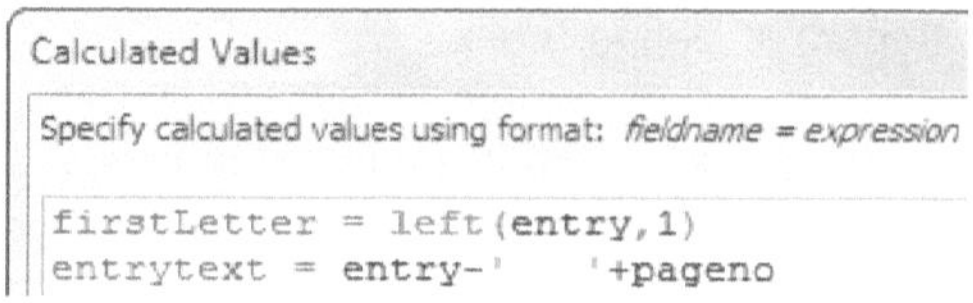

Figure 8-16 Index layout expressions

The **FIRSTLETTER** expression displays the first letter of the data in the content. In this exercise, that is the first letter of the last name field.

The **ENTRYTEXT** expression displays the data selected for the last report section on the Edit Index for Report dialog box. In this exercise the last report section is the Customer ID group. In another report it could be the Detail section. The **PAGENO** field is the page number that the value in the **ENTRY** field is on, in the report.

Believe it or not, you can't add fields to these calculated fields. If you look in the Drag Drop List panel, you will not see any of the tables that the main report uses. This means that you have to create the expression as part of the index entry to add data from a table.

Add Fields To The Entry Text Calculated Field

In this part of the exercise you will add the customer first name and order date field to the calculated field. You will also delete the state index entry. If you look at the index shown earlier in Figure 8-14, you will see the states in the index. You have decided that displaying the states in the index does not provide any value.

1. Close the aIndexCustomLayout report, then open the aIndexCustom report.

2. Report ⇒ Define Index.

3. Click on the State report section, then click the **REMOVE ENTRY** link. Click Yes to remove the entry.

4. Click on the Customer ID section, then click the Index entry expression field button. Modify the expression, as shown in Figure 8-17.

```
trim(Last_Name) + " " + trim(First_Name)  + " " + orders->order_date
```

Figure 8-17 Modified Customer ID section index entry modified

5. Save the changes to the aIndexCustom report, then close it. Open the aIndexCustomLayout report in Design mode.

Change The Number Of Columns

In this part of the exercise you will change the number of columns to two, which is often used in an index. The other reason you are changing the number of columns is because the Entrytext calculated field has more content.

1. Right-click on the Group Letter section bar and select Properties.

2. On the Region tab, change the **COLUMNS IN GROUP** option to 2.

3. Make the Entry text field wider. Change the width of the field on the Properties panel to 40. Save the changes, then close the report.

4. Preview the aIndexCustom report, then display the index. It should look like the one shown in Figure 8-18.

   Compare this version of the index to the one shown earlier in Figure 8-14.

A
Aaron, Zalapski 04/06/2012 1
Alex, Smith 07/31/2012 14
Alexa, Quartermain 07/23/2012
Alexander, Mast 07/29/2012 1
Alexandra, Burris 07/31/2012
Amos, Fred 05/10/2011 4
Andersen, Elizabeth 05/09/2012
Andrea, Dixon 01/30/2012 28
Andrew, Dong 08/12/2012 18
Annie, Harper 08/01/2012 9
Anthony, Shoemaker 07/31/2012
Chris, Christianso 07/25/2012
Christianson, Brent 06/11/2012
Christine, Manley 07/27/2012
Christopher, Carmine 08/03/201
Cindy, Forester 04/16/2012 2
Colin, White 05/03/2012 6
Colts, Marvin 06/02/2011 19
Craig, Jacobson 02/01/2012 1
Cunningham, Brent 06/07/2012
D
Dan, Simpson 08/10/2012 8
Danielle, Rubens 04/05/2012

Figure 8-18 Revised custom index

For me, it is a little difficult to see the page numbers for the entries, so I modified the expression to display three periods before the page number, as shown in Figure 8-19. Doing this is optional. Figure 8-20 shows the modified index.

```
trim(Last_Name) + " " + trim(First_Name)  + " " + orders->order_date + ". . ."
```

Figure 8-19 Modified index expression

A
Aaron, Zalapski 04/06/2012 ... 16
Alex, Smith 07/31/2012 ... 14
Alexa, Quartermain 07/23/2012 ... 13
Alexander, Mast 07/29/2012 ... 1
Alexandra, Burris 07/31/2012 ... 30
Amos, Fred 05/10/2011 ... 4
Andersen, Elizabeth 05/09/2012 ... 22
Andrea, Dixon 01/30/2012 ... 28
Andrew, Dong 08/12/2012 ... 18
Annie, Harper 08/01/2012 ... 9
Anthony, Shoemaker 07/31/2012 ... 3
Chris, Christianso 07/25/2012 ... 13
Christianson, Brent 06/11/2012 ... 29
Christine, Manley 07/27/2012 ... 11
Christopher, Carmine 08/03/2012 ... 28
Cindy, Forester 04/16/2012 ... 25
Colin, White 05/03/2012 ... 6
Colts, Marvin 06/02/2011 ... 19
Craig, Jacobson 02/01/2012 ... 14
Cunningham, Brent 06/07/2012 ... 26
D
Dan, Simpson 08/10/2012 ... 8
Danielle, Rubens 04/05/2012 ... 15

Figure 8-20 Modified index

Deleting The Bookmarks, Table of Contents Or Index

If you have the need to delete all of the bookmarks, the entire index or Table of Contents, follow the steps below.

1. Open the main report (not a custom report) that has entries that you want to delete.

2. Report ⇒ Clear Bookmarks/TOC/Index.

3. The dialog box shown in Figure 8-21 displays which options the report has.

   Clear the check mark for the type of entry that you want to delete from the report.

Figure 8-21 Remove TOC/Bookmark/Index dialog box

4. Click OK, then save the changes to the report.

Report Cover Page

In the previous exercises in this chapter you learned how to add bookmarks, a Table of Contents and index to a report. Another feature that you can add to a report is a cover page. It can be as basic or elaborate as needed.

As you know, the Report Header prints at the top of the first page. By adding a **PAGE BREAK CONTROL** to the Report Header section, anything above the page break will print on a page by itself.

Exercise 8.6: Add A Cover Page To A Report

1. Save the aGroupedByOrderDate report as `aCoverPage`.

2. Make the Report Header section four inches long, then drag the top line object, report title, date field and bottom line object down to the middle of the section.

3. Add the Page Break control at the four inch mark in the Report Header section.
   Change the background color of the Report Header section to a light color.

4. Use the Bitmap control to add an image to the Report Header section. On your own, you could add a company logo to the cover page.

5. Delete the Page number field in the Page Footer section, then add the Page X of Y System field.

Remove The Page Number From The Cover Page

More than likely, you do not want a page number of the cover page of a report. The steps below show you how to remove the page number from this page of the report, but keep it on the other pages of the report. The easiest way to do this is to add a Page Footer section to the Report Header section. Doing this will overwrite, if you will, the default Page Footer section that you added the page number system field to.

1. Right-click on the Report Header section bar and select Properties. On the Head/Foot tab, check the Has Page Footer option. You should see the Page Footer for Report Header section below the Report Header section (which changed to Body for Report Header).

2. When you preview the report, it should look similar to the one shown in Figure 8-22.

   You will not see the page number on the cover page, but the other pages in the report will have a page number, which is what should happen.

Figure 8-22 Report Cover page

ENHANCING REPORTS WITH ARGUMENTS

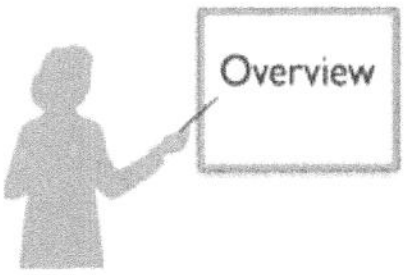

In this chapter you will learn how to create and attach arguments to reports.

CHAPTER 9

Using Arguments To Get Information At Run Time

In my opinion, this is one of the most useful report features. The reports that you have learned to create so far in this book did not require any input from the people that would run them. Often, different users may need slightly different versions of the same report. Based on the report creation techniques that you have learned so far, if one group of people needed to see a customer report for a specific date range and another group of people need to see the same report for specific customers, you would have to create two reports. This is the largest downside to the reports that you have created so far. Using arguments to pass data to the report is a much better solution.

Think about this. If a user requested a report to only show data for one year, the date range would be entered as the filter criteria on the report. Now, the same user or a different user needs the same report, but for a different date range and specific customers. The easiest thing to do based on the report techniques that you have learned so far is to open the existing report and save it with a new file name and change the filter criteria to the new date range and add customer criteria. As you can see, this could get out of hand quickly. If the original report used prompts to get the criteria from the person running the report, the report could be used for any date range and any customer. Another thing to think about is maintaining all of these reports. If a field needs to be added, you would have to add the field to more than one report.

If you created two argument fields for the report, one for a date range and another one to select customers, both groups of people could use the same report. An argument field can also pass data to conditional and other types of expressions. The argument fields allow the person running the report to have control over the records that will appear on the report without having to know how to create formulas or modify reports. The reports that you have already created that have criteria in the Filter expression field can be enhanced by using argument fields in place of specific (hard coded) values from a table or the value that you type in the Filter expression field. This would give reports a lot more flexibility.

To help the person that will run a report that has argument fields, you can include features like default values and drop-down lists. For example, if you were creating an argument field to select a country, you could set a default country if the report is often run using a specific country. You could also create a drop-down list field that contains all of the countries and let the user select the country that they wanted to run the report for. In the workplace you may hear the term drop-down list referred to as a **PICK LIST**.

Arguments in Alpha Five are known as **PARAMETERS** or **PARAMETER FIELDS** in other software packages.

How Argument Fields Work

When a report is run that has an argument field, it prompts the user to select options, which creates all or part of the criteria that is needed to run the report. The information that is gathered from the argument field is passed to various components of the report like the filter expression. The data in the argument field is used to run the report.

Argument fields ask questions that will determine what data will be retrieved for the report. Using argument fields, the following questions can be answered: Which three months do you want to see the sales reps totals for? Which country do you want to see sales for? Which customers ordered hats in December?

In addition to using argument fields to gather the report filter criteria, argument fields can be used to customize and format the report. For example, argument fields can be used to select the sorting or grouping options or highlight records that meet a certain condition. If a report has confidential information, one of the argument fields can require the person running the report to enter their User ID. Based on the User ID, parts of the report would be hidden.

The argument values are added to an **SQL SELECT STATEMENT** when the report is run to fill in the **WHERE CLAUSE** (the filter), **ORDER BY CLAUSE** (sorted by) or **GROUP BY CLAUSE** of the SQL Select statement.

Define/Edit Arguments Dialog Box

Now that you know what argument fields are, how useful they are and how they work, it is time to learn about the dialog box shown in Figure 9-1, which is used to create the arguments.

Tables 9-1 and 9-2 explain the options on the Define/Edit Arguments dialog box. Reports can and often do need more than one argument field.

This dialog box is used to create and customize the prompt (argument) that the user will see when they run the report.

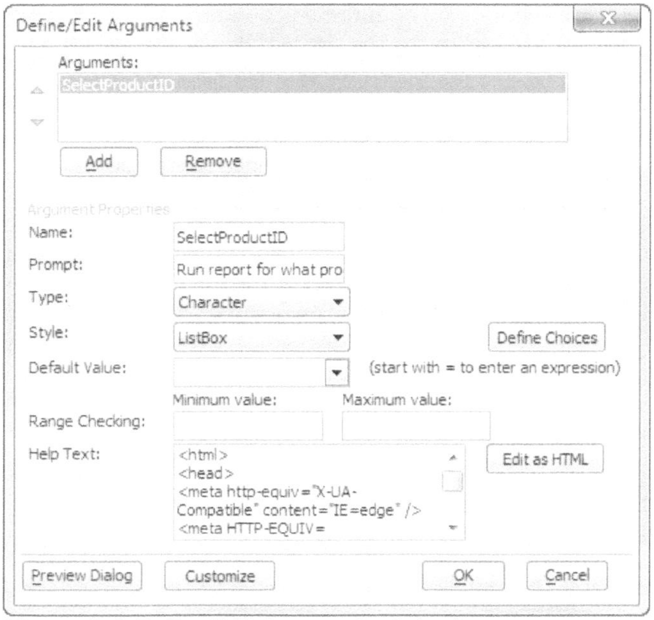

Figure 9-1 Define/Edit Arguments dialog box

Opening The Define/Edit Arguments Dialog Box
There are two ways to open this dialog box when a report is open in Design mode, as explained below.

① Edit ⇒ Define Arguments, opens this dialog box.

② Click the **SELECT RECORDS** button on the toolbar. On the Select Records To Print dialog box, click the **DEFINE FILTER ARGUMENTS** link.

Option	Description
Arguments	This list displays the name of the arguments attached to the report. The triangle buttons to the left of the list are used to change the order that the arguments will appear in on the dialog box.
Add button	Opens the dialog box shown later in Figure 9-6. It is used to enter the name for the argument and select the data type for the argument.
Remove button	Deletes the selected argument in the Arguments list.
Name	Displays the name of the argument. (1)

Table 9-1 Define/Edit Arguments dialog box options explained

Option	Description
Prompt	This is the text that will be displayed with the argument field on the dialog box that is displayed at run time. You should enter something that will make it easy for the user to know what to enter or select for the argument field. (1)
Type	Is the data type of the field in that table that the argument will be attached to. The type selected should be the same as the field that will be used to create the filter. (1)
Style	[See Style Options For An Argument]
Default Value	If there is a value that will be selected more than the other values for the prompt, enter it here. Doing so will automatically display the value in the prompt field, so that the user does not have to select it.
Define Choices button	Opens the dialog box shown later in Figure 9-7. This button is not available if the Text Box, Calculator or Calendar style is selected.
Range Checking	Is used to enter the minimum and maximum values that the prompt value must be between.
Help Text	Is used to enter more information to help the person running the report select an appropriate value. When the user clicks on the prompt, the help text is displayed, as shown later in Figure 9-12.
Edit as HTML button	Opens the dialog box shown in Figure 9-2. This dialog box is an HTML editor that is used to format the help text in HTML format.
Preview Dialog button	Is used to view the dialog box that is created based on the options selected on the Define/Edit Arguments dialog box. This is what the user will see when they run the report. Figure 9-11 shows the dialog box created in Exercise 9.1.
Customize button	Opens the dialog box shown later in Figure 9-10. It is used to change properties of the dialog box shown later in Figure 9-11, which is what users will see when they run the report.

Table 9-1 Define/Edit Arguments dialog box options explained (Continued)

(1) This field is automatically filled in from the Add Argument dialog box. You can change it here if you need to.

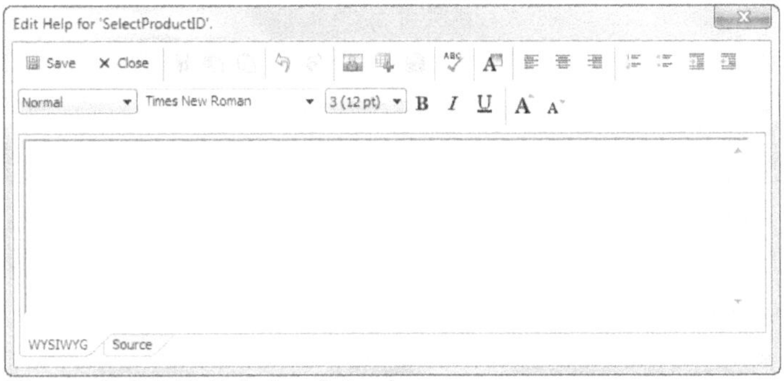

Figure 9-2 Edit Help for dialog box

Style Options For An Argument

The options shown in Figure 9-3 are used to select the type of field that the prompt will use.

The purpose of the style options is to make it as easy as possible for the person running the report to select the data for the filter.

Table 9-2 explains the options. Many of the styles are shown in Figure 9-4.

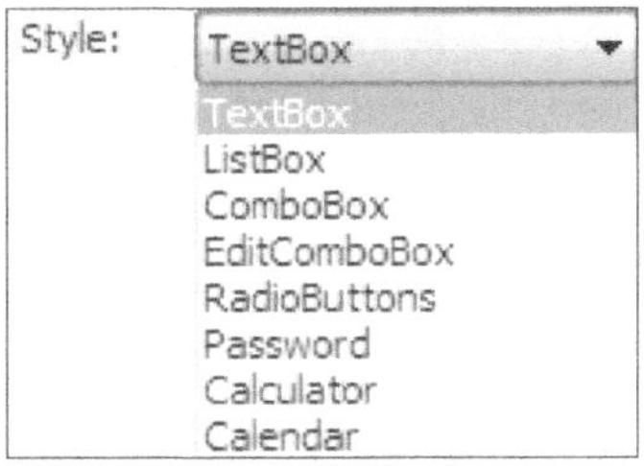

Figure 9-3 Style options

Option	Description
Text Box	This is the default style. Select this option if the data for the prompt does not exist in any field in a table and the data needs to be typed in.
List Box	Is used to create a drop-down list that contains the values that the user can select from. (2)
Combo Box	Works like the List Box style. The difference is that you have to scroll to see more options in the list.
Edit Combo Box	Works like the List Box style. The difference is that if the value needed is not in the list, the user can type it in, like you do in a Text Box.
Radio Buttons	Is used to display a few values that the user must select from. (2)
Password	Is used to let the user enter a password.
Calculator	Displays a calculator with the field, as shown in Figure 9-5. (3)
Calendar	Displays a calendar with the field, as shown later in Figure 9-16. (3)

Table 9-2 Style options explained

(2) The values displayed in this list usually come from a field in a table. Selecting this option displays the Define Choices button on the Define/Edit Arguments dialog box.
(3) This style adds a button to the end of the field to display the object (calculator or calendar).

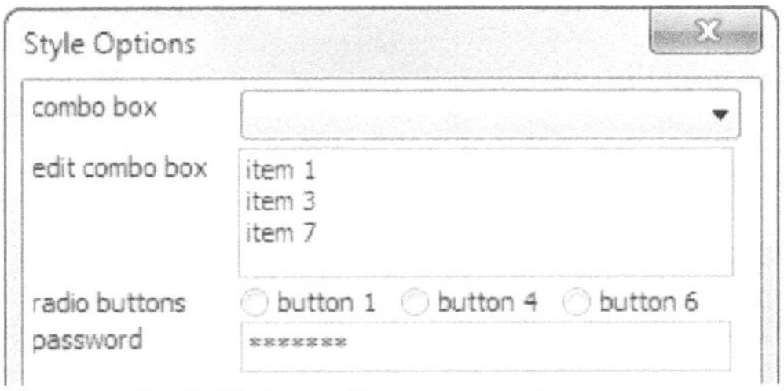

Figure 9-4 Style option examples

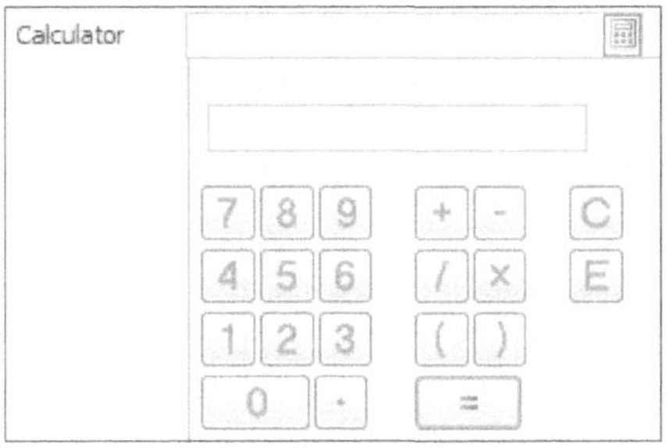

Figure 9-5 Calculator style

Exercise 9.1: Create A Single Prompt For Information

In this exercise you will create an argument that prompts the user to select a product number. The report will display all order line items that match the product number that is entered in the argument. It is helpful to know the field type for the field(s) that will be used in an argument before getting to step 3 below.

1. Save the Line Item Total report as `aSingleUserPrompt`.

2. Open the Define/Edit Arguments dialog box, then click the Add button.

3. On the Add Argument dialog box in the Argument name field, type `SelectProductID`, then select the **CHARACTER** option, as shown in Figure 9-6.

You can name the argument anything you want, as long as it is not a reserved word.

I find it helpful to use the field name as part of the argument name. Doing this is optional.

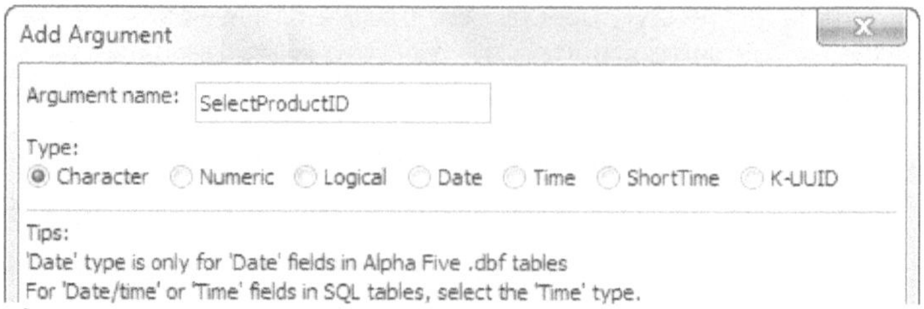

Figure 9-6 Add Argument dialog box

Selecting Data For The Argument

The majority of style options (the options that display the **DEFINE CHOICES** button on the Define/Edit Arguments dialog box) are used to select or create the data, so that the user does not have to type it in manually. There are two options for getting the data: Type in the list of values or use the values in a field. These options are explained below.

Define Choices Dialog Box

The dialog box shown in Figure 9-7 is used to manually type in the values for the argument field.

Use this dialog box when the values are not in a table.

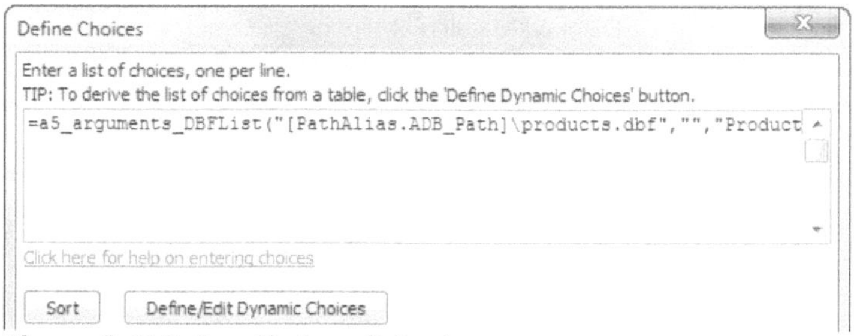

Figure 9-7 Define Choices dialog box

Define Dynamic Choices Dialog Box

To open the dialog box shown in Figure 9-8, click the Define/Edit Dynamic Choices button on the dialog box shown above in Figure 9-7. The Define Dynamic Choices dialog box is used to select the values from a field in a table, an Excel file, Access database or an SQL data source.

Select The Style Options

In this part of the exercise you will set up the list box style to get its values from a field in the table. The values displayed in the list box will be the product name, while the filter will use the Product ID field, because that is the field on the report. If the table had hundreds or thousands of records, using a numeric field is faster than a character field.

1. Open the Style drop-down list and select List Box.

2. Click the Define Choices button. On the Define Choices dialog box, click the **DEFINE/EDIT DYNAMIC CHOICES** button.

Select The Data Source For The Argument

1. Open the Type drop-down list and select DBF.

2. Click the Table name field button, then select the Products table.

3. Open the **DISPLAY VALUE** drop-down list and select the Product Name field.

4. Open the Stored value drop-down list and select the Product ID field. Change the **MAXIMUM NUMBER OF ENTRIES** field to zero.

   Changing this option to zero removes the limit of the number of values that will be displayed in the list. I don't recall creating or seeing a list of values that had more than 1,000 entries, but just in case you do, I wanted to let you know how to display as many values as you need.

   You should have the options shown in Figure 9-8.

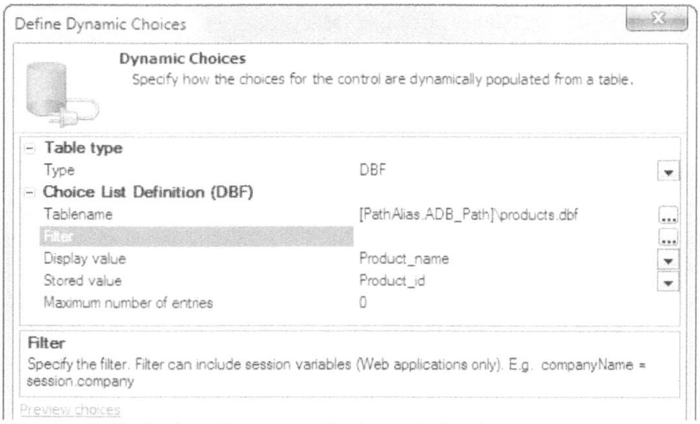

Figure 9-8 Define Dynamic Choices dialog box

   The **FILTER** option displays the **FILTER BUILDER**, so that an expression can be created to keep some data from being displayed in the argument field.

5. Click the **PREVIEW CHOICES** link. You should see the values shown in Figure 9-9.

   The **DISPLAY VALUE** column contains the values that will appear in the drop-down list.

   The related value in **STORED VALUE** column is the field that the report will be filtered on.

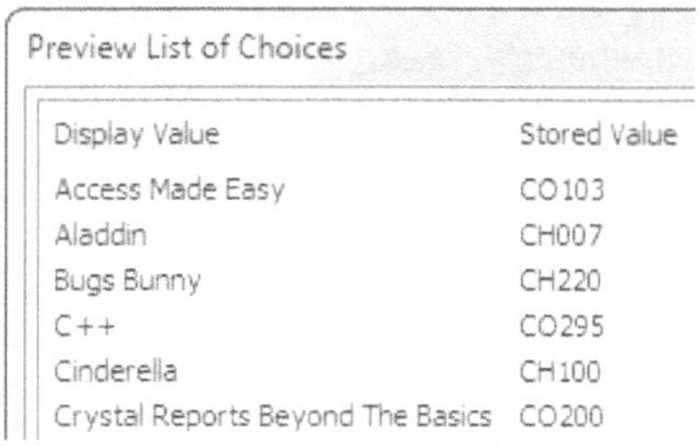

Figure 9-9 Preview List of Choices dialog box

6. Click OK. You should see the code shown earlier in Figure 9-7 on the Define Choices dialog box. Click OK.

Finish Selecting The Argument Properties

1. Change the Prompt field to `Run report for what product?`

2. Click the Edit as HTML button, then type `Select the product to display on the report`. Make the text bold and change the font color to red. Click the Save button.

Customize The Prompt Dialog Box

In this part of the exercise you will learn how to change features of the dialog box that will appear with the prompt (argument) when the report is run.

Customize Dialog Box

The options shown in Figure 9-10 are used to change the appearance of the dialog box displayed when the report is run.

The Customize button on the Define/Edit Arguments dialog box opens this dialog box. The options are explained below.

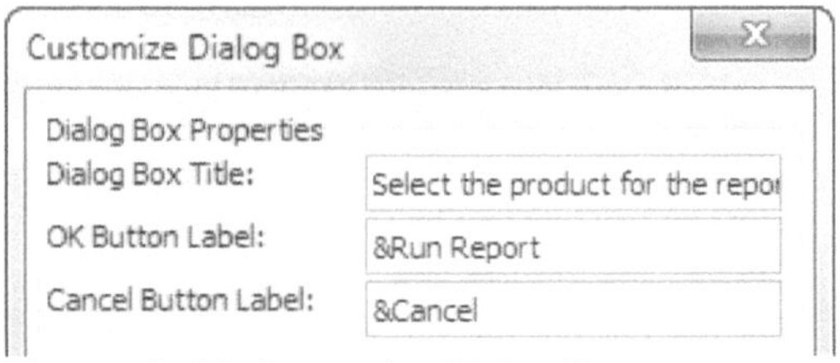

Figure 9-10 Customize Dialog Box

The **DIALOG BOX TITLE** field is used to change the text in the Title bar of the dialog box.
The **OK BUTTON LABEL** field is used to change what is displayed on the OK button on the dialog box.
The **CANCEL BUTTON LABEL** field is used to change what is displayed on the Cancel button on the dialog box.

1. Click the **CUSTOMIZE** button on the Define/Edit Arguments dialog box.

2. In the Display Box Title field type `Select the product for the report.`

3. Change the OK Button Label to `&Run Report`, as shown above in Figure 9-10.

4. You should have the options shown earlier in Figure 9-1 on the Define/Edit Arguments dialog box. Click the **PREVIEW DIALOG** button. The prompt dialog box should look like the one shown in Figure 9-11. Notice that the label changed for the OK button. This is the dialog box that will be displayed when the report is run. If you click on the prompt text, you will see the help text illustrated in Figure 9-12.

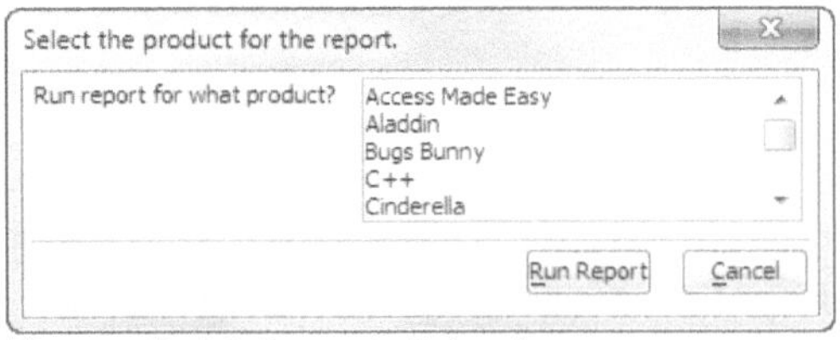

Figure 9-11 Prompt dialog box

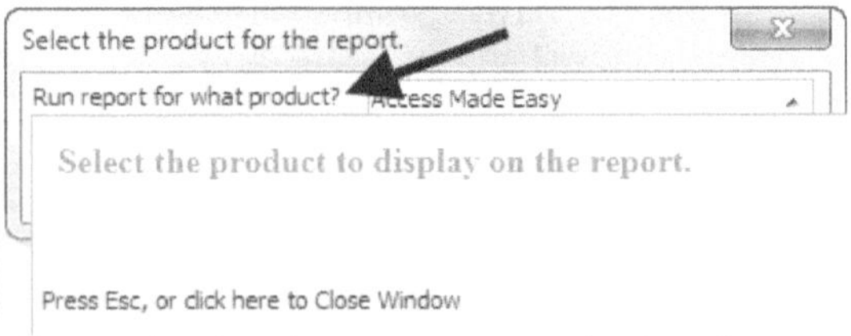

Figure 9-12 Help text message displayed

5. Click OK to close the Define/Edit Arguments dialog box.

Create The Filter For The Argument

By itself, the argument that you just created does not do much. It needs a way to be activated and added to the report. Adding a filter to the report, which includes the argument as part of the expression, is how the argument is added to the report.

1. Click the Filter field button on the Select Records to Print dialog box. Add the Product ID field to the expression, then type an equal sign.

2. Click on the Argument option in the list on the left, then click the Insert button. The Argument option in the list is only available when a report has an argument.

   On the dialog box shown in Figure 9-13, select the argument that you created, then click OK.

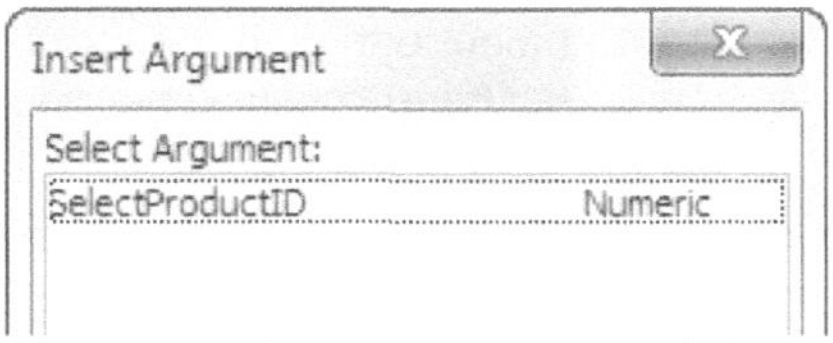

Figure 9-13 Insert Argument dialog box

3. Notice that a colon was added before the argument name in the expression shown in Figure 9-14. This is what denotes that the field is an argument field. Click OK.

   You should see the expression in the Filter field, as shown in Figure 9-15. Click OK.

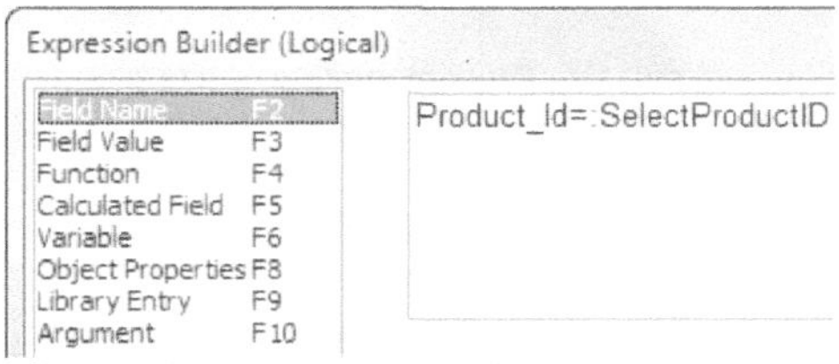

Figure 9-14 Expression that uses argument

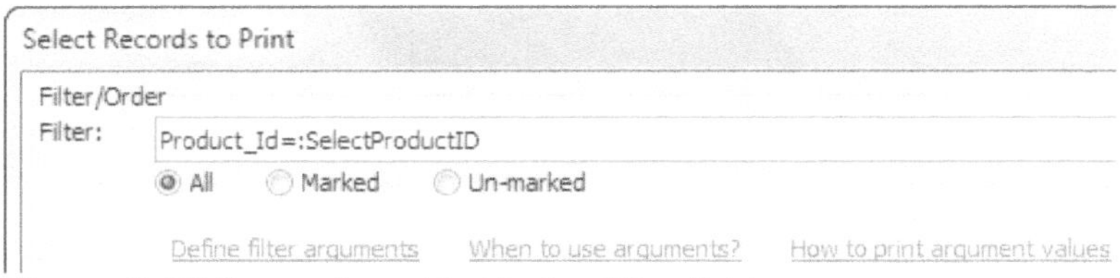

Figure 9-15 Expression added to the Filter field

4. Save the changes. When you preview the report, you should see the dialog box shown earlier in Figure 9-11. Run the report a few times, selecting different products.

Exercise 9.2: Create A Date Prompt

One of the most popular ways to filter data on a report is by date. In this exercise you will create an argument that allows the user select a date. The argument will display records with a date equal to or greater than the date that the user selects.

1. Save the Prompts report as `aOrderDatePrompt`.

2. On the Define/Edit Arguments dialog box, click the Add button.
   Type `SelectOrderDate` as the argument name, then select the Date type.

3. Select the following options on the Define/Edit Arguments dialog box.
   Prompt - `Select the earliest date that you want to see orders for`
   Style - Calendar
   Minimum Value - `01/01/2011`
   Help Text - `Enter a date >= 01/01/2011`

4. Click the Customize button. Change the Dialog Box Title field to `Select the order date`.

Create The Filter For The Argument

1. On the Select Records to Print dialog box, click the Filter field button.

2. Add the Order Date field to the expression, then type `>=`.

3. Select the Argument option in the list on the left, then click the Insert button. Select the SelectOrderDate argument on the Insert Argument dialog box.

4. Select the Order Date field to sort (order) the records by.

Test The Argument

1. Run the report.

   You will see the Prompt dialog box that you created.

   Click the button at the end of the field. You will see the calendar shown in Figure 9-16.

   You can select the date on the calendar or type the date in the field.

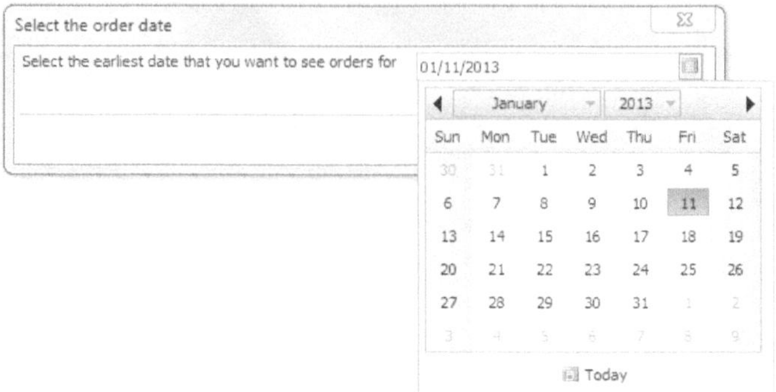

Figure 9-16 Prompt dialog box

2. After you type in or select a date on the calendar and run the report, you will see records on the report with an order date equal to or greater than the date that you selected.

Exercise 9.3: Create Three Prompts For A Report

In the previous exercise you created one prompt for a report. In this exercise you will create three prompts that will allow the user select a sales rep, state and order date greater than 1/1/2011. The report that you will modify in this exercise has filters that need to be deleted.

Create The Sales Rep Filter Argument

1. Save the Prompts report as `aMultipleUserPrompts`.

2. On the Define/Edit Arguments dialog box, click the Add button. Create a character argument named `SelectSalesRep`.

3. Select the argument properties in Table 9-3 for the sales rep argument.

Property	Value
Prompt	Select a sales rep
Style	Combo Box
Help Text	Select the sales rep to display orders for

Table 9-3 Sales rep argument properties

4. Define the choices for the sales rep argument by using the Order Takers table.

5. Create the expression shown in Figure 9-17 for the Display value field on the Define Dynamic Choices dialog box.

```
trim(Repfirstname) + " " + trim(Replastname)
```

Figure 9-17 Display value expression

6. Select the Rep ID field for the Stored value, as shown in Figure 9-18.

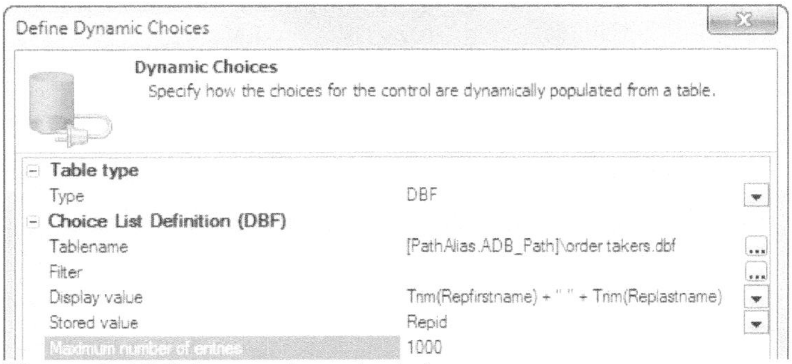

Figure 9-18 Sales rep dynamic choices

Create The State Filter Argument

1. Create a character argument named `SelectState`.

2. Select the argument properties in Table 9-4 for the state argument.

Property	Value
Prompt	What state do you want to see orders for
Style	List Box
Default Value	Type in your home state
Help Text	Select the state that you want to see orders for

Table 9-4 State rep argument properties

3. Define the choices for the state argument by using the Customers table.

4. Select the State field for the Display value and Stored value fields.

   You should have the argument properties shown in Figure 9-19.

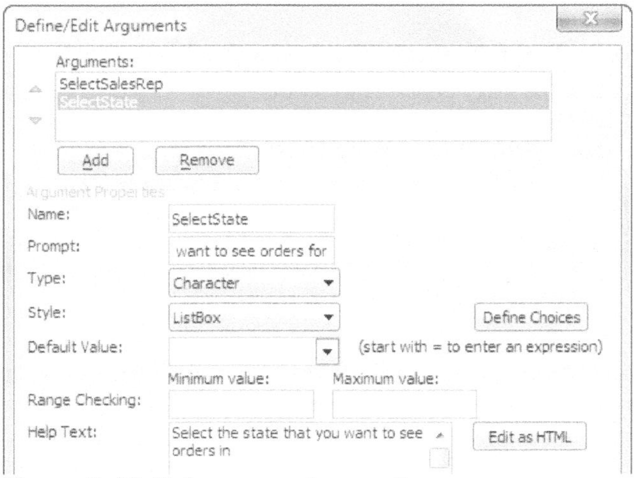

Figure 9-19 State argument properties

Create The Order Date Filter Argument

1. Create a date argument named `WhatOrderDate`.

2. Select the argument properties in Table 9-5 for the order date argument.

Property	Value
Prompt	Select the date to view orders for in this format mm/dd/yyyy.
Style	Text Box
Minimum value	01/01/2011
Help Text	What date do you want to see orders for? You have to enter the date in the format shown at the end of the prompt.

Table 9-5 Order date argument properties

Customize The Prompt Dialog Box

1. Click the Customize button.

2. Change the Dialog Box Title to `Select the sales rep, state and order date.`

3. Change the OK Button Label to `&Run Report.`

   The dialog box should look like the one shown in Figure 9-20.

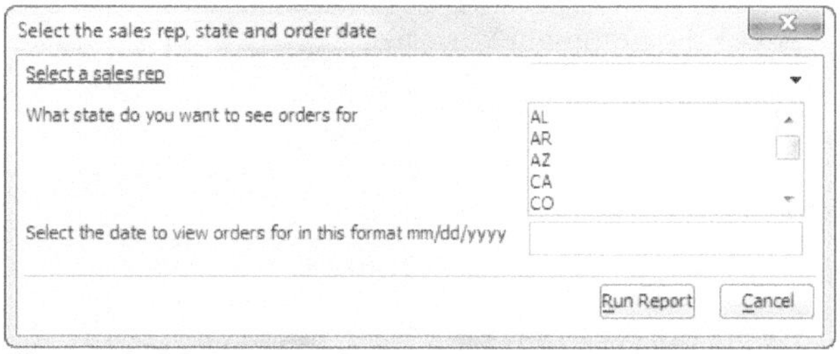

Figure 9-20 Prompts for report

Create The Filter For The Argument

1. Click the Filter field button on the Select Records To Print dialog box, then create the expression shown in Figure 9-21.

```
Orders_Multi_Prompt->Salesrep_Id = :SelectSalesRep
.and. State = :SelectState
.and. Orders_Multi_Prompt->Order_Date = :WhatOrderDate
```

Figure 9-21 Filter expression with the arguments

2. Save the changes to the report. When you run the report, you will see the dialog box shown earlier in Figure 9-20. Select the Sales rep Veronica Smith, State = CT and Order date 02/06/2011. You will see two records on the report.

Exercise 9.4: Create A Prompt For A Date Greater Than Or Equal To

In this exercise you will modify a report that has arguments to allow the person running the report to see records with an order date greater than or equal to the date that they select.

1. Save the aMultipleUserPrompts report as `aPromptDateGreaterThan.`

2. Delete the Select Sales Rep and Select State arguments.

3. Change the Order Date prompt to `What is the oldest order date that you want to see data for?`

4. Delete the Help Text message.

5. Click the Customize button. Change the Dialog Box Title to Select the oldest order date.

6. Delete the filter expression.

   Use the Filter Builder to create the criteria below.

   Table - Orders Multi Prompt
   Field - Order Date
   Criteria - Is on or after the date
   Argument - WhatOrderDate

   You should have the criteria shown in Figure 9-22.

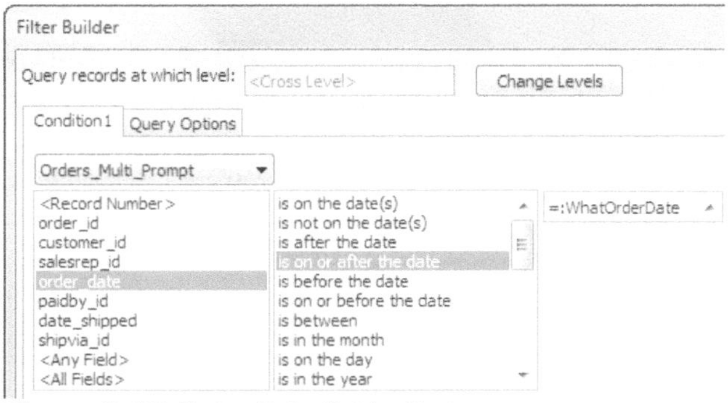

Figure 9-22 Order Date field criteria

7. Sort the records by the Order Date field.

8. Run the report. All of the records on the report should have an order date the same or greater than the date that you entered. The date you entered should be displayed at the top of the report, as shown in Figure 9-23.

Current filter Orders_Multi_Prompt->order_date >= {05/01/2011}

Customer id	First name	Last name	State	Order id	Salesrep id	Order date
14	Louis	Riker	CT	37	2	05/01/2011
15	Brian	Bark	NY	42	2	05/01/2011
19	Carrie	Downing	NV	67	2	05/01/2011
22	Donald	Davis	PA	24	2	05/01/2011

Figure 9-23 Order date greater than or equal to report

Exercise 9.5: Create Prompts For Orders Between Two Dates

In this exercise you will create two date arguments that will let the user select a date range for the orders that they want to see.

1. Save the aMultipleUserPrompts report as `aPromptDateRange`.

2. Open the Define/Edit Arguments dialog box. Change the WhatOrderDate argument name to `SelectStartDate`. Change the prompt to `Enter the first date to see orders for`. Delete the Help text.

3. Delete the Sales Rep argument.

4. Create a date argument named `SelectEndDate`.
   Change the prompt to `Enter the last date to see orders for.`

When I am creating a report with arguments, I enter a default value for each argument so that I do not have to enter or select anything on the Prompt dialog box each time I run the report while testing. When the report is ready to go live, I remove the default values.

5. Click the Customize button. Change the Dialog Box Title to `Select the state and date range`.

6. Delete the current filter expression, then create the filter expressions in Table 9-6. The OrderDate expression should look like the one shown in Figure 9-24.

Field	Criteria	Argument
State	Is equal to	SelectState
OrderDate	Is between	StartDate and EndDate

Table 9-6 Filter expressions

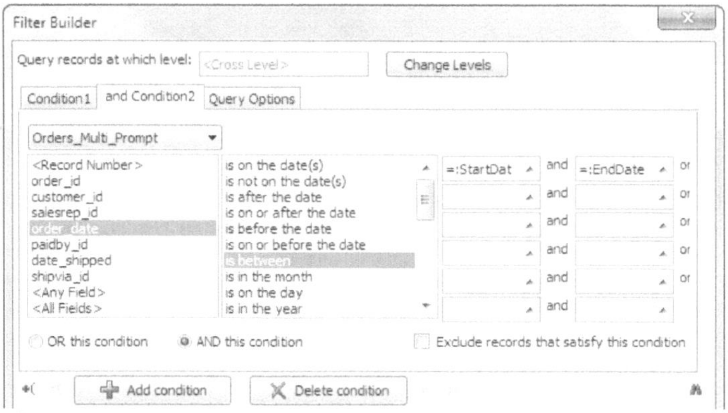

Figure 9-24 Order Date criteria

7. Sort the records by the Order Date field.

8. When you run the report, select a state, start date and end date. The report should look similar to the one shown in Figure 9-25.

Current filter (state = "FL") .and. (between(Orders_Multi_Prompt->order_date,{01/01/2011},{12/15/2011}))

Customer id	First name	Last name	State	Order id	Salesrep id	Order date
40	Charles	Harrison	FL	71	4	02/01/2011
1	Tina	Jones	FL	5	10	02/02/2011
4	Todd	Green	FL	7	9	02/03/2011
16	Robert	Emerson	FL	29	2	02/03/2011

Figure 9-25 Report with a date range

Use The A5_GetArgumentValue Function

At the top of the report shown above in Figure 9-25, you see the Current Filter system field, which displays the arguments and the values selected on the prompt dialog box. This field is okay for displaying some values.

There is another way to display the argument values. The way to display the argument value is to create a calculated field. The **A5_GETARGUMENTVALUE() FUNCTION** is used in the calculated field to display the value in the argument. The expression shown in Figure 9-26 displays the criteria shown in Figure 9-27. This looks better than the Current Filter system field shown above in Figure 9-25.

Type this formula on one line on the Calculated Values dialog box.

```
Criteria selected to run report = "- State = "
+ a5_GetArgumentValue("SelectState")
+ ",  Date Range = "
+ a5_GetArgumentValue("SelectStartDate")
+ " to "
+ a5_GetArgumentValue("SelectEndDate")
```

Figure 9-26 A5_GetArgumentValue function

Criteria selected to run report - State = FL, Date Range = 01/01/2011 to 12/31/2012

Customer id	First name	Last name	State	Order id	Salesrep id	Order date
40	Charles	Harrison	FL	71	4	02/01/2011
1	Tina	Jones	FL	5	10	02/02/2011
4	Todd	Green	FL	7	9	02/03/2011

Figure 9-27 Expression with A5_GetArgumentValue function displayed

Argument Restrictions

① Currently, there is no built-in option to allow multiple values from the same field to be selected in a single argument. This is the equivalent of the **IS ONE OF OPERATOR.**

② There is also no built-in option to make an argument prompt optional. That means that each prompt must have an option selected. After the next exercise you will learn a work around to make an argument optional at run time.

Exercise 9.6: Create Multiple State Prompts

In this exercise you will modify the aPromptDateRange report to allow the user to select two states to run the report for.

1. Save the aPromptDateRange report as `aPromptMultipleStates`.

2. Open the Define/Edit Arguments dialog box, then add a character argument named `Select2ndState`.

3. Select the options below.
   Move this argument up in the Arguments list above the Select Start Date argument.
   Prompt - `Select the 2nd state to include on the report`
   Style - List Box

4. Define the choices for the Select2ndState argument by using the Customer table.

5. Display the Filter expression in the Expression Builder. Type the following after the state portion of the expression, as shown in Figure 9-28. `.OR. (State=:Select2ndState)`

```
(state = :SelectState) .OR. (state = :Select2ndState) .and.
(between(Orders_Multi_Prompt->order_date,:SelectStartDate,:SelectEndDate))
```

Figure 9-28 Modified expression to include the 2nd state argument

6. Run the report.

   The prompt dialog box should look like the one shown in Figure 9-29.

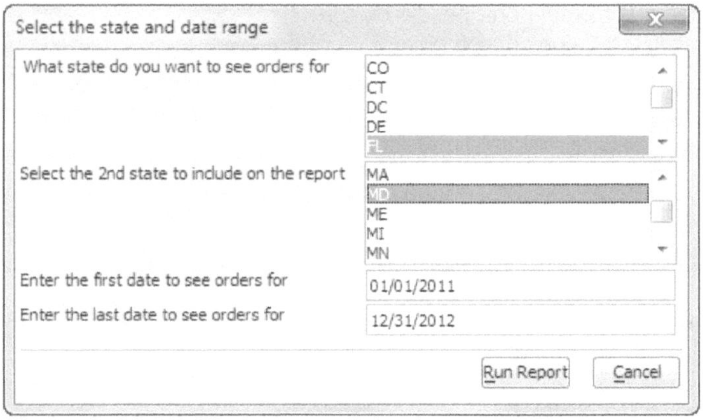

Figure 9-29 Modified prompt dialog box

Making Prompts Optional

All of these prompts provide a lot of options to run the report. The prompts, as they are now are all required, meaning that you have to select a value for each prompt. If you leave one empty, you will see an error message similar to the one shown in Figure 9-30.

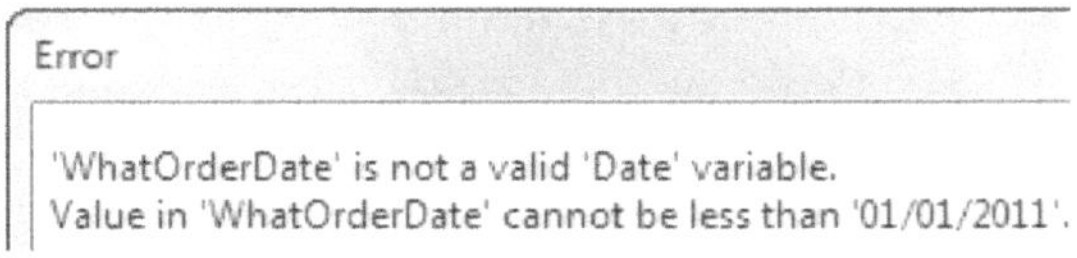

Figure 9-30 Error message

Exercise 9.7: Use The Null Value Function To Make A Prompt Optional

In this exercise you will modify a report to make one of the arguments optional. The report in Exercise 9.6 has four prompts, as shown earlier in Figure 9-29. There will be times when the report only needs to be run for one state. Using the **NULL VALUE FUNCTION** as the default value will allow a prompt to be optional.

1. Save the aPromptMultipleStates report as `aPromptStateOptional`.

2. On the Define/Edit Arguments dialog box, select the Select2ndState argument.

   In the Default Value field type `null_value()`, as shown in Figure 9-31.

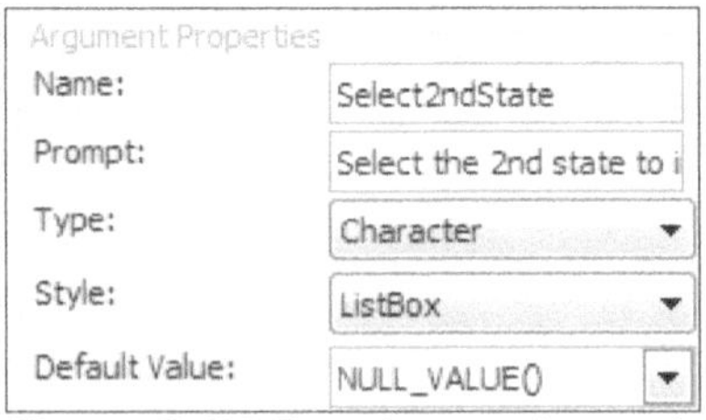

Figure 9-31 Function used to make an argument optional

3. Run the report and do not select an option for the second state field. You will not get the error shown earlier in Figure 9-30. You will see that the report runs and selects the correct records.

Exercise 9.8: Create A Top N Percent What If Prompt

Earlier, you learned how to create Top and Bottom N reports. They work as intended. Often, people have the need to do **WHAT IF ANALYSIS**. The reports created earlier do not allow the value of N to be changed each time the report is run. In this exercise you will create an argument that will let the user select the percent of sales that they want to see on the report. Because the user will probably print the report several times using different percents, you will print the percent selected on the report so that they can easily tell what percent was selected.

Create The Top N Percent Report

1. Save the Last Years Sales report as `aPromptTopNPercent`.
2. Click the Select Records button, then click the Create Filter/Order Using Genie button. In the Order Expression field, select the Last Years Sales field.
3. Open the Sub-select options drop-down list and select **TOP N % OF SELECTED RECORDS**. Because you are going to create an argument for N, you do not need to select a value for it on this dialog box.
4. On the Select Records to Print dialog box, select the Descending option.

Create The Top N Percent Argument And Add It To The Filter

1. On the Select Records To Print dialog box, click the Define filter arguments link.
2. Create a numeric argument named `TopPercent`.
3. Select the argument properties in Table 9-7 for the Top Percent argument.

Property	Value
Prompt	What percent of last years sales do you want to see?
Style	Text Box
Default Value	10
Minimum value	1
Maximum value	100
Help Text	Type the percent of sales that you want to see. The range is 1 to 100. Do not type the % percent sign.

Table 9-7 Top Percent argument properties

4. On the Customize Dialog box, change the Dialog Box Title field to `Top N Percent Report`.
5. On the Select Records To Print dialog box, in the Filter field, change the 10 to `:TopPercent`, as shown in Figure 9-32.

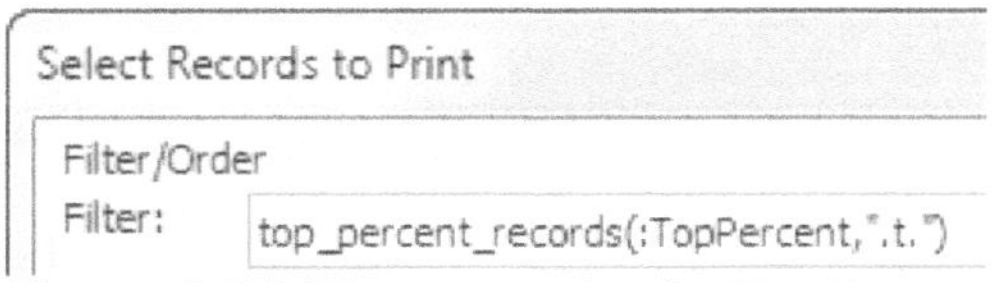

Figure 9-32 Filter expression for Top Percent argument

Add The Argument To The Report

1. Open the Calculated Values dialog box, then create the formula below.

```
PrintPercent = "Top " + a5_GetArgumentValue("TopPercent") +
"% of Last Years Sales"
```

2. Add the PrintPercent calculated field to the report below the Last Years Sales title.

   When you preview the report, it should look like the one shown in Figure 9-33.

Last Years Sales

Top 19% of Last Years Sales

Customer #	Name	State	Last years sales
200	Anna Bedecs	WA	500000.00
239	Tim Smith	MI	500000.00
311	Lee-Johnson Laurie	CA	401000.00
236	Laura Callahan	VA	300000.00
341	Zalapski Aaron	NC	298356.22

Figure 9-33 Top N Percent report

CREATING CHARTS

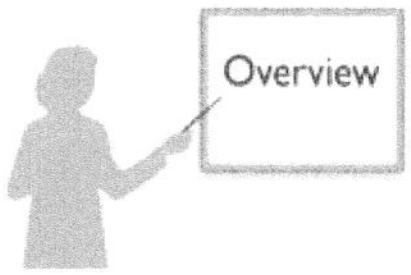

Alpha Five has a control for creating charts. This control supports over 15 types of charts, including pie, bar, scatter and line. In this chapter you will learn how to create a variety of chart types.

CHAPTER 10

Overview

In addition to being able to format data in reports, charts are used to present data in a graphical format. Charts often make the data easier to understand because the relationship between the data is displayed visually. Charts also allow data to be presented in formats that text-only reports cannot do as well. For example, charts can show trends over time, relationships or how one set of data compares to another set of data. It is very easy to get carried away when creating charts. Try to create charts that present the data in a meaningful way. Remember that sometimes, less is more.

Chart Considerations

There are two areas that need to be addressed before you start to create the chart: The chart type and the source of the data for the chart. You will select the chart type on the Graph Data dialog box, which is explained below. Changing the chart type is easy. If you are not sure which chart type is the most appropriate, with a few mouse clicks, you can try out a few chart types and variations to see which chart type is best for the data.

Charts should enhance the ability to understand the data and make it easy to see differences in the data. While a report can have more than one chart, keep in mind that charts are memory intensive.

I use to teach a technical writing class and one of the assignments had students create three charts to visually present data. Overall, the students did a good job on the charts. However, it was easy to tell which students had never created a chart before, for at least one of the reasons listed below.

① The wrong chart type was selected. Newsflash: Bar charts are not the best option for all types of data <smile>, especially data that shows trends or needs to show how data has changed over time.
② The values on the X and Y axes were on the wrong axis. Dollar amounts, quantity and percents usually go on the Y axis and time, dates, quantities, percents and categories usually go on the X axis.
③ Not understanding the data that was used to create the chart.

> **Where Are The X And Y Axis?**
> If you are new to creating charts, it is imperative that you understand the following. Many of the options on the Graph Data dialog box are used to select how the chart will display the data values that you see across the bottom of the chart (the **X AXIS**, also known as the **HORIZONTAL AXIS**) and on the left side of the chart (the **Y AXIS**, also known as the **VERTICAL AXIS**).

Graph Data Dialog Box

To create a chart, the **EMBEDDED CHART CONTROL** has to be added to the form or report. After this control is added, the dialog box shown in Figure 10-1 opens. This is the tool used to create charts. Charts can be created from the same data source that the form or report uses or it can be created from a different data source.

As you can see, there are a lot of options on the Graph Data dialog box. It is important that you understand the options on this dialog box, so that you will be able to create the charts that you need. The majority of options are explained in Table 10-1.

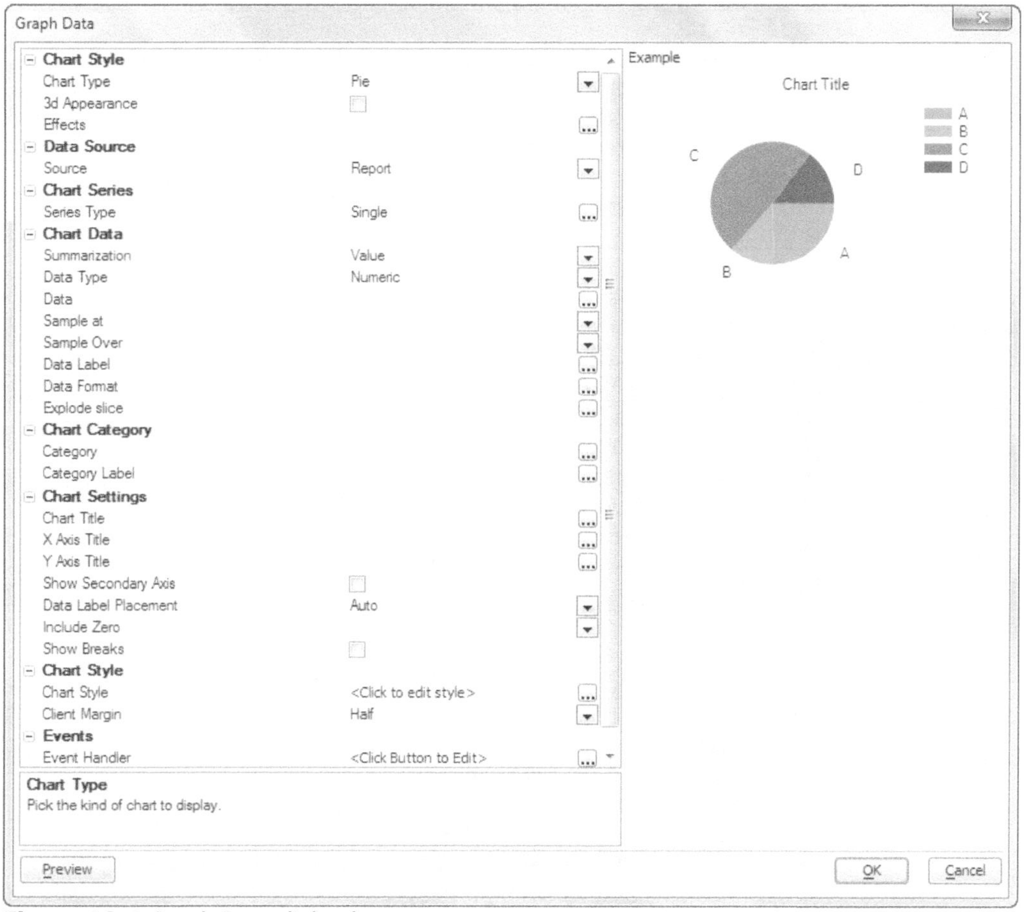

Figure 10-1 Graph Data dialog box

Option	Is Used To . . .
Chart Type	[See Chart Type Options]
3D Appearance	Change the look of the chart by displaying it in 3D format. [See 3D Appearance Option]
Effects	Add other appearance options. This option is not available for all chart types. The button displays a list of options, as shown later in Figure 10-14. The options displayed in the list depend on the chart type that is selected and whether or not the 3D Appearance option is selected.
Source	Select where the data for the chart is coming from. The options are Report (uses data on the report), Table, SQL and Custom. [See Data Source Options]
Table or Set	Select the table or set that has the data for the chart. (1) (2)
Arguments	Opens the Define/Edit Arguments dialog box to create an argument (filter) for the chart. [See Chapter 9, Define/Edit Arguments Dialog Box] (1)
Argument Bindings	Attach the argument to a field or expression. [See Argument Bindings] (1)
Filter Records	Create a filter to select the data that will be displayed on the chart. [See Specify Filter], [See Chapter 2, Filter Builder] (1) (2)

Table 10-1 Graph Data dialog box options explained

Option	Is Used To . . .
Series Type	Select how many series of data will be plotted on the chart. Some chart types like line and area support multiple series of data. The button opens the dialog box shown later in Figure 10-19. [See Series Type Options]
Plot Series on Axis	Select whether the category or series will be plotted on the X axis. The one that is not selected is used in the legend. This option is only available when the Multiple Record Series Type option is selected on the Select Chart Series Type dialog box. (1)
X Data Type	Select the X values data type. (1)
Y Data Type	Select the Y values data type. (1)
Summarization	Select how the data for the chart will be calculated (summarized). The options are Value (the default option), Total, Count, Average, Standard Deviation, First, Last, Min and Max.
Data Type	Select the type of data that will be plotted on the Y axis. The options are Number, Date and Time.
Data Columns	Open the dialog box shown later in Figure 10-21. This option is only available when the Multiple Column Series Type option is selected on the Select Chart Series Type dialog box. (1)
Data	Select the field that the Summarization option will be applied to. This option is only available when the Multiple Column Series Type option is not selected.
Sample at	Select a group on the report. The group selected must be lower than the group selected for the Sample over option. Often, this is the data that is displayed across the bottom of the chart. (3)
Sample over	Select a group on the report. Usually, the Grand option is appropriate because it is the largest group. Often, this is the data that is displayed vertically on the left side of the chart. (3)
Sample unique	Create an expression that will be used on unique summary values. This option is available if the Data Source is Table or SQL. (1)
Data Label	Create an expression for the data point labels on the chart. By default, the value in the Sample at field will be displayed across the bottom in the chart. The Data Label field overrides the Sample at value for what is displayed across the bottom of the chart. [See Data Label Expression Dialog Box Options]
Data Format	Open the Display Format dialog box, which is used to format numeric or text data.
Explode Slice	Move one part away from the rest of the pie chart.
Category	Select the field that will be used to group the elements on the chart.
Category Label	Override the label for the field selected in the Category field. For example, if the Category field has the Order ID field, that is also the title that would be displayed on the chart. If you wanted Order # to be displayed, type it in quotes in this field.
Chart Title	Enter the text that will appear above the chart. (4)
X Axis Title	Enter the text that will appear below the chart. (4)
Y Axis Title	Enter the text that will appear to the left of the chart. (4)
Show Secondary Axis	Display a third axis. If checked, the **SECONDARY X AXIS TITLE** and **SECONDARY Y AXIS TITLE** options are available on the dialog box to create labels for the X and Y secondary axis.
Data Label Placement	Select one of the following for where the labels for the actual values on the chart are placed. The options are Auto, None, Legend and Chart.

Table 10-1 Graph Data dialog box options explained (Continued)

Option	The Option Is Used To . . .
Include Zero	Select whether or not the number zero is displayed on the Y axis.
Show Breaks	Visually show where there is less data than expected. [See Use The Show Breaks Option]
Y Interval	Select the amount that the tick marks on the Y axis are incremented. Setting this option to zero automatically selects the best increment value. (1)
Minimum Y Interval	Set the smallest limit for the Y axis interval. This option is only available if the Y interval option is set to zero. (1)
Chart Style	[See Chart Style Options]
Client Margin	Select where the X axis starts printing. [See Changing The Client Margin]
Event Handler	View or edit the mouse event handlers. [See Mouse Events]

Table 10-1 Graph Data dialog box options explained (Continued)

(1) This option is not shown in Figure 10-1.
(2) This option is only available if the Data Source is Table.
(3) The options are the group name(s) on the report, Detail and Grand. The Detail option cannot be used when the summarization is based on a group. [See Chapter 8, Report Sections]
(4) The title must be enclosed in quotes.

Previewing The Chart
If the Data Source is Report, you cannot view the chart by clicking the Preview button on the Graph Data dialog box.

Error Messages
When you click OK and see a message similar to the one shown in Figure 10-2, it means that what you selected or typed in the field listed in the error message is not correct. In this example, there is something wrong with what I typed in the Chart Title field. What bothers me about this error system is that it only lists one error at a time, even if there is more than one error on the Graph Data dialog box.

Figure 10-2 Chart error message

Formatting Numeric Values
The built-in formatting options did not work, at the time this book went to print. Trying to find a work around is difficult. After completing the exercises in this chapter, you will be able to see if the numeric data that you will use to create charts will work.

Chart Type Options

The options shown in Figure 10-3 are the types of charts that can be created.

If you have created charts in spreadsheet software, you are probably familiar with many of the chart types in Alpha Five.

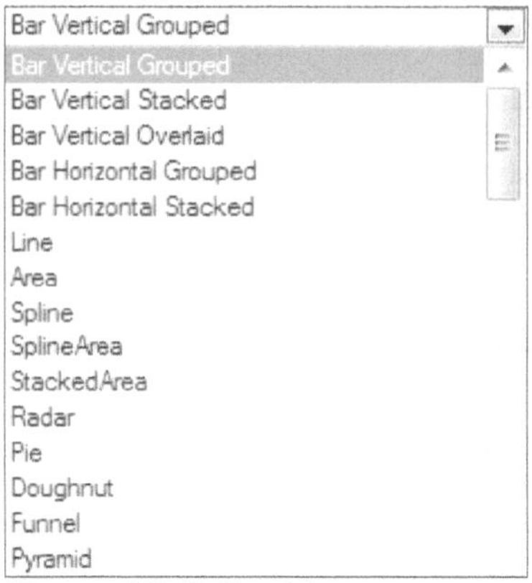

Figure 10-3 Chart types

Figure 10-3 Chart types (Continued)

When selecting the chart type, the most important consideration should be to select the chart type that will best display the data that will be presented on the chart. If you are not sure what a chart type looks like, select it and a sample will appear on the right side of the Graph Data dialog box. The chart types are explained in Table 10-2.

Chart Type	This Chart Type . . .
Bar	Shows differences between items and relationships between groups of data, as shown in Figure 10-4. This is probably the most used chart type. The types of bar charts are **BAR VERTICAL GROUPED**, **BAR VERTICAL STACKED**, **BAR VERTICAL OVERLAID**, **BAR HORIZONTAL GROUPED** and **BAR HORIZONTAL STACKED**. Stacked bar charts show each item as a percent of the total.
Line	Shows trends and changes for groups over a period of time. The markers on the bottom of line charts indicate the exact values. Unlike XY and Bubble charts, Line charts are not required to only use all numeric values on the axes. A good use of **3D LINE CHARTS** is when the data lines cross each other often. This makes a line chart easier to read.
Area	Shows how the data has changed over a period of time. Figure 10-5 shows how four types of income (mail order, store, kiosk and Internet) make up the total income and how the income changes over the months. Area charts are almost identical to line charts. The difference is that area charts are filled in below the **TRENDLINE**. Area charts are probably best suited for a few groups of data. The other area chart type is **STACKED AREA**.
Spline	Is a combination of area and line charts. The difference is that Spline charts do not use straight lines to connect the data points like line charts do. Instead, spline charts plot the data points on a curve, as shown in Figure 10-6. There is also a **SPLINE AREA** chart type.
Radar	Compares sets of data relative to a center point and shows how far the data value is from the standard (the center point value). The values that are often used are group subtotals. The data from the X axis is usually plotted in a circle and the Y axis values are plotted from the center of the circle out. Radar charts are also known as **SPIDER CHARTS**.

Table 10-2 Chart types explained

Chart Type	This Chart Type . . .
Pie	Only displays data for one point in time. Figure 10-7 shows various types of income for July. Each slice of the pie represents the percent for the item. (5)
Doughnut	Is similar to pie charts. The difference is that there is a hole in the center of the chart. (5)
Funnel	Is similar to stacked bar charts because each bar on the funnel shows each item as a percent of the total. The difference is that the bars are in the shape of a funnel. The height of the bar represents the percent of the data. The width of the bar does not represent anything.
Pyramid	Is similar to funnel charts. The difference is that the pyramid displays the smallest number at the top, as shown in Figure 10-8.
Stock	Is similar to bar charts. Stock charts plot the first and last trade of the day or the high and low values for each element. The difference is that the items (values) for stock charts usually do not touch the bottom of the chart because they are used to display stock data. They will remind you of **OHLC CHARTS** (which stands for Open High Low Close) because the values are represented by **HASH MARKS**. The hash marks represent the values selected in the **DATA HIGH**, **DATA LOW**, **DATA OPEN** and **DATA CLOSE** options that are displayed on the chart.
Candlestick	Is similar to stock charts. Figure 10-9 shows a Candlestick chart.
Bubble	Is similar to XY charts because the bubbles plot individual points. The difference is that bubble charts use plot points (bubbles) based on the data value. Use a bubble chart when there are three interdependent numeric values that need to be displayed on the chart. Figure 10-10 shows a bubble chart. (6)
Box Plot	Is similar to stock and candlestick charts. The difference is that they display the spread in a batch of data through its five number summary. The following fields are used to select the high and low values: **DATA LOWER WHISKER**, **DATA UPPER WHISKER**, **DATA LOWER BOX**, **DATA UPPER BOX**, **DATA AVERAGE** and **DATA MEDIAN**. This chart type is often used for various types of analysis, including test results, scientific and marketing. Multiple batches of data can be displayed on one chart. For example, you can compare the spread (high and low values) of student grades for the same course that is taught by different professors. This chart type is also known as a **WHISKER CHART**.
Scatter	Is a combination of bubble and XY charts.
XY	Shows how two values are related (like month of year and order amount) and how a change in one value affects the other value, as shown in Figure 10-11. This chart type is used to show the correlation between two interdependent items. Other XY chart types are **XY SPLINE**, **XY AREA**, **XY SPLINE AREA**, **XY BAR VERTICAL GROUPED**, **XY BAR VERTICAL STACKED**, **XY BAR VERTICAL OVERLAID**, **XY BAR HORIZONTAL GROUPED** and **XY BAR HORIZONTAL STACKED**. (6)

Table 10-2 Chart types explained (Continued)

(5) This chart type only uses one value because it shows how the whole (100%) is divided.
(6) The X and Y axis must display numeric data. If data like dates or months can be converted to numeric data, it can be used in this chart type.

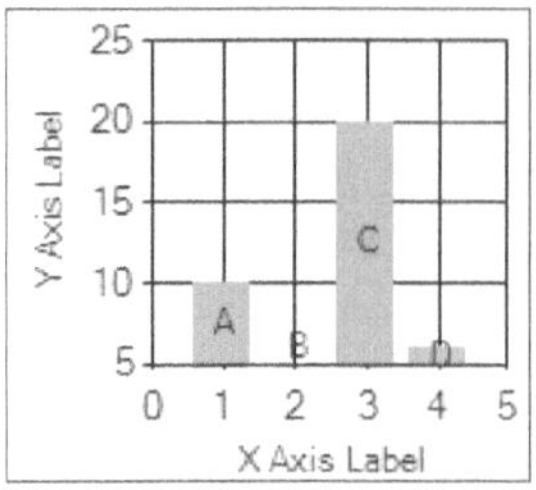

Figure 10-4 Bar chart

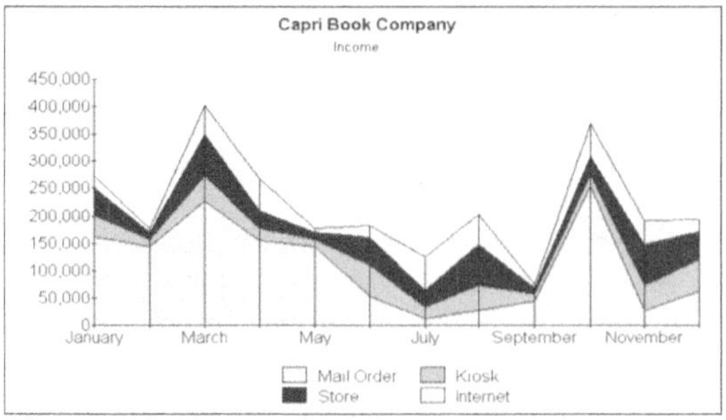

Figure 10-5 Area chart

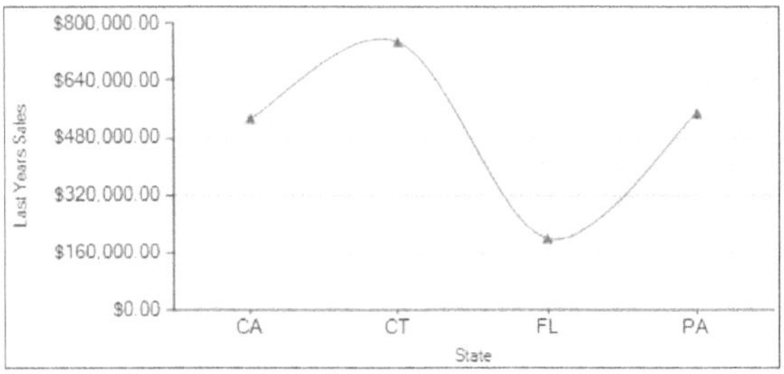

Figure 10-6 Spline chart

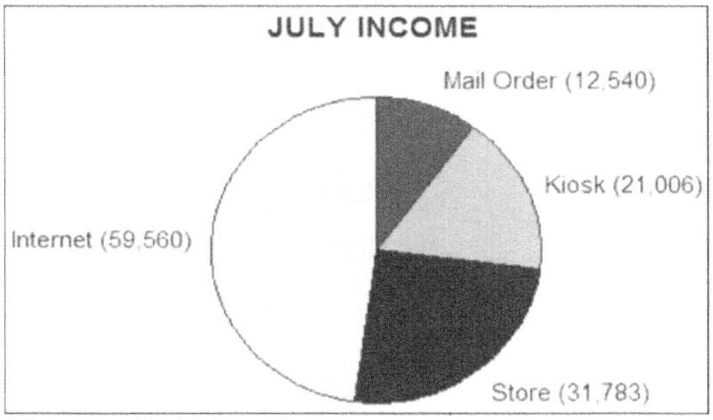

Figure 10-7 Pie chart

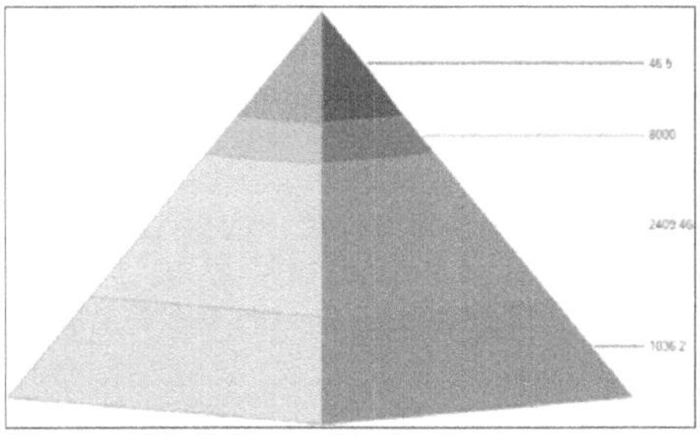

Figure 10-8 Pyramid chart

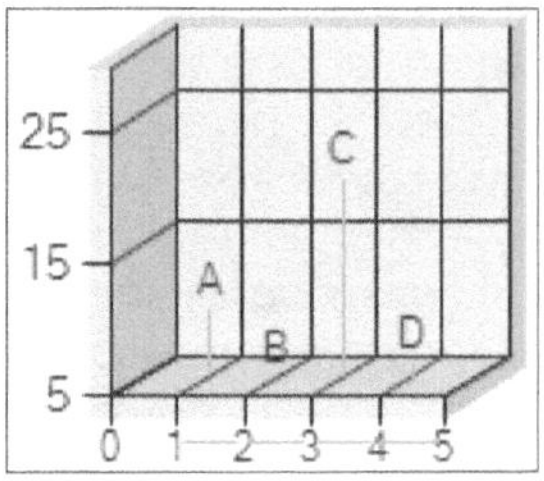

Figure 10-9 Candlestick chart

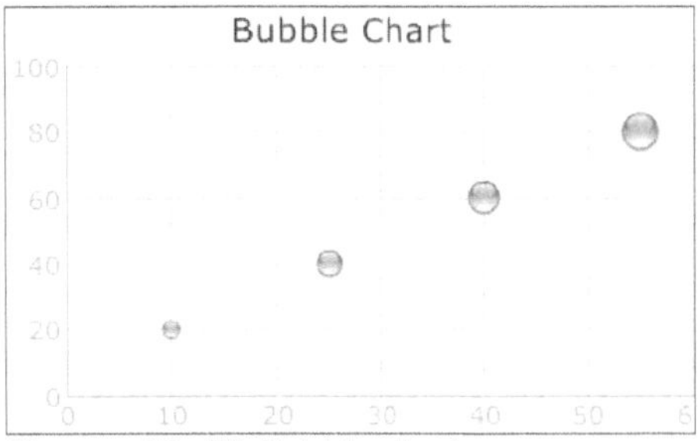

Figure 10-10 Bubble chart

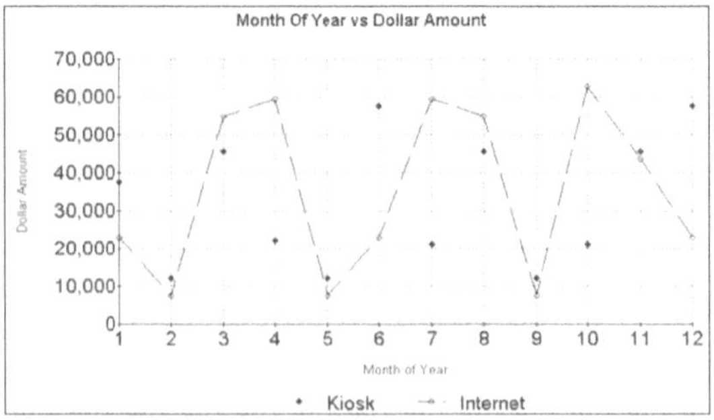

Figure 10-11 XY chart

3D Appearance Option

By applying this option, the chart changes from the one shown in Figure 10-12 to the one shown in Figure 10-13.

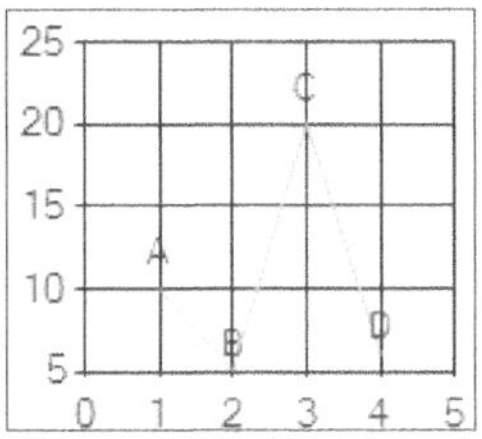

Figure 10-12 Line chart without 3D option

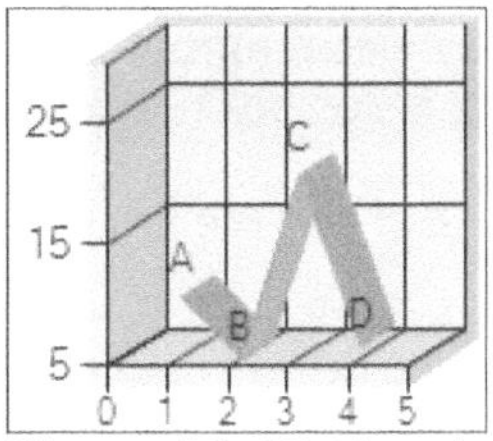

Figure 10-13 Line chart with 3D option

Effects Options

Figure 10-14 shows the effects options for a radar chart.

Different chart types have different effects.

None
Circle
Polygon
Line
Marker
Area

Figure 10-14 Effects options for a radar chart

Data Source Options

Each data source type has slightly different options, as explained below.

The **REPORT DATA SOURCE** option does not have any other options. The benefit that this option has is that fields on the report, including calculated fields can be used to create the chart.

Figure 10-15 shows the **TABLE DATA SOURCE** options.
Figure 10-16 shows the **SQL DATA SOURCE** options.
Figure 10-17 shows the **CUSTOM DATA SOURCE** options. Select this option when you need to create an expression to retrieve the records for the chart, including a data source like an Excel spreadsheet or Access database. This option can also be used to get data from an Xbasic function.

Data Source	
Source	Table
Table or Set	
Arguments	<Click Button to Edit>
Argument Bindings	<Click Button to Edit>
Filter records	

Figure 10-15 Table data source options

Data Source	
Source	SQL
Connection	
Select Statement	
Use Portable SQL	✓
Arguments	<Click Button to Edit>
Argument Bindings	<Click Button to Edit>

Figure 10-16 SQL data source options

Data Source	
Source	Custom
Custom Source	<Click Button to Edit>
Custom Watch	<Click Button to Edit>

Figure 10-17 Custom data source options

Argument Bindings

Click the **ARGUMENT BINDINGS** button on the Graph Data dialog box to open this dialog box.

Figure 10-18 shows the arguments that can be bound.

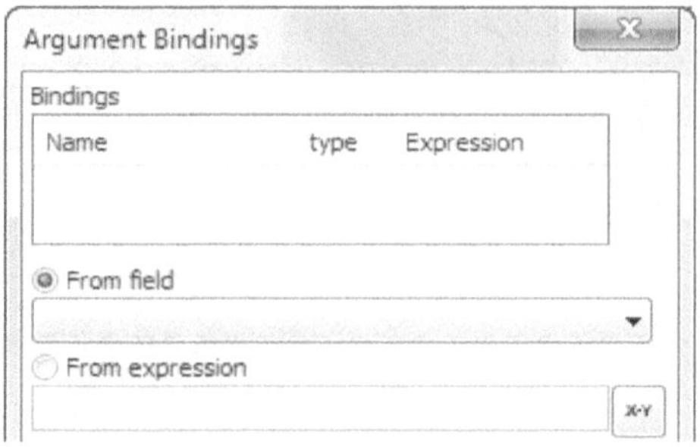

Figure 10-18 Argument Bindings dialog box

Series Type Options

Click the **SERIES TYPE** button on the Graph Data dialog box to open this dialog box.

Figure 10-19 shows the series type options for charts.

Selecting the **MULTIPLE RECORD** option displays the Chart Series options shown in Figure 10-20 on the Graph Data dialog box.

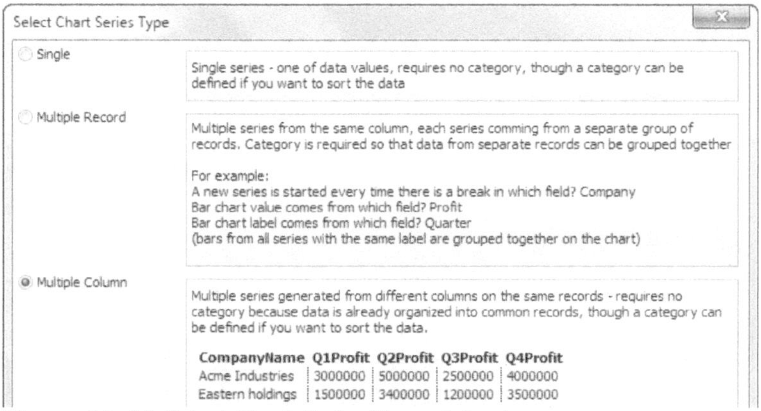

Figure 10-19 Select Chart Series Type dialog box

Selecting the **MULTIPLE COLUMN** option shown above in Figure 10-19 only displays the **PLOT SERIES ON AXIS** option shown in Figure 10-20.

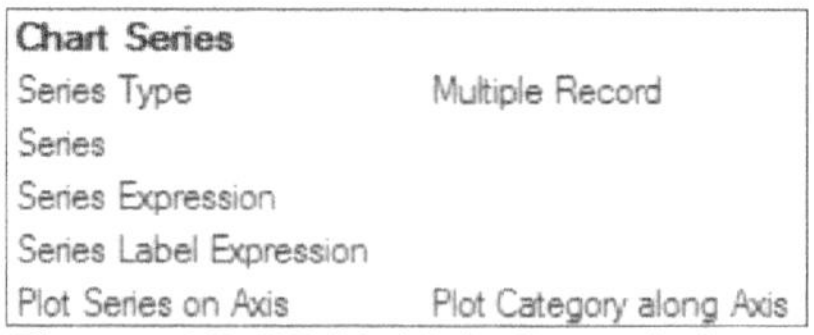

Figure 10-20 Multiple Record chart series options

Data Columns Options

Click the **DATA COLUMNS** button on the Graph Data dialog box to open this dialog box.

Figure 10-21 shows the options to create the series for columns.

Figure 10-21 Define Chart Series Columns dialog box

Data Label Expression Dialog Box Options

The dialog box shown in Figure 10-22 is accessed by clicking the Data Label field button on the Graph Data dialog box. It is used to select the field that has the labels for the data points on the chart. The default data label is the field in the Sample at or Sample unique field. You can also type in what you want for the data labels. Doing this is optional.

The **USE PREDEFINED FORMAT** link displays formats that you can use. Most of the options display the fields in the data and category fields on the Graph Data dialog box.

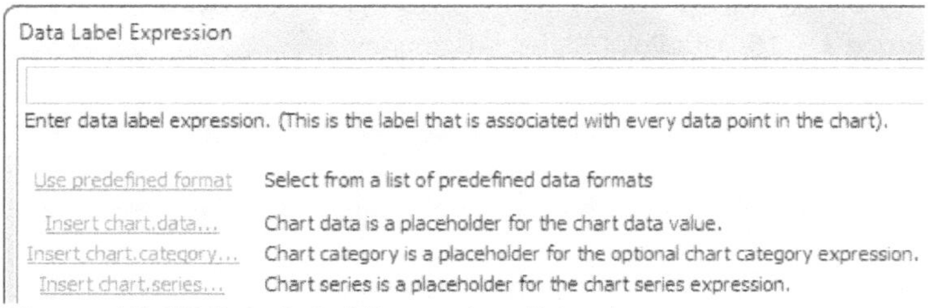

Figure 10-22 Data Label Expression dialog box

The **INSERT CHART DATA** link uses the Data field as the data for the data points.
The **INSERT CHART CATEGORY** link uses the Category field as the data for the data points.
The **INSERT CHART SERIES** link uses the Series field as the data for the data points.

Chart Style Options

Click the **CHART STYLE** button on the Graph Data dialog box to open the dialog box shown in Figures 10-23 to 10-27. You can select a pre-defined option or edit the style sheet and create your own style.

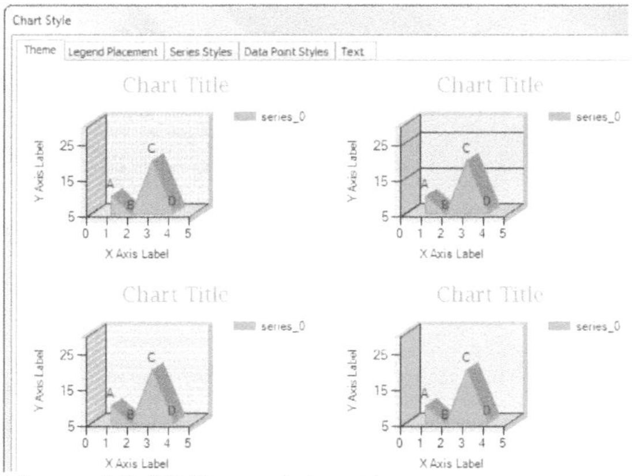

Figure 10-23 Theme tab options

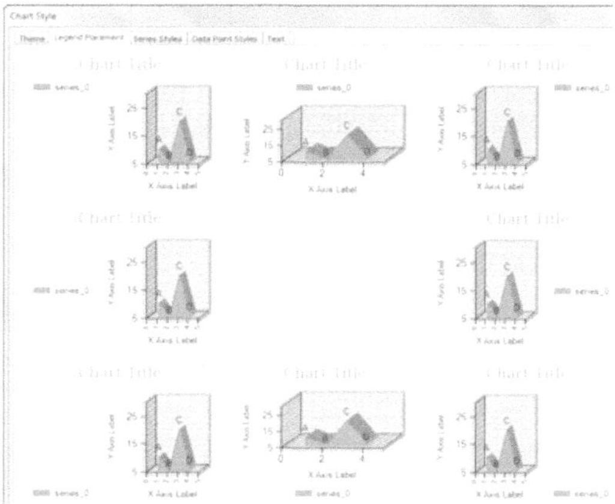

Figure 10-24 Legend Placement tab options

Figure 10-25 Series Styles tab options

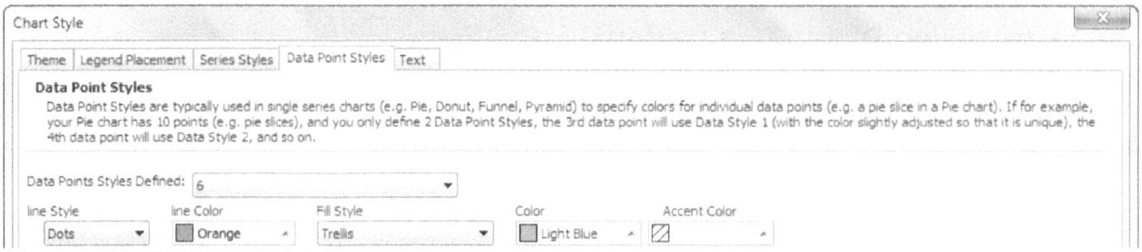

Figure 10-26 Data Point Styles tab options

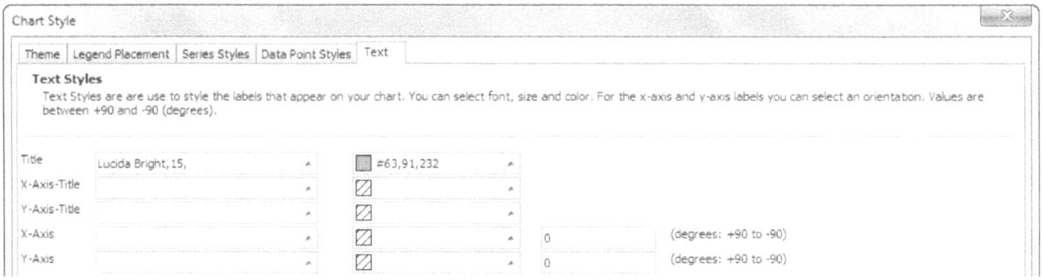

Figure 10-27 Text tab options

Chart Style Dialog Box
The problem with this dialog box, at least on a 15.6 inch laptop screen is that it is too big to see the buttons at the bottom of the dialog box and currently, the dialog box cannot be resized. If you cannot see the buttons at the bottom of the dialog box, press the ALT+O keys to emulate clicking the OK button.

Mouse Events

Click the **EVENT HANDLER** button on the Graph Data dialog box to open this dialog box.

The default mouse events for the chart are shown in Figure 10-28.

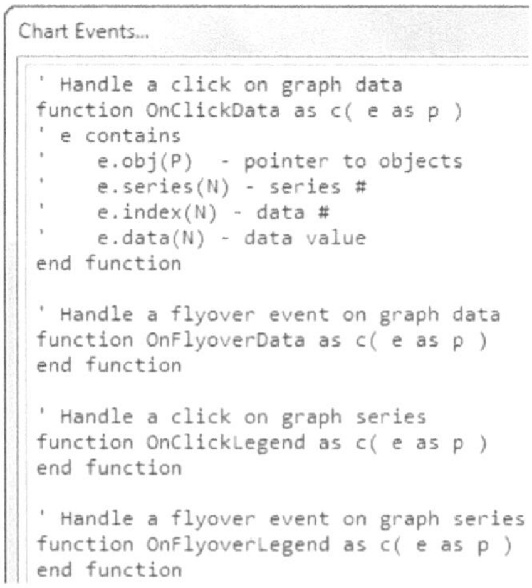

Figure 10-28 Chart Events dialog box

Chart Tips For Exercises
① Before starting the step (this step instructs you to select the options in a table) that has the options to create the chart, drag the **EMBEDDED CHART CONTROL** to the Report Header section of the report, unless stated otherwise. Make the chart as large as needed.
② After making changes on the Graph Data dialog box, save the changes before previewing the report.

Exercise 10.1: Create A Bar Chart

In this exercise you will create a chart that displays the daily order total amount for specific days.

1. Save the Chart Orders By Date report as `aBarChart`.

2. Create a filter that selects order dates between 2/1/2011 and 2/5/2011.

3. Select the options in Table 10-3.

   Leave the dialog box open to complete the next part of the exercise.

Option	Change To
Chart Type	Bar Vertical Stacked
3D Appearance	Yes
Source	Report
Summarization	Total
Data	Order amount
Sample at	Order Date
Sample over	Grand
Category	Order Date
Chart Title	"Orders By Date"
X Axis Title	"Order Date"
Y Axis Title	"Order total amount per day"

Table 10-3 Bar chart options

Formatting Data Values

If you viewed the chart, it would look like the one shown in Figure 10-29.

It would look better if the values on the Y axis were formatted.

Figure 10-29 Bar chart without formatting

1. Click the Data Format field button, then click the Select Pre-Defined Format button.

> **Cannot Suppress Decimal Places**
> The **SELECT PRE-DEFINED FORMAT BUTTON** is used to select a numeric formatting option. You can also select the number of decimal places. Setting the decimal places option to zero did not work for me. I also tried the **INTERNATIONAL CURRENCY FORMAT OPTIONS** to see if I could suppress the decimal place, but that did not work either. Later in this chapter, you will learn how to use the **INT FUNCTION** to hide the decimal places.

> **Reopening The Graph Data Dialog Box**
> If you need to reopen this dialog box, double-click on the chart in Design mode on the form or report. You can also click the arrow button in the upper right corner of the chart control to open it.

2. Select the first option in the list that has a dollar sign, as shown in Figure 10-30.

   If the **DECIMALS** option worked, you would set it to zero, as shown in the figure.

   You should have the expression shown in Figure 10-31.

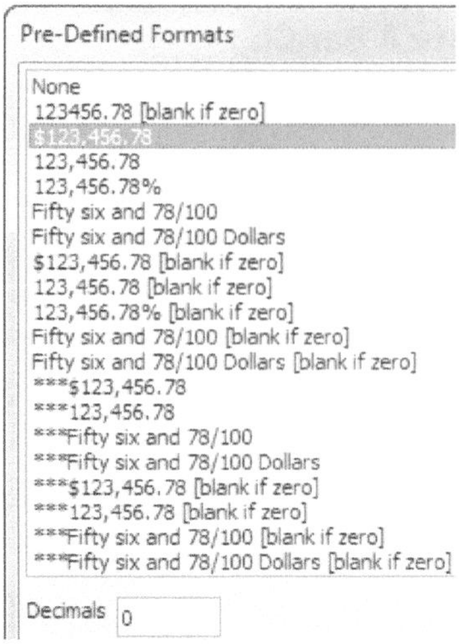

Figure 10-30 Pre-Defined Formats dialog box

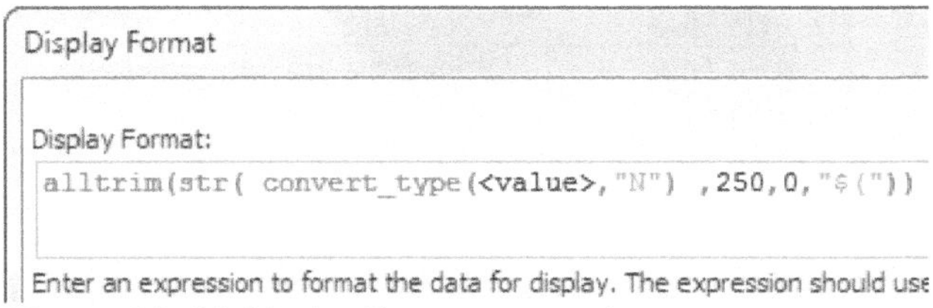

Figure 10-31 Display Format expression

The chart will look like the one shown in Figure 10-32.

As you can see, the values are displaying the cents.

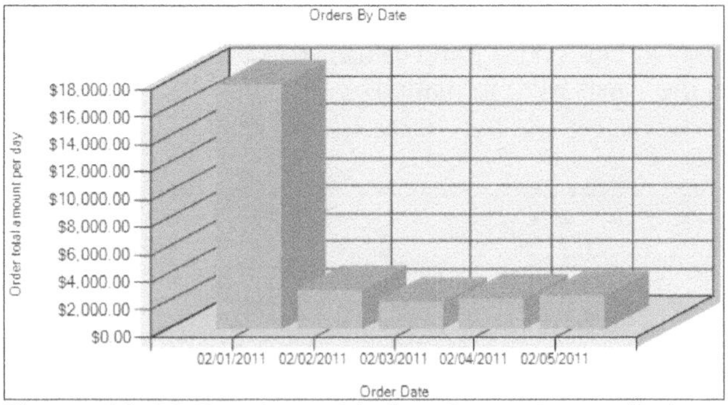

Figure 10-32 Bar chart with data formatting applied

Exercise 10.2: Create A Line Chart

In this exercise you will create a line chart that displays the order total amount by month for a specific year. To create the report you will need to use a calculated field to display the monthly total amount. The month names will be displayed across the bottom of the chart.

1. Save the Chart Order By Month report as `aLineChart`.

2. Change the filter to select order dates in 2011.

3. Select the options in Table 10-4.

   The chart should look like the one shown in Figure 10-33.

Option	Change To
Chart Type	Line
Source	Report
Summarization	Value
Data Type	Numeric
Data	Select the Total order amount by month calculated field
Sample at	By Month
Sample over	Grand
Data Format	Select the Pre-defined format $123,456.78.
Category	cmonth(Chartorders->order_date)
Chart Title	"2011 Monthly Order Totals"
Y Axis Title	"Total for the month"
Include Zero	Yes

Table 10-4 Line chart options

The reason that there is no data on the chart for January is because there are no orders in the table for that month.

Figure 10-33 Line chart

Exercise 10.3: Create A Spline Area Chart

In this exercise you will create a report that only has a chart. The chart will display the total amount of last years sales by state.

1. Create a blank free-form report based on the Chart Customers table.

2. Create a group for the State field.

3. Create a filter that selects customers in FL, CA, PA or CT.

4. Open the Calculated Values dialog box and create the expressions below.

```
StateSales = total(chartcustomers->last_years_sales,
grp->State,grp->detail)

GrandSales = total(chartcustomers->last_years_sales,
grp->Grand,grp->detail)
```

5. Save the report as `aSplineAreaChart`.

6. Select the options in Table 10-5.

   The chart should look like the one shown in Figure 10-35.

Option	Change To
Chart Type	Spline Area
Source	Report
Summarization	Total
Data Type	Numeric
Data	Last Years Sales
Sample at	State
Sample over	Grand
Data Format	Select the Pre-defined format $123,456.78.
Category	(7)
Chart Title	"Last Years Sales for FL, CA, PA and CT"
X Axis Title	"State"
Y Axis Title	"Last Years Sales"
Chart Style	Select the Series Styles options shown in Figure 10-34.

Table 10-5 Spline Area chart options

(7) Type this expression. `State + " ($" + calc->StateSales + ")"`

Figure 10-34 Series Styles options

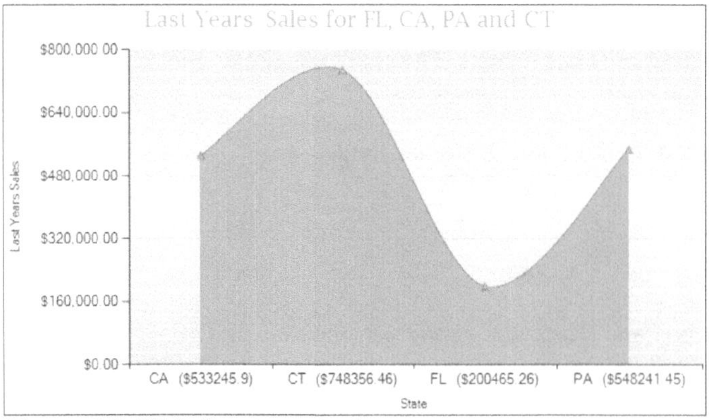

Figure 10-35 Spline Area chart

Use The Show Breaks Option

If you wanted to display where there is less data in the chart, check the **SHOW BREAKS** option on the Graph Data dialog box.

When applied to the spline area chart shown above in Figure 10-35, the chart would look like the one shown in Figure 10-36.

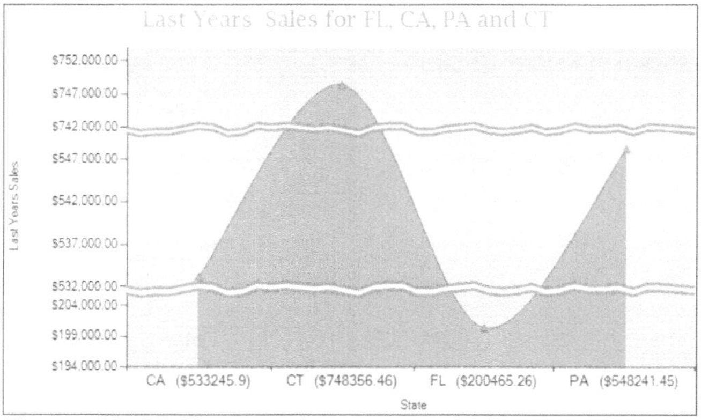

Figure 10-36 Show Breaks option applied to the spline area chart

Changing The Client Margin

The options explained below are used to select how far from the left of the grid area that a chart is displayed.

① **FLUSH** The chart starts all the way to the left. This option spreads the chart out over the entire background area, as shown in Figure 10-37.
② **HALF** This is the default option. An example is shown above in Figure 10-36.
③ **FULL** This option does not seem to work, regardless of the chart type that I tried.

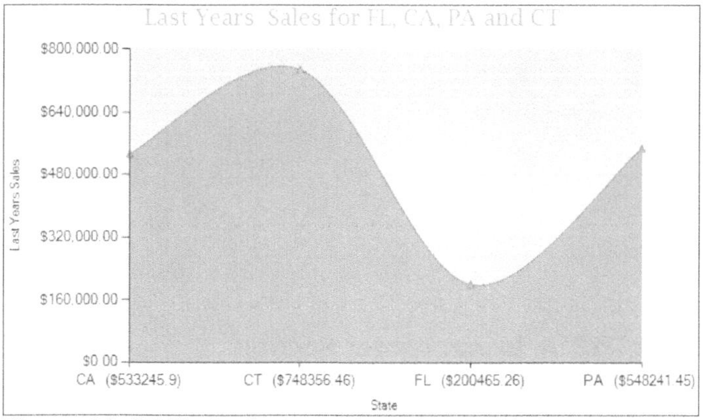

Figure 10-37 Flush client margin option enabled

Exercise 10.4: Create A Pie Chart

In this exercise you will create a pie chart that displays a total dollar amount of orders per sales rep in 2012.

1. Save the Chart Orders By Rep report as `aPieChart`.

2. Select the options in Table 10-6.

   The chart should look like the one shown in Figure 10-38.

Option	Change To
Chart Type	Pie
3D Appearance	Yes
Source	Report
Summarization	Total
Data Type	Numeric
Data	Order Amount
Sample at	Sales Rep
Sample over	Grand
Category	(8)
Chart Title	"2012 Orders By Sales Rep"
Data Label Placement	Chart

Table 10-6 Pie chart options

One Way To Hide Decimal Places
If by the time that you read this book, the Pre-Defined Formats Decimal Places option has not been fixed, you can use the **INT() FUNCTION**, as shown in footnote (8) below.

(8) Type this expression. `Left(Chartsalesreps->rep_first_name,1) + " " + Trim(Chartsalesreps->rep_last_name) + "($" + Int(calc->run_tot_chartorders_orderamount_for_order date)+ ")"`

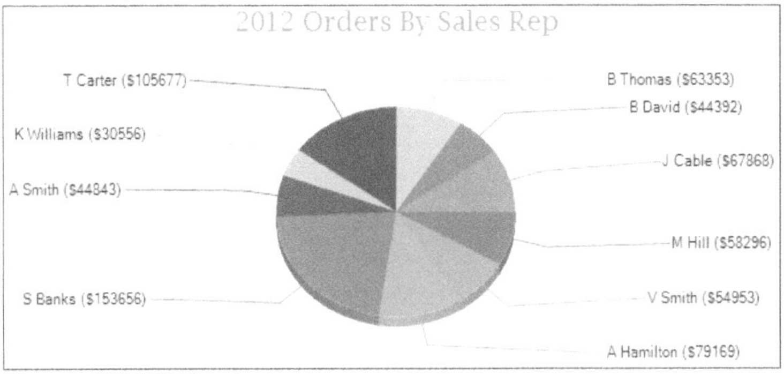

Figure 10-38 Pie chart

Exercise 10.5: Add A Chart To The Group Footer Section

So far, all of the charts that you have created were placed in the Report Header section of the report. This means that the data displayed on the chart (if the chart is based on data displayed on the report) is for all of the data on the report. Placing a chart in a group section means that the data displayed is only for the group. As you will see, this means that the data displayed on the chart will change for each group.

1. Save the Chart Invoice Total report as `aChartInGroupFooter`.

2. Sort the data on the Order ID field in the Chart Orders table by typing the following expression in the Break on change in field on the Order Number Group Properties dialog box.

```
val(remspecial(chartorders->Order_ID))
```

3. Add the chart control to the Group Footer section below the Order Total field, then select the options in Table 10-7.

   The chart for Order #3 should look like the one shown in Figure 10-39.

   The chart for Order #4 should look like the one shown in Figure 10-40. Notice the difference in the pie charts.

Option	Change To
Chart Type	Pie
Source	Report
Series Type	Single
Summarization	Value
Data Type	Numeric
Data	Line total calculated field
Sample at	Detail
Sample over	Order Number
Data Label	(9)
Chart Title	"Items Ordered"
Data Label Placement	Chart

Table 10-7 Chart in Group Footer section options

(9) Type this expression. `trim(products->product_name) + " (Qty " + Chartorderdetail->Qty + ")"`

Another Way To Create An Expression For The Data Label Field
If you find that you are getting errors when creating an expression for the Data Label field and want to create the formula on the Expression Builder, you can click the **DATA LABEL** field button, then click the button at the end of the field on the Data Label Expression dialog box to open the Expression Builder.

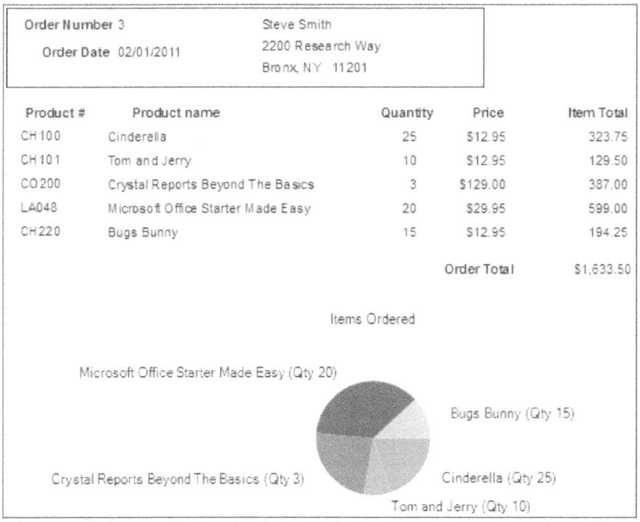

Figure 10-39 Chart in Group Footer section of order #3

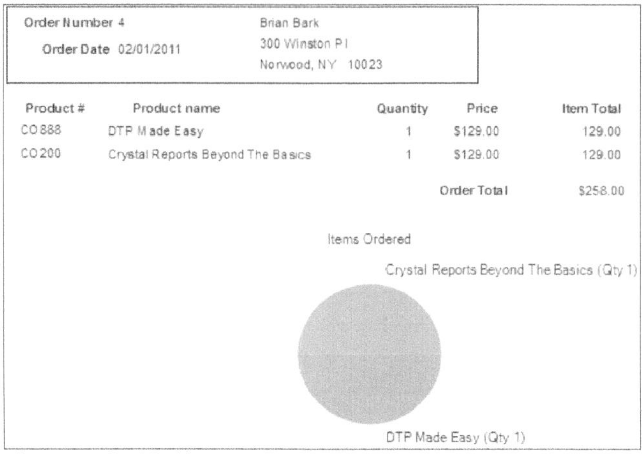

Figure 10-40 Chart in Group Footer section of order #4

Exercise 10.6: Use The Table Data Source Option To Create A Chart

So far, all of the charts covered in this chapter were created using the Report data source option. In this exercise you will learn how to use the Table option. You will create a chart that displays a count of students per state, per class.

1. Save the Chart Class Roster report as `aTableChart`.

2. Add the chart control to the Group Footer section.

   Select the options in Table 10-8.

   Leave the dialog box open to complete the rest of the exercise.

Option	Change To
Chart Type	Pie
Source	Table
Table or Set	ChartStudents
Series Type	Single
Summarization	Count
Data Type	Numeric
Data	Student Name
Sample unique	State
Data Label	State + " (" + chart.data + ")"
Category	State
Category Label	"State"
Chart Title	"Count of students by state in the class"
Data Label Placement	Legend

Table 10-8 Table data source chart options

Create The Argument And Binding

Creating an argument for a chart is the same process as creating one for a report.

1. Click the Arguments field button, then create an argument that has the properties in Table 10-9.

Property	Change To
Name	classfilter
Type	Numeric
Style	Text Box

Table 10-9 Argument properties

2. Click the Argument Bindings field button on the Graph Data dialog box. Select the **FROM FIELD** option, then select the Classnbr field from the drop-down list. Click OK.

Create The Filter

1. Click the **FILTER RECORDS** field button. On the Filter Builder, create the condition Classnbr is equal to.

2. Click the button at the end of the last field.

   On the dialog box shown in Figure 10-41, select the **SELECT AN ARGUMENT** option, then click on the argument.

   You should have the options shown in Figure 10-42.

   The chart should look like the one shown in Figure 10-43.

   Like the chart that you created earlier in Exercise 10.5, each chart on the report will display different values.

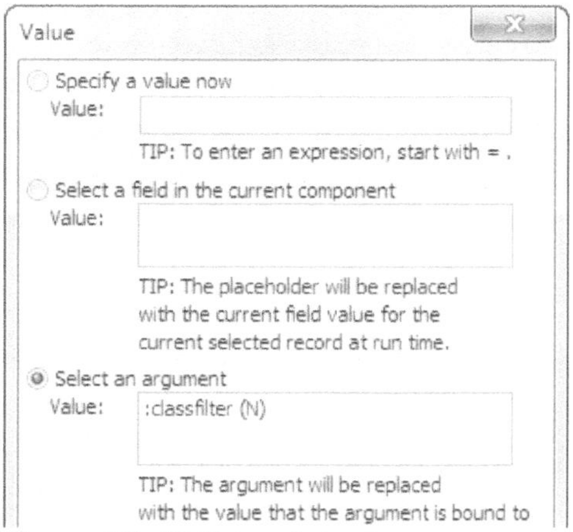

Figure 10-41 Value dialog box

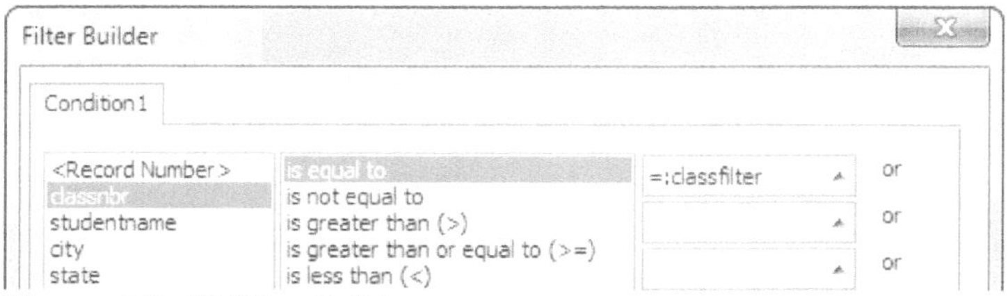

Figure 10-42 Filter Builder

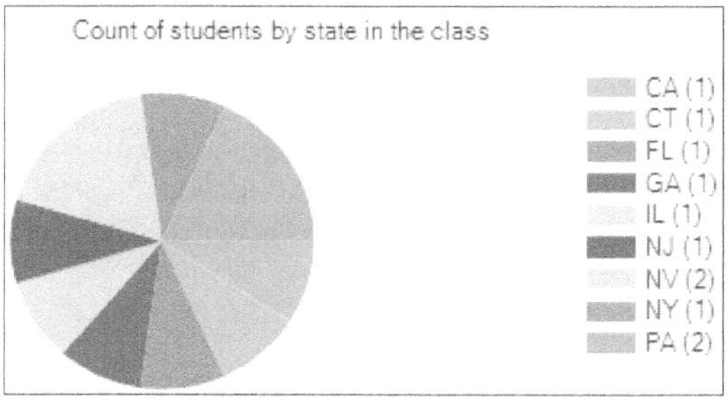

Figure 10-43 Chart based on a table data source

> **Change The Filter Records Option**
> Once you save the changes to the report, you may have the need to change how the records are filtered. When you click the **FILTER RECORDS** field button on the Graph Data dialog box, you will see the dialog box shown in Figure 10-44 instead of the Filter Builder shown earlier in Figure 10-42.

Figure 10-44 Specify Filter dialog box

Exercise 10.7: Use The Explode Slice Option

In this exercise you will modify a pie chart to have a slice of the chart to be detached, if the condition is met.

1. Save the aTableChart report as `aPieChartExplode`.

2. In the Explode Slice field, type `State="PA"`.

   This will detach a slice of the pie chart when its slice is equal to PA, as shown in Figure 10-45.

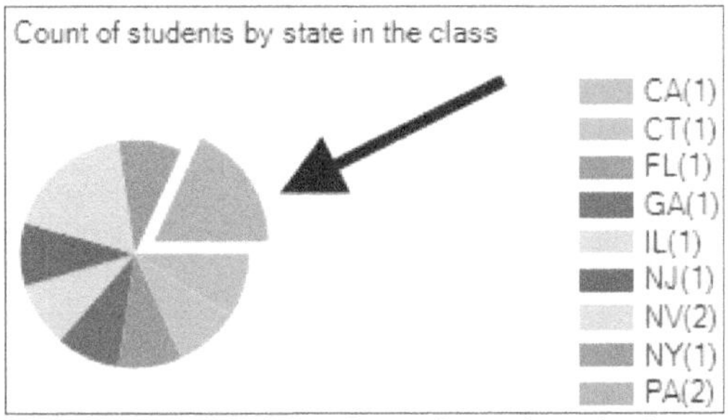

Figure 10-45 Slice of pie chart detached

Exercise 10.8: Create A Radar Chart

In this exercise you will display quarterly totals on a radar chart.

1. Save the aOrdersByQuarter report as `aRadarChart`.

2. Select the options in Table 10-10. The chart should look like the one shown in Figure 10-46.

Option	Change To
Chart Type	Radar
3D Appearance	Yes
Effects	Area
Source	Report
Series Type	Single
Summarization	Value
Data Type	Numeric
Data	(10)
Sample at	By Quarter
Sample over	Grand
Category	(10)
Data Label Placement	Chart

Table 10-10 Radar chart options

Figure 10-46 Radar chart

(10) Select the Total order amount by quarter calculated field.

Exercise 10.9: Create A Bubble Chart

In this exercise you will learn how to display order totals by day.

1. Save the Chart Orders By Date report as `aBubbleChart`.

2. Select the options in Table 10-11.

   In this exercise the **Y INTERVAL** option will display the values in $500 increments.

   Leave the dialog box open to complete the next step.

Option	Change To
Chart Type	Bubble
Source	Report
Series Type	Single
Summarization	Total
Data Type	Numeric
Data	Order Amount
Data Shape Size	Order Amount
Sample at	Order Date
Sample over	Grand
Data Format	Display a dollar sign
Category	Order Date
Chart Title	"Daily Order Totals"
Y Interval	500
Client Margin	Flush

Table 10-11 Bubble chart options

Rotate The Text On The X Axis

There may be times when the text on an axis is too large to fit. If that is the case, the **TEXT ROTATION** option may be a solution.

1. Click the Chart Style field button. On the Text tab, change the **TEXT X-AXIS ROTATION** field to 30, as illustrated in Figure 10-47. The chart should look like the one shown in Figure 10-48.

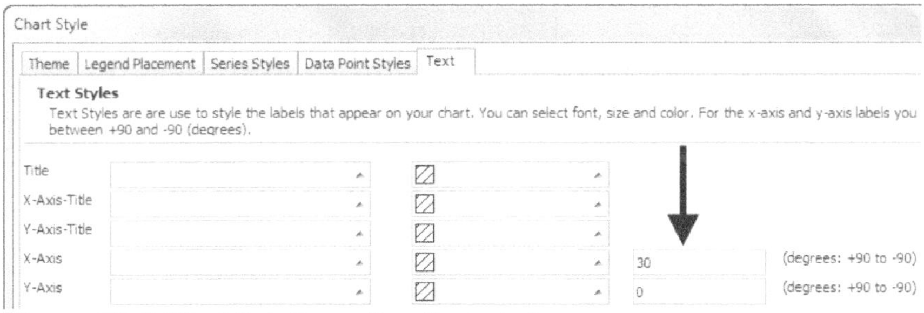

Figure 10-47 Text Rotation option illustrated

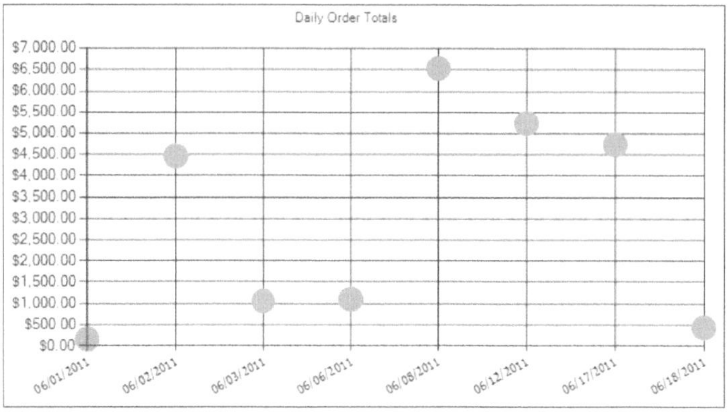

Figure 10-48 Bubble chart with text on the X axis rotated

Exercise 10.10: Display Quarterly Totals On A Chart

In Chapter 7, Exercise 7.14, you created a report that grouped the data by quarter. In this exercise you will display the quarterly data on a chart.

1. Save the aOrdersByQuarter report as `aChartByQuarter`.

2. Select the options in Table 10-12. The report should look like the one shown in Figure 10-49.

Option	Change To
Chart Type	Pie
3D Appearance	Yes
Source	Report
Series Type	Single
Summarization	Value
Data Type	Numeric
Data	Order Amount
Sample at	By Quarter
Sample over	Grand
Data Label	(11)
Data Label Placement	Chart

Table 10-12 Quarterly totals chart options

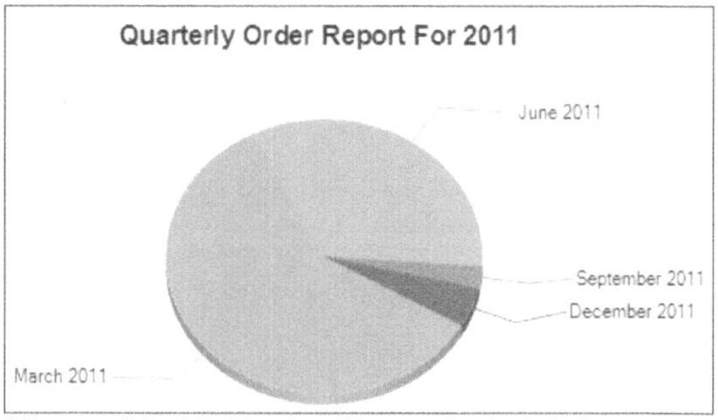

Figure 10-49 Chart with quarterly totals

(11) Type this expression. `cmonth(chartorders->order_date) + " " + cyear(chartorders->order_date)`

Exercise 10.11: Create A Chart Based On Top N Percent Data

In this exercise you will create a chart based on data from a Top N Percent report.

1. Save the aPromptTopNPercent report as `aTopNPercentChart`.

2. Make the Report Header section longer, then move the field headings down to the bottom of the section.

3. Add the chart control to the Report Header section.

   Select the options in Table 10-13.

Option	Change To
Chart Type	Bar Horizontal Stacked
3D Appearance	Yes
Effects	Cylinder
Source	Report
Series Type	Single
Summarization	Value
Data Type	Numeric
Data	Last Years Sales
Sample at	Detail
Sample over	Grand
Data Label	(12)
X Axis Title	"Percent Rank - 1 is high"
Y Axis Title	"Dollar Amount"
Data Label Placement	Chart

Table 10-13 Top N chart options

(12) Type this expression. `"$" + Last_Years_Sales + " - " + trim(first_name) + " " + last_name`

Customize The Data Point Styles

The bars on the chart would look better if they were different colors. The way to change the color is to use the **DATA POINT STYLES** options on the Chart Style dialog box.

1. Click the Chart Style field button. On the Data Point Styles tab, define three data point styles, by selecting the options shown in Figure 10-50.

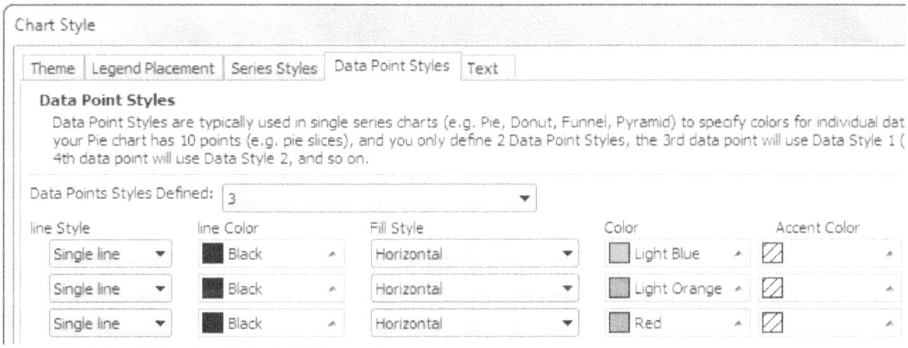

Figure 10-50 Data Point Style options

2. When you run the report, select 5% or less when prompted.

   The reason is because a higher percent means more customers will appear on the chart, making it hard to read. The reason that I selected this report was so that you could see a chart that is partially created from an argument.

   The report should look like the one shown in Figure 10-51.

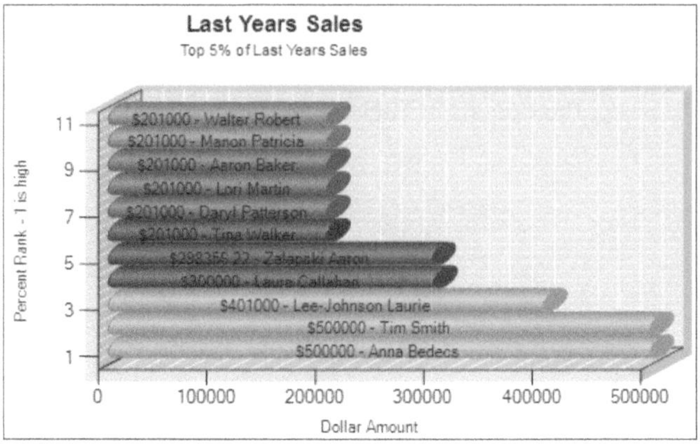

Figure 10-51 Chart based on Top N percent data

INDEX

D

E

F

S

T

Made in United States
Cleveland, OH
05 November 2026

47659899R00110